Asian Flavors

Changing the Tastes of Minnesota since 1875

Phyllis Louise Harris

With Raghavan Iyer

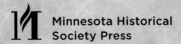

Minnesota Historical
Society Press

www.mhspress.org

The Minnesota Historical Society Press is a member of the Association of American University Presses.

Manufactured in Canada

10 9 8 7 6 5 4 3 2 1

∞ The paper used in this publication meets the minimum requirements of the American National Standard for Information Sciences—Permanence for Printed Library Materials, ANSI Z39.48–1984.

International Standard Book Number

ISBN: 978-0-87351-864-2 (cloth)

Library of Congress Cataloging-in-Publication Data
Harris, Phyllis Louise.
Asian flavors : changing the tastes of Minnesota since
    1875 / Phyllis Louise Harris ; with Raghavan Iyer ;
    Designer, Wendy Jedlička; Photographer Tom Nelson.
        p. cm.
Includes bibliographical references and index.
ISBN 978-0-87351-864-2 (cloth : alk. paper)
1. Cooking, Asian. 2. Cooking—Minnesota. I. Title.
TX724.5.A1H37 2012
641.595—dc23
                          2012010521

Cover design: jedlicka.com
Cover images: tnphoto.com

The publication of this book was supported through a generous grant from the Bean Family Fund for Business History.

Abe's egg rolls and Mena-li's empanadas from the Philippines represent the many versions of filled rolls, wraps, puffs, and buns throughout the Asia Pacific Rim.
Platter by Richard Bresnahan, St. John's Pottery, Collegeville.

Contents

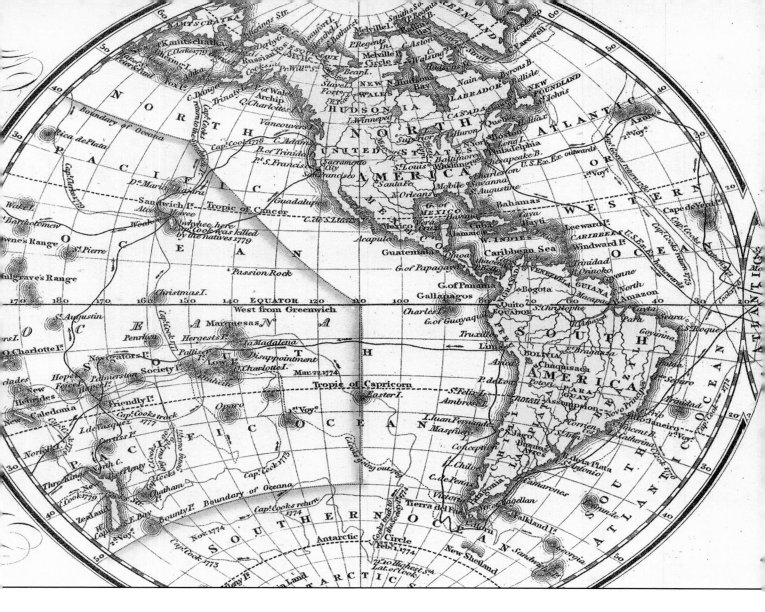

Preface

This book is a tribute to the countless men and women who made the often arduous journey halfway around the world to live in Minnesota. It is for the refugees fleeing from oppression, persecution, and the threat of death. For the immigrants looking for work to support themselves and their families. For the students seeking a higher education and finding Minnesota a good place to learn and live. For those who came to start a new life with their partner or spouse. And for the many Minnesotans who make the food of Asia an important part of their lives and ours.

It is for all those people who shared their own home cooking and Asian culinary traditions with us and opened up a whole new world of flavors and food for us to enjoy.

While this book is able to feature only a few of these exceptional, talented, and generous people, we thank them all for introducing us to these centuries-old culinary heritages and changing forever our own culinary history.

Phyllis Louise Harris
CEO, Asian Culinary Arts Institutes, Ltd. (ACAI)
Food Editor, *Asian Pages*, 1991–2011

Above: The world as the first Asian immigrants to Minnesota knew it, c 1856.

Introduction

The history of Asian food in Minnesota comes full circle with two restaurants: the Canton Restaurant, the first Chinese restaurant in the state, which opened in 1883, and Thom Pham's Wondrous Azian Kitchen, one of the new Asian fusion restaurants, which opened in 2010 on the same street. The people responsible were both teenage immigrants to Minnesota from Asia, both were talented entrepreneurs, both created unique culinary opportunities for Minnesotans to experience the flavors of their homelands, and both offered the fusion food of their day.

Woo Yee Sing was just eighteen in 1880 when he left China to establish a business in Minneapolis. First was a laundry, then an import firm, and three years later he sent for his younger brother Woo Du Sing to join him. Together they opened the Canton Restaurant, later moving it to 28 South Sixth Street and changing its name to Yuen Faung Low, commonly known as "John's Place." They understood their market so well that, with the dedication and support of their families, the restaurant survived eighty-four years and its offshoot, John's No. One Son, another twelve.

A century after Woo Yee Sing's arrival, another teenager, this time from Vietnam, sought refuge from the tragedies of his war-torn homeland. He came to Minnesota to complete his education and eventually to open a restaurant. Ten years after his arrival, Thom Pham bought the Kowloon Chinese Restaurant in St. Louis Park, changed it into a modern café featuring his creative version of fusion foods with Asian influences, and called it ThanhDo. He went on to open four more restaurants, including, in 2010, Thom Pham's Wondrous Azian Kitchen on Sixth Street in Minneapolis, just a hundred yards from the former John's Place.

From the Woo brothers' Canton Restaurant to Thom Pham's Wondrous Azian Kitchen and beyond, the story of Asian food in Minnesota includes more than eleven hundred restaurants established by people representing dozens of countries. It includes cookbook authors who often spend years re-creating the recipes of their homeland. It includes companies that produce, package, and market Asian food. It includes merchants who import Asian food to Minnesota and make it available for everyone to enjoy. And it includes the talented home cooks who share their family recipes with friends and neighbors and pass them down to the next generation, keeping age-old traditions alive. We bring you just a few of their stories and their amazing Asian flavors.

Facing page: May Yia Lee of Mhonpaj's Garden in Oakdale, representing the many Asian farm families in Minnesota.

Below: Canton Restaurant, 246–48 Marquette Avenue, Minneapolis, ca. 1883.

Thom Pham's Wondrous Azian Kitchen, Minneapolis, 2012.

The flavors of...
China

Woo Yee Sing, a merchant from Hoy Ping district (now Kaiping) in the Sei Yup area of Canton Province (Guangdong), was a teenager when he traveled to San Francisco to build a business in America's land of gold and opportunities. The gold rush had ended and railroads now spanned the country, and instead of opportunity he found a strong anti-Chinese sentiment in California. Rather than return to China, in 1880 he moved to Minneapolis, where Chinese people appeared to be more easily accepted. Just eighteen years old, Woo Yee Sing first opened a laundry on Nicollet Avenue and then an import shop on Glenwood Avenue. In 1883 he sent for his younger brother, Woo Du Sing, and together they started the Canton Restaurant on Marquette Avenue South. In 1903 they changed the name to Yuen Faung Low (Café of Exotic Fragrance from Afar), "John's Place," and moved to 28 South Sixth Street, on the second floor above two stores. It was the first Asian restaurant in Minnesota and continued operations for eighty-four years.

The 250-seat restaurant was furnished with tall, ornately carved Chinese teakwood tables inlaid with mother-of-pearl. Colorful Chinese lanterns hung throughout the large dining room, with glass-enclosed panels of painted silks and camphorwood carvings imported from China decorating the walls. It was indeed an exotic place with fragrances from afar.

Woo Du Sing's granddaughter Honnay Chinn Molloy remembers it well. Since her father, Howard Chinn, was sometimes a host and other times a chef, and her mother, Margaret Woo Chinn, also worked in the restaurant part time, Honnay occasionally tagged along with her parents to work. Sometimes she was allowed to help make fresh noodles by beating a bucket of fifty eggs with a wire whip. The eggs were poured into a large mound of wheat flour and hand blended until the dough was pliable enough to run through the noodle machine. The finished strips were steamed and cooled before being deep-fried in lard for crisp chow mein noodles. They were so popular with John's Place diners that the process had to be repeated three to four times each week to keep up with demand. Honnay recalls they were so good she would take a few of the warm, freshly fried noodles and sprinkle them over ice cream. When the noodle machine broke in 1960 and replacement parts were not available, the restaurant bought its noodles from an outside supplier.

The food at John's Place was distinctly different from its closest competitor, the Nankin, which opened in 1919 a block away on Seventh Street. Stir-fried beef dishes were always made with beef tenderloin, not cheaper cuts. The Chicken Subgum Chow Mein contained no soy sauce or bead molasses, resulting in a pale color and a lighter flavor than its competitors. And the restaurant had a complete American menu cooked by Honnay's Uncle Willie (Margaret's brother). One of the most popular dishes was John's Special Chow Mein, made of Chicken Subgum Chow Mein with tomatoes, green peppers, and cashews added. The restaurant was so popular that at one point John's Place opened a second location in the Uptown area of Minneapolis, but it closed after a year.

Facing page: John's Special Chow Mein served on a John's Place plate and Wo Hop tea in a John's Place cup. Both plate and cup are from the 1960s.

Bottom left: Woo Yee Sing, ca. 1893.

Bottom right: Woo Du Sing at Yee Sing and Company, 22 Western Avenue, Minneapolis, 1920–29.

A menu from 1953 lists the usual chow mein, egg rolls, egg foo young, and wonton soups but also features John's specialties, including Pressed Duck and Sweet and Sour Wontons. The American menu made up one-third of the dishes served and included omelets, sandwiches, oysters in season, fried chicken, and several types of steak. Tea cost ten cents, Egg Drop Soup was thirty cents, and John's Special Chow Mein (cooked to order) was $1.30 including rice and tea. The most expensive item on the menu was Choice Cut T-Bone Steak with soup, salad, long-branch potatoes, beverage, and ice cream or sherbet for $4.50.

In the early 1900s, the Woo brothers ran one of the most prosperous restaurants in Minneapolis. Woo Yee Sing, who managed the John's Place dining room and served as its host, became a well-known leader in the community and often invited business and community leaders to dine at the restaurant. Woo Du Sing was the force behind the outstanding food, creating a menu of Chinese food acceptable to the market along with a long list of American dishes. He managed the kitchen and the many Chinese cooks brought in to handle the growing volume of diners.

Woo Yee Sing died in 1925 and Woo Du Sing in 1933, but many of their children, grandchildren, and relatives continued to operate John's Place for decades, making it truly a family business. They included Woo Yee Sing's wife, Liang May Seen (the first woman born in China to live in Minnesota), and son Howard with his wife, Lolita, and Woo Du Sing's sons Charles and William and daughter Margaret with her husband, Howard Chinn, and their daughter Honnay. But in 1967 when the lease was not renewed, the family decided to close John's Place. It was the year Honnay graduated from West High School. She went on to attend the Illinois Institute of Technology to pursue an engineering degree; she married Greg Molloy, and after a career with Procter and Gamble retired in 2000. In the tradition of the family business, she still has a standing wok in her kitchen and often cooks family recipes. And one of those beautifully carved John's Place tables resides in her basement.

Michael Wong and Honnay Molloy.

As John's Place was closing, the family announced the dates of their final two weeks of operation. Immediately they were deluged with diners. "So many longtime customers wanted to come back for a last meal," recalled Honnay, "that we were swamped with reservations for those final days." They put on extra staff to handle the crowds. "My eleven-year-old brother, Howard, was assigned the task of keeping people at the door downstairs and would only let them come up to the dining room once there was a table available," she added. "I was so busy at the cash register and answering phones that I never had time to go downstairs to see how long the line was out on the sidewalk." Howard, it appears, made quite a few tips from people wanting to get in. But the customers were not the only ones who sought a last glimpse of John's Place: former staff members who had worked for the restaurant twenty, thirty, or forty years before retiring came back to help out in the final week. After closing day, the family held one last dinner for special guests. It was a fitting farewell to the restaurant that had introduced Asian food to Minnesota nearly a century before.

After the restaurant closed, Honnay's father, Howard Chinn, became the front-of-the-house manager at the Nankin, where he stayed for more than fifteen years. Her Uncle Charles Woo had already opened John's No. One Son on Linden Avenue, eventually moving to Wayzata Boulevard, where he operated it with his daughter Myrna, her husband, John Wong, and their son Michael until 1979. The restaurant was sold when Michael Wong, Woo Du Sing's great-grandson, chose architecture as his career instead of staying in the restaurant business.

At our request, Woo Du Sing's granddaughter Honnay Molloy and great-grandson Michael Wong worked together to re-create the signature dish from John's Place, John's Special Chow Mein (page 4). They agree that the most important part of cooking this dish is in the preparation and careful cutting of ingredients. And while it may not include some of the pork flavor used in making the restaurant's homemade chicken broth or the handmade egg noodles fried in lard, it will be a close replica of the dish served at the first Chinese restaurant in Minnesota.

At John's Place, cooks made large batches of this chow mein several times a day, keeping it warm on the steam table, ready to fill diners' orders. It was never cooled and reheated because the cornstarch mixture would break down and the sauce would become watery.

John's Chicken Subgum Chow Mein

Serves 6

Dice each ingredient into pieces about 1/2 inch square and 1/3 inch thick and set aside on separate plates.

6 cups diced celery (about 14–18 large stalks)

1 tablespoon vegetable oil

1 tablespoon rendered chicken fat

1 teaspoon minced garlic

1 pound chicken, white and dark meat, skin and bones removed, diced

2/3 cup canned tiny button mushrooms, drained and rinsed, quartered if larger than 1 inch

1/2 cup canned bamboo tips, drained and rinsed, diced

2/3 cup canned whole water chestnuts, drained and rinsed, diced

4 cups chicken stock

1 1/2 tablespoons cornstarch combined with 1 1/2 tablespoons water

deep-fried egg noodles

5–6 egg crepe strips (recipe folows)

steamed white rice

1. Blanch the celery in a large pot of boiling water. Let the water return to a boil and cook until celery color begins to deepen, about 1 minute. Remove celery from water and plunge into a bowl of ice water to stop the cooking process and refresh the color. The celery will have a sweeter flavor than raw celery.

2. Heat a large skillet or wok over medium-high heat until hot and coat with the vegetable oil and then the chicken fat; add the garlic. Quickly stir-fry the garlic to flavor the oil, about 10 seconds, then add the chicken pieces and quickly stir-fry for 1 minute, until the chicken begins to color.

3. Add the blanched celery and mix with the chicken; then add the mushrooms, bamboo tips, and water chestnuts. Mix together and add the chicken stock. Quickly bring to a boil and reduce the heat to low. Simmer uncovered for about 15 minutes, until the celery is tender.

4. Push the ingredients to the edge of the pan, leaving a pool of broth in the middle. Stir the cornstarch mixture to blend and then slowly add it to the liquid, stirring until it begins to thicken, about a minute. Then mix the thickened sauce into the rest of the ingredients and stir-fry until the sauce becomes clear and coats all of the ingredients. Remove from heat.

5. Serve on a plate over deep-fried egg noodles and top with egg crepe strips. Garnish with a scoop of steamed white rice at the side.

Egg Crepe Strips

Makes 2 crepes (60–80 strips)

1 egg

1/2 pinch salt

1/4 teaspoon cornstarch

1 teaspoon vegetable oil

1. Combine egg, salt, and cornstarch in a bowl and beat well with a wire whisk. Do not make it frothy. Pour mixture through a fine strainer.

2. Heat a nonstick 8-inch skillet or crepe pan and lightly grease with the vegetable oil. Pour half the egg mixture into the pan and immediately tilt pan to swirl mixture around to form a very thin crepe. Cook over low heat about a minute, until the egg is firm enough to turn over. Do not brown the crepe. Cook the other side about 30 seconds and remove to a board or plate to cool.

3. Cut into strips about 1/4 inch wide and 2 inches long. Set aside. They will keep for several hours.

John's Special Chow Mein

Re-created by Honnay Chinn Molloy and Michael Wong

Serves 1

1 cup John's Chicken Subgum Chow Mein (page 3)

1/4 tomato, peeled with seeds removed, diced into 1/2-inch squares

1/8 medium green pepper, seeds and membranes removed, diced into 1/2-inch squares

deep-fried egg noodles (chow mein noodles)

approximately 20 cashew halves, roasted and salted

2–3 egg crepe strips (page 3)

steamed white rice

Take one cup of John's Chicken Subgum Chow Mein and stir in the chopped tomato and green pepper. Pour over deep-fried egg noodles. Top with cashews and garnish with a few egg crepe strips. Add a scoop of steamed white rice at the side and serve immediately.

Three kinds of rice are used in Chinese cooking. Glutinous or sticky rice is used for stuffing or coating for pearl balls (page 40) or sometimes ground into flour for sweet pastries. Long-grain or oval-grain rice is used for everyday cooking, with long-grain rice the most popular. This type of rice was served at John's Place. Rinse the rice several times in cold water to remove any starch coating. When the water runs clear, the rice is ready to cook. Drain off all water.

Chinese Boiled Rice

Makes 3 cups cooked rice

1 cup rice, rinsed and drained

1 3/4 cups water

Place the rice and water in a heavy saucepan. Bring to a boil over moderate heat and simmer until small craters appear in the surface. Cover with a tight-fitting lid and lower heat to slow simmer. Cook for 20 minutes. Turn off heat and remove the pot from the burner without removing the lid. Let it rest for 10 minutes, and then fluff the rice with chopsticks or fork. Serve hot.

Interior photo postcard of John's Place.

I grew up during the Depression of the 1930s, when money for eating in restaurants was very scarce. But John's Place was one restaurant we were able to afford for an occasional treat. By "we" I mean my grandmother, mother, and me, and in later years my sister and brother—never my father. Dad refused to eat "foreign food" because "you don't know what's in it!"—a sentiment held by many people even in later years.

As a child I remember struggling up the long flight of stairs to John's Place on the second floor, but once we were there it was like another world, with the subdued lighting from the colorful Chinese lanterns, the ornate wood carvings on the walls, and the large mirrors making the spacious dining room (250 seats) seem even larger. Even the aromas were from another world. I would climb onto a wooden chair and then kneel in order to see over the tall, carved teak tables. Until I could read I thought John's Place served only one dish, chow mein, for that's the only meal that was ordered for me. Pale green and containing mysterious food piled on top of crisp noodles and served with steaming white rice, it was far removed from the food I got at home, or from my father's restaurant.

My dad, Lewis S. Igo, ran a small (about thirty-seat) restaurant on the ground floor of the apartment building owned by his father, Ernest B. Igo, the Roof Garden on Harmon Place near Thirteenth Street in downtown Minneapolis. His menu was strictly down-home-Iowa-farm-meat-and-potatoes cooking, and his mother, Myrtle Igo, made wonderful pies with flaky lard crusts and heavenly, light yeast rolls. Everything was made fresh daily from scratch to the delight of the nearby firemen, auto mechanics and used car salesmen who stopped in every day. Until I was six we also lived in the building, so going out for dinner often meant heading downstairs to sit at the counter where dad would serve us whatever was left in the kitchen that day, which was always good. It was a wonderful adventure for a six-year-old but nothing as exotic as John's Place.

Ironically, the recipe for that "foreign" food my dad refused to eat contains mostly ingredients he often used in his own restaurant. — PLH

Growth of Chinese Food Across the State

Initially the Twin Cities attracted the most Chinese immigrants to the state, with an estimated fifty-two in 1900, 150 in 1910, and 300 by 1920. One early settler, Moy Ju Hee, from the Taishan area of Guangdong Province, opened a restaurant in St. Paul called Kwong Tung Low Co. Café in 1903 and soon after established another restaurant in Minneapolis. His businesses were very successful, and he became prominent in the Twin Cities business community. One of the most well-known Chinese immigrants was Kin Wah, better known as Walter James, whose Nankin Café opened in 1919 next to the Radisson Hotel on Seventh Street in Minneapolis. With a variety of owners and locations, the Nankin operated on the same street for eighty years.

By 1920, the Chinese population had expanded throughout the state and totaled nine hundred to one thousand. Bernard Wong, known as Bon Wong, chose St. Cloud as the place to settle down and in 1918 opened the O. K. Café on St. Germain Street. In a 1978 oral history interview by the Stearns County Historical Society, Wong's son Edward talked about this early endeavor. His father and eldest brother, William, ran the restaurant

and "served mostly meat and potatoes," he recalled. There were six other restaurants in St. Cloud at the time, but only the O. K. Café and one other allowed women to enter through the front door. "The rest were saloons where ladies were not allowed," he explained.

In 1923 Bon Wong sent for Eddie to come to St. Cloud to work at the restaurant. They were the city's first Chinese settlers. Eddie's mother and sister remained in China, and he never saw them again, a typical story of the era. By the 1930s, the restaurant was open twenty-four hours a day, with the staff taking turns sleeping in the back rooms. Meals cost twenty-five cents, but it was the Depression and competition was very stiff. Somehow they managed to survive, and eventually Eddie's five children also worked in the O. K. Café, using their wages for tuition as they each earned a college degree. Eddie was active in St. Cloud community affairs and retired in 1974.

The Huie Family Creates Two Chinese Restaurants in Duluth

Two more teenage immigrants came to Minnesota and built popular Chinese restaurants and outstanding reputations in their community. The first was Joe Huie, who at age seventeen left his native Guangzhou in 1909 and settled in Duluth, where his relatives owned the St. Paul Café. Success did not happen overnight. For forty-two years, he worked his way up in the restaurant business from dishwasher to kitchen help and finally to cook and manager. Initially his salary for working fourteen hours a day, seven days a week was sixty dollars per month, and most of that was set aside to help his family back in China. Since he spoke no English, his first investment was in language classes that took half of his salary for several months.

Over the years, Joe divided his time between Duluth and China, where he built a thriving pharmacy and made several medicines to sell throughout Canton City. In 1948, when the communist government began confiscating land and companies, Joe lost all of his holdings in China. He moved his family to Duluth and made it their permanent home.

In 1951 Joe Huie borrowed some money and along with two brothers bought the Shangri La restaurant, changing the name to Joe Huie's Café. It was open twenty-four hours a day, seven days a week, and its Chinese and American menu became so popular that sometimes he had to hire a policeman to control the lines of diners waiting to get into the café, especially after the bars closed at one in the morning.

His eldest son, Wing Ying Huie, remembers it well. "My thirteen-year-old brother Wing Jung and I worked sixteen hours a day, seven days a week," he recalled, "and there was little time for anything else." Wing Ying was sixteen when he came to Duluth and would have entered the ninth grade had he stayed at the private school he attended in China. "I wanted to continue my education here," Wing Ying said, "and finally convinced my dad to let me go to school when I wasn't working in the café." The Duluth school system placed him in the fourth grade due to his difficulty with the English language. But Wing Ying persisted, advancing to junior high, high school, and then the University of Minnesota–Duluth. After college he served in the armed forces, stationed in Korea, and finally returned to settle in Duluth.

"I was still working for my dad and had some ideas to improve the café," he said. "But my father and uncles were not interested. They were happy with the restaurant as it was." Wing Ying had no money to start his own restaurant, so he looked around for an existing restaurant that was large but had no business. After a year he found the failing Gourmet House on Superior Street and made a

deal with the landlord. He changed the name to Chinese Lantern and in 1964 opened his own restaurant. His dad thought it was a mistake, but Wing Ying forged ahead with his concept of a menu that would attract all levels of diners, from low to high incomes. Part of his philosophy was to make each of his dishes the best possible and to serve large portions. When a cook tried to serve a steak that was less than the two-pound minimum Wing Ying had set, he sent it back to the kitchen.

The restaurant became famous for its beef prime ribs as much as its Chinese dishes. In fact, several Minnesota governors and senators made a point to eat at the Chinese Lantern when in Duluth and helped spread the word about the restaurant's outstanding food. Diners were soon coming in for both the Chinese and American

Chinese Lantern exterior photo ca. 1990, and a postcard showing the restaurant's interior (above).

dishes, and the business grew. After a decade, Wing Ying moved to a larger space where he could serve a thousand customers at a time. He successfully operated there for twenty more years, until a fire destroyed the restaurant in 1994. His children had graduated from college and were living in the Twin Cities; rather than rebuilding, Wing Ying retired and moved closer to them. Now his time is spent doing the things he couldn't during those sixteen-hour workdays, such as golfing, bowling, and visiting grandchildren. He still likes to cook and has provided three recipes from the Duluth restaurants.

Joe Huie operated his café until 1972, when at the age of eighty he finally retired. Rather than sell the restaurant, he closed it and sold off all the contents. Many of his customers bought everything from dishes to woks just to have a piece of the place they loved. He died in 1989. His youngest son, Wing Young Huie, who also worked in the restaurant while growing up, became an award-winning photographer whose acclaimed exhibits include *Frogtown* (1996), *Lake Street U.S.A.* (1996–99), and the *University Avenue Project* (2007–10).

Joe Huie with two of his sons who worked in his restaurant. Left to right: Kwong, Joe, and Ying, ca. 1950.

The following recipe for Joe Huie's Shrimp is the only one in the book that is not Asian. It is an example of the "American" food that many Chinese restaurants served (and some still serve today) to bring in customers who might eventually sample their Chinese cooking. It was so popular at Joe Huie's that Wing Ying Huie also served it at the Chinese Lantern.

Joe Huie's Shrimp

Re-created by Wing Ying Huie

Serves 2–3

1 pound large shrimp, shells removed (about 16)	2 eggs
1/8 teaspoon salt	1 1/2 cups vegetable oil
1 cup flour	tartar sauce

1. Make a deep cut into each shrimp through the back and remove the vein, keeping the shrimp in one piece. Open up the shrimp and press down with your hand to flatten. Sprinkle with salt.

2. Place the flour on a plate or in a pie plate. Place the eggs in a bowl and beat with a fork for about 30 seconds, until mixed but not frothy. Take each shrimp and dip into the flour, covering it completely. Shake off excess flour and dip shrimp into the beaten eggs. Put the shrimp back into the flour and press flour onto each side. Set coated shrimp aside, keeping each one flat.

3. Preheat oven to 250°. In a large pan or wok at least 6 inches deep, heat the oil over medium-high heat to 350°. Add the shrimp one at a time, cooking 4 to 6 at a time for approximately 4 minutes, until coating turns golden brown and shrimp turns pink. Remove shrimp from oil and drain on a paper towel to remove excess oil. Place cooked shrimp on a wire rack in the warm oven. Repeat with remaining shrimp. Serve hot with tartar sauce.

Dar Cheen Chicken

Wing Ying Huie's Chinese Lantern
Serves 3–4

2 teaspoons vegetable oil

1 teaspoon minced garlic

1/2 teaspoon salt

1 1/2 cups boneless chicken (white or dark meat or both) diced into 1/3-inch pieces

2 teaspoons cooking wine

1 1/2 cups onion cut into 1-inch cubes (1 jumbo onion)

2 cups canned button mushrooms, halved

2 cups green pepper cut into 1-inch squares

1 1/2 cups broccoli cut into 1-inch squares

1 1/2 cups canned chunk pineapple cut into 1-inch cubes

1 1/2 cups diced water chestnuts (fresh or canned)

1/4 cup chicken broth

2 teaspoons sugar

2 teaspoons oyster sauce

1 teaspoon thin soy sauce (Chinese light soy sauce)

1 teaspoon Tabasco sauce

4 teaspoons hoisin sauce

4 teaspoons cornstarch mixed with 1/4 cup water

1. Heat a wok or large frying pan over medium-high heat and add oil, then garlic and salt. Stir-fry for 20 seconds to season the oil. Add the chicken and stir-fry for 2 minutes.

2. Add wine and stir-fry 10 seconds; then add onion, mushrooms, green pepper, broccoli, pineapple, and water chestnuts and stir together.

3. Add the chicken broth, sugar, oyster sauce, soy sauce, Tabasco, and hoisin sauce. Mix together and stir-fry for 20 seconds. Cover the pan to cook for about 3 minutes. Remove lid, stir cornstarch mixture, and add to pan, stirring to cook and blend for about 20 seconds. Remove from heat and serve hot.

Chicken Chow Mein

Wing Ying Huie's Chinese Lantern
Serves 2

2 teaspoons vegetable oil

1 teaspoon garlic, ground or minced

1/2 teaspoon salt

1 cup chicken breast cut into 1/4-inch by 1/2-inch by 1-inch pieces

1 teaspoon cooking wine

1 medium-size stalk celery, shredded into strips 1 1/2 inches long

1/2 cup sliced water chestnuts

1 cup canned button mushrooms, halved

1/4 cup chicken broth

20 snow pea pods, stems and strings removed

1 cup fresh bean sprouts

1/2 teaspoon sugar

1/2 teaspoon sesame oil

1 teaspoon oyster sauce

2 teaspoons Chinese light soy sauce

4 teaspoons cornstarch combined with 1/4 cup water

1 1/2 cups chow mein noodles

1. Heat a large skillet or wok over medium-high heat. Coat with oil and add garlic and salt. Stir-fry for 10 seconds to season the oil. Add the chicken and stir-fry for 2 minutes. Add cooking wine and stir for 10 seconds.

2. Add celery, water chestnuts, mushrooms, and chicken broth. Mix well; cover and cook for 4 minutes.

3. Add pea pods and bean sprouts; stir for 10 seconds. Cover and cook for 40 seconds. Add sugar, sesame oil, oyster sauce, and soy sauce and stir-fry for 10 seconds. Stir the cornstarch mixture and add it to the pan, stirring for another 20 seconds or until sauce is no longer cloudy. Serve hot over chow mein noodles.

Marvel and Stanley Chong, 1975.

Chinese Food Takes on New Dimensions

As the Chinese population grew in Minnesota, so did the number of restaurants serving Chinese food. Getting supplies for this expanding market continued to be a problem because so many ingredients had to be imported from the West Coast or directly from China. Stanley Chong recognized this business opportunity when he moved to Minneapolis from Yakima, Washington, in 1934 to further his education. To earn some money and to supply food and other cooking needs to local restaurants, Chong created the International House of Foods. After serving in the U.S. Army in World War II, he expanded the company into a nationwide Chinese food mail-order service, and by 1961 it was believed to be the largest such business in the country.

Along with his wife, Marvel, Stanley Chong operated the International House of Foods near the University of Minnesota's Minneapolis campus. The only store in the area to carry Chinese food items, it became a favorite place for Chinese students. The husband and wife team also created a line of frozen products called Marvel Foods and produced the first frozen Chinese chow mein sold throughout the Midwest, along with frozen fried rice. The firm also produced more fortune cookies annually than any bakery outside the East and West coasts.

The Chongs offered cooking classes at their production plant, which operated on Nicollet Island in Minneapolis until 1981, when a fire destroyed the building. After they retired, Stanley continued as a leader in a number of community organizations, including the Shriners and the Chinese American Association of Minnesota. Marvel passed away in 2003, and three years later Stanley died. In 2007, Stanley Chong was posthumously named a Chinese Minnesotan of Note by the Chinese Heritage Foundation.

Marvel Chong's Chinese and International Cooking School offered a series of five classes for twenty-five dollars. Teachers were Stanley and Marvel as well as Lolita Woo, from John's Place. A 1978 flyer instructed students to "bring a 2 1/2–5 pound whole raw chicken" to a class on boning chicken. Other lessons featured shu my, Mongolian hot pot, pressed duck, and lotus root chop suey, to name just a few.

The Chongs' daughter Siu-Linn recalled that early offerings attracted about ten students, but when the numbers increased to fifty or sixty per class they limited registrations to twenty-four students. Siu-Linn later offered Chinese cooking classes at the Creative Learning Center in Richfield, where she taught for twenty-one years. When she decided to move to Iowa, she convinced a local seamstress, Leeann Chin, to continue the program.

The Italian Bean Sprout King

Settlers from Asia brought to Minnesota some of their favorite foods, including mung bean sprouts. The sprouts grow indoors, mature in five days, provide continuing crops throughout the year, and are used in many Asian dishes. But mung bean sprouts do not grow from soybeans, something Jeno Paulucci learned the hard way.

It was the early 1940s, and Jeno was traveling the Midwest selling wholesale garlic and looking for a business to start on his own. The son of Italian immigrants living on the Iron Range in northern Minnesota, Jeno began peddling at an early age, first selling iron ore samples to tourists, then working as a produce hawker outside a grocery store, and later serving as a traveling salesman out of Duluth.

While on a sales trip to Minneapolis, he happened to see a group of Japanese American farmers raising bean sprouts in hydroponic gardens. It seemed simple enough to Jeno to take the beans, put them in tubs that had holes in the bottoms, and constantly add water for germination. After only a few days, the beans would sprout and be ready for market. Since the process could be repeated again and again, the result was an ongoing cash crop.

On his return to Duluth, Jeno got a tub, punched a few holes in it, and added some beans, but nothing happened. He had used mature soybeans instead of mung beans, and the result was nothing but smelly, rotting beans. Realizing his mistake, he tried mung beans and found success. Now he needed money to start the business. Duluth banks were not very eager to lend an Italian from the Iron Range $2,500 to start a bean sprout business. Finally an Italian food broker, Antonia Papa, advanced him the money, and soon Jeno and partner Dave Persha were growing bean sprouts in the back of Persha's food store. They began selling their Shantung brand bean sprouts to East Coast food processors, who packed them in jars to sell to the public. Shantung was the first commercial bean sprout producer in the country, and by the time semi-trucks were backing up to their loading docks to handle the volume of shipments, Jeno knew he wanted to process the sprouts himself in order to grow their business even bigger.

After several false starts, the partners began canning sprouts, soon outgrew their original location, and opened a processing plant outside of Duluth. To develop their line, they began to mix in celery, pimientos, and other items that could be used to make chop suey, tagging these products with the Foo Young brand name. When they expanded into canned chow mein, Jeno asked his mother, Michelina, a native of Italy, to help liven up the flavor and she did, with garlic and her favorite seasonings. Soon the brand was changed to Chun King and became popular throughout the United States; the business was so successful that in 1966 Jeno sold the company to R. J. Reynolds Tobacco Company for $63 million. He went on to create a variety of other food businesses, including Jeno's Pizza Rolls. He tells his story in an autobiography written with Les Rich in 1969 entitled *HOW (it was) to MAKE $100,000,000 IN A HURRY* and in an expanded version in 2005, *Jeno: The Power of the Peddler.*

Bean Sprout Salad

Florence Lin

Adapted by ACAI

Serves 4–6

1 pound fresh mung bean sprouts, rinsed and drained	1 tablespoon rice wine vinegar
1/2 teaspoon salt	1 teaspoon sesame oil (roasted oil)
1 teaspoon sugar	hot pepper oil to taste, optional
1 tablespoon Chinese light soy sauce	

1. Discard any browned or limp sprouts. Place sprouts in a colander and pour boiling water over to blanch, stirring or shaking colander to reach every sprout. Immediately plunge sprouts into a bowl of ice water. Drain sprouts and dry with paper towels. Place in a bowl.

2. In a separate small bowl combine salt, sugar, soy sauce, vinegar, sesame oil, and hot pepper oil (if using) and mix well. Pour dressing over bean sprouts, tossing well to coat. Serve immediately.

United Noodles Reflects Changing Times

When Teddy Wong, Herb Wong, and Ramon Tan opened United Noodles in 1972, they made chow mein noodles and grew bean sprouts for the expanding Chinese restaurant market. But it wasn't long before the partners began seeing changes in the Twin Cities food climate.

I met with Teddy Wong in 1994 to talk about Minnesota's everchanging Asian food industry. As we sat in his Roseville restaurant, House of Wong, the noontime crowd ordered everything from chow mein to Szechuan stir-fries to burgers and sodas. He recalled the early days of United Noodles: "We were seeing Vietnamese, Cambodian, Laotian, and then Hmong refugees coming in [to the area], and with them a de-

mand for Asian markets carrying their native foods."
So in 1976 they sold the noodle business to Everfresh
Food and United Noodles became Everfresh's sole
distributor of chow mein noodles in the Twin Cities.
United Noodles also discontinued the bean sprout
operation, and in 1983 sold the wholesale division to
H. Brooks. Partner Tan moved to H. Brooks for four
years to help grow their Asian division while continu-
ing his role with United Noodles. For many years
United Noodles was the only distributor of Asian food
to American grocery stores in the area.

A native of Fargo, North Dakota, Teddy Wong moved
to the Twin Cities, opened the restaurant in 1957,
and regularly traveled to China on business. "Tastes
are changing," he commented as he looked around his
busy restaurant. Originally diners came for House of
Wong's chow mein, chop suey, fried rice, and a few
American dishes. "Now they are looking for stir-fries
and exotic tastes," he added. "People today are better
educated about food," and they are enjoying greater
options in Asian foods than ever before. — PLH

United Noodles focused on this expanding market by
importing a wider variety of foods from many Asian
countries and by finding domestic growers for fresh
Asian ingredients. In 1980 it was relocated to its own
building at 2015 East Twenty-fourth Street in Minneapolis. Despite two recessions and a damaging tornado in
1981, United Noodles continued to grow. The operation
expanded several times and eventually added a meat
department, a takeout deli in 2006, and then an area
for in-store dining. In 2007 the deli was featured on
Rachael Ray's television show *Tasty Travels*. In 2011 the
deli added a Japanese section offering sushi and other
popular dishes.

In 2005 Teddy Wong sold his shares in United Noodles
to Ramon and his new partner Alice Fung. Through
their leadership the company continues to respond to
the everchanging market. Today, customers come from
all areas of the community, not just the Asian sectors,
and from all areas of the state.

Huang Lanh Duong surrounded by only a few of the herbs and
products available at Truong Thanh. She holds a photograph of her
father, Xuong Mau Duong.

Chinese Herbalist Comes to Minneapolis

Living in Minnesota is usually by choice, but sometimes
it is by chance. Such was the case for Xuong Mau Duong
in 1979 when he and his family were sent to Minnesota
from a Malaysian refugee camp. It was the final destination on a journey that had started in 1948.

A native of China, after World War II Xuong fled with
his family to Vietnam, where they operated a successful
food and herb store for thirty years. When the conflict
in Vietnam again forced them to move, they escaped by
sailing over the treacherous South China Sea to Malaysia. There Xuong and his family lived in a refugee camp
for nearly a year, until a Minneapolis Catholic church
sponsored their relocation to Minnesota.

Xuong had been a successful herbalist in China and Vietnam, but in Minnesota there were no opportunities to continue his trade, so he and his wife went to work for the Leamington Hotel. His eldest daughter, Huang Lanh Duong, and her siblings also found jobs to help support the family and work toward opening their own business. By 1988, Xuong and Huang Lanh were able to open a small store on Fifteenth Street off Nicollet Avenue in Minneapolis, once again providing the special ingredients and herbs his customers sought. While other stores carried Asian herbs, Xuong was believed to be the state's first commercial Chinese herbalist.

Truong Thanh (Great Wall) also offered a wide assortment of fresh produce, canned goods, dried ingredients, fish, and other items for Asian cooking. But the predominant wares were the two to three hundred Asian herbs stored in jars, plastic containers, and wooden drawers at the front of the store. Customers would meet with Xuong, describe their needs or bring in their lists, and take home a square of paper folded around a combination of herbs to be steeped into a soothing broth.

In 1993, Truong Thanh moved to a larger space at 2520 Nicollet Avenue. Xuong and Huang Lanh were able to expand the number of Asian items they offered, and the store became a reliable source for fresh water chestnuts, live crabs, Shanghai bok choy, lotus root, tree ears, and hundreds of other items necessary for traditional Asian cooking and, of course, a large selection of herbs. When Xuong died in 1998, Huang Lanh Duong continued to operate the business, and her son Thang Nguyan and daughter Thien Nguyan also helped in the store. Another daughter, Christina Nguyan Le, opened Lake Wine and Spirits in Minneapolis and St. Paul.

While Truong Thanh carries frozen periwinkle meat, once in a while it will receive a box of these tiny fresh snails. Popular in England and Asia, this mini version of escargot is delicious with a black bean dipping sauce. A word of caution: cook the periwinkles until they come out of their shells; otherwise, they are still inside and very much alive.

Periwinkles with Black Bean Sauce / Chao Luo Si

Florence Lin

Adapted by ACAI

Serves 4–8

1 pound periwinkles (choose the ones that appear to be moving)

2 teaspoons black beans, rinsed in water to remove salt

1 clove garlic, minced

1 small fresh chili, seeds removed, sliced into thin rings

1/4 cup water mixed with 1 teaspoon cornstarch

2 teaspoons sugar

2 teaspoons brown bean sauce

Additional Ingredients:

2 teaspoons oyster sauce

1 teaspoon Chinese light soy sauce

1 teaspoon sesame oil

2 tablespoons corn or peanut oil

3/4 cup chicken broth

1/4 cup dry sherry

1. Wash the periwinkles in cold water several times, drain, and set aside.

2. Combine black beans with garlic and chili slices by briefly mashing together. Set aside.

3. In another bowl mix the water and cornstarch until blended and add sugar, bean sauce, oyster sauce, soy sauce, and sesame oil. Mix well. Set aside.

4. Heat a wok or saucepan over medium heat, add corn or peanut oil and then the black bean–chili mixture, and stir-fry for 30 seconds. Add the broth and sherry and bring to a boil. Add the periwinkles and return to a boil. Cover pan and let cook for about 1 minute, until periwinkles come out of their shells. Using a slotted spoon, remove the periwinkles to a serving bowl, leaving the liquid in the pan.

5. Continue simmering the liquid over medium heat. Add the sauce, stirring constantly until it thickens and forms a glaze on the spoon. Pour sauce into individual dipping bowls or cups to serve with periwinkles.

Notes: Each diner holds the periwinkle by its shell and uses a pointed bamboo skewer or toothpick to pull out the cooked meat, dipping it into the sauce before eating. The sauce is also good with fresh small or large clams that have been baked in a 400° oven for about 5 minutes or until they open.

Fortune Cookies: More Than Little Treats with Prophecies

"Fortune cookies bring much success." The phrase could be a fortune that came true for Kwan Shu-Sun (Sunny) and his wife, Pauline. Natives of Hong Kong, they moved to Canada in 1974 and initially worked in his family's baking business. In 1979 they relocated to Chicago, where the Keefer Bakery originated. In 1982 they moved to Minneapolis, and the following year the family opened Minnesota's first Chinese bakery, at Riverside and Cedar avenues. Keefer Court Foods offered traditional Chinese treats, including almond cookies, baked buns, moon cakes—and fortune cookies.

At the bakery in 1993, Sunny demonstrated the mostly hand-operated machine turning out about five thousand fortune-filled cookies a day. It took a request from McDonald's for eleven million fortune cookies to push Sunny into expanding his operation. Clearly he could not fill the order in the required three months, and he went looking for an automated machine. When he could not raise the $250,000 to buy the piece of equipment, he took the order anyway and subcontracted it to a number of bakeries around the country. As it turned out, McDonald's ordered fifty-six million fortune cookies to promote its Shanghai Chicken McNuggets. This high-profile order inspired Sunny to find other promotional contracts, and with them in hand he was able to secure bank financing for his own automated fortune cookie maker. In 1995, he built a separate building to house the fortune cookie operation.

One of his first contracts was from Leeann Chin: 140,000 cookies containing special coupons for a summer-long campaign for free food or beverages at

Sunny and Pauline Kwan in their Keefer Court Foods bakery and café.

Leeann Chin locations and a chance to enter a free drawing to win a trip to China. The cookies were a huge success, generating twenty thousand repeat customers for the restaurant chain. This contract led to a continuing flow of orders for Sunny to make cookies for special promotions and events. "We make green fortune cookies for St. Patrick's Day," he admitted, "with shamrock-decorated fortunes," and even special cookies for political campaigns and a wide variety of businesses. In fact, the fortune cookie volume grew so large that Sunny added another automated cookie baker and was able to produce more than half a million fortune cookies a week. While fortune cookies are an American invention, they became popular in China in 1985, and initially Sunny exported his Golden Plaque fortune cookies to Hong Kong. Today, KC Fortune Cookies are sold throughout the nation and world, with orders shipped to London, Switzerland, and Canada.

With the fortune factory working in its own separate building, Pauline operates the bakery and café, drawing customers from the nearby University of Minnesota campus for noodle soups, congee, roast duck, barbecue pork buns, almond cookies, coconut rolls, wintermelon cookies, lotus pastry, buttercream cones, custard tarts, and moon cakes—just a few of the foods made at Keefer each day.

MOON FESTIVAL '95

Moon cakes are a Chinese tradition during the Moon Festival, celebrated on the fifteenth day of the eighth lunar month, usually in September but sometimes in October. According to legend, the jade rabbit and the three-legged toad live on the moon. Others say it is home to the beautiful fairy Change E, her pet jade rabbit, and a woodcutter named Wu Gang. Why and how they got there seems to differ; nevertheless, once a year the Chinese pay tribute to them and to the moon with symbolic food such as moon cakes.

Pauline continues to make moon cakes by hand. First she mixes the outside dough, stretching it around a special filling wrapped around a hard-boiled egg yolk. She pushes the filled cake into a mold to make the moon cake shape and then quickly taps it out onto the baking sheet. Her molds were carved in Hong Kong and leave the imprint of Chinese symbols representing the name of the bakery, the type of filling, and the Moon Festival symbol. The cakes are made year-round, but during the Moon Festival the bakery turns out about two thousand to meet customer demands.

Another popular item at Keefer Court Foods is house-made roast duck. Traditionally in China bakeries roasted ducks and pigs because many homes did not have ovens. Keefer also makes barbecued pork to fill their baked buns and sells the pork for takeout.

Building a Multimillion-Dollar Business One Wok at a Time

A seamstress from Canton (Guangzhou) China moved to Minneapolis in 1956 and built a multimillion-dollar company by cooking. She spoke no English, had learned the food business by working in her parents' grocery store, raised five children, and became one of the best-known entrepreneurs in Minnesota.

While Leeann Chin's story may seem like a fairy tale, it was anything but. Wai-Hing (Leeann's Chinese name) first met Tony Chin when she was seventeen and her parents sent her to Hong Kong for a prearranged marriage. She married Tony and had their first child, Linda; then he moved the family to Minneapolis, where he first worked in his sister's restaurant, the Canton, and later at the University of Minnesota's photo lab. As her family grew to also include Bill, Laura, Jean, and Katie, Leeann learned English and used her skills as a seamstress to take in sewing and handle alterations for upscale fashion stores.

As her clientele expanded, she began cooking special Chinese dishes for them and was soon catering Chinese food for their parties. A few of her customers approached her to open a restaurant, and with their backing (and a second mortgage on her house), in 1980 she opened the first Leeann Chin Chinese Restaurant, in the Ridgedale Bonaventure shopping mall in Minnetonka. "I didn't start the company to have a big business or to make lots of money," she once said. "I started the business because I wanted to have a good job and because my husband thought I couldn't do it!"

Her daughter Laura, recently graduated with a degree in sociology, pitched in to help her mother launch the new restaurant. Laura had also been working part time with her mother in Leeann Chin's catering business, so the transition was natural. She recalled that Leeann wanted to take the dishes her catering clients liked best and offer them on a full menu in an upscale restaurant. The location was considered a risk because it was still in the "country," not far from Wayzata on busy Highway 12. To add to the

Moon cakes with bean paste filling from Keefer Court Foods.

ambience and perhaps attract more crowds, they created menu covers out of ultrasuede and stitched the Leeann Chin logo on each. They had a calligrapher print each of the hundred menu items and then used cording to tie the paper menus into the covers. They also sewed matching ultrasuede aprons for the waitstaff.

"We spent at least a week before the opening to prep enough food for the first week of business," Laura recalled. Their selections included Cantonese classics such as whole steamed fish and other items popular with their catering clientele. "So we opened the doors that first night and in one hour we ran out of food," Laura exclaimed. "We were in shock! We had to turn people away, and when we finally locked the doors Mother decided right then to set up a buffet for the second night." While many people had warned Leann Chin about how bad the business could be, no one told her how to handle too much business.

They worked through the night to prep food for the rest of the week. They opened the second night with the first Leeann Chin signature buffet and still offered to cook special dishes off the menu. But once again they ran out of food in an hour. And there were only two requests off the menu—the rest were buffet orders. It took them a week to finally gauge the right amount of food and to learn that the buffet was the star of the show. "My daughter and I were working eighteen hours a day, day after day, to get all the work done," Leeann recalled. "There were times when I was cooking with three woks at a time just to keep up with the orders."

Several people in the industry, including her sister-in-law, told her the restaurant would not last a year, but by the end of that first year, sales in her small, eighty-seat restaurant totaled $1.3 million. It was so successful that Leeann bought out her investors and struck out on her own. She added restaurants at the Union Depot in St. Paul and in the International Centre in downtown Minneapolis. Her signature Chinese buffet fed the crowds of diners quickly and efficiently. And while the food was not the traditional dishes she had cooked in China, it was clearly what the market wanted. In 1985, she sold her growing chain to

Leeann Chin restaurant in Golden Valley, just one of more than forty in several states.

General Mills, but when the food giant did not build on her operation, she bought it back three years later. She expanded again and restructured six times, always keeping her vision in sight until there were fifty-two Leeann Chin locations in four states—Minnesota, Wisconsin, Kansas, and Washington. Among them was a carryout service in Dayton's Department Store and in each Byerly's food store. In 1994, she started Leeann Chin carryout operations in Seattle and the following year, in Eden Prairie and Burnsville, Minnesota, opened Asia Grille by Leeann Chin, featuring the cuisine of several Asian countries. Leeann once said she originally wanted a partner in the business "so I would have someone to talk to"; later, when she had silent partners, she reported, "they weren't always so silent!"

The public voted the Leeann Chin restaurants Best Restaurant, Best Fast Food, Best Takeout, Best Ethnic Food, a Top 50 Twin Cities Restaurant, and Best Chinese Food year after year. In 1986, Leeann was elected to the Minnesota Business Hall of Fame. In 1988, she was named Business Woman of the Year by the Minnesota Chapter of Women Business Owners and also declared a Minnesota Woman of Distinction. In 1993, she was the first woman to receive the Minnesota Entrepreneur of the Year award.

Leeann Chin created a foundation to help support the arts, children's causes, and Chinese American organizations. In 1995, Laura Chin left the company to manage the foundation; she and her husband, David, a business consultant, were also raising their three children, Logan, Katie, and Griffin.

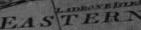

Leeann and Katie Chin.

Before her death in 2010, Leeann had closed Asia Grille and had sold the Leeann Chin operation to a group of investors and was no longer active in its management. But, according to Laura, she still had plans to write another cookbook or two and maybe even try another venture.

Leeann Chin was, perhaps, the single most important person in Minnesota to promote the enjoyment of Asian food throughout the region. She was an outstanding example of how a woman from a traditional Chinese family could turn the American dream into a reality. She did it through talent, hard work, enthusiasm, determination, and, most of all, grace.

In 1981, Leeann Chin wrote *Betty Crocker's Chinese Cookbook*, which by 2001 had more than 500,000 copies in print worldwide. In 2000 with her daughter Katie Chin, she wrote *Everyday Chinese Cooking* for families to share the fun of cooking Chinese food at home. Leeann once told me her favorite part of the business was teaching. She initially gave Chinese cooking classes in her home and then in community centers. Over the years she trained hundreds of Leeann Chin employees and occasionally taught home cooks at Byerly's School of Culinary Arts in St. Louis Park. There, this talented, energetic woman explained the techniques for creating traditional Chinese food—something she truly loved. In this type of setting, her exceptional cooking skills could be most appreciated. She gave me permission to reprint her recipes from that class, and we have adapted two for this book. When a student asked how

difficult the dumplings were to make, she replied, "It is a recipe I often make when my grandchildren come to visit because they have so much fun helping me."

Leeann Chin's Shrimp and Cilantro Dumplings

Adapted by ACAI

Makes 40 dumplings

1 pound raw shrimp, shells removed	1 teaspoon sugar
	1/4 teaspoon white pepper
2 ounces fresh cilantro (see note)	1 teaspoon sesame oil
	2 teaspoons cornstarch
1/2 teaspoon salt	1 egg white

For the skins:

1 pound wonton skins	1/2 cup water—1 tablespoon at a time
1 egg white, lightly beaten	
4 teaspoons vegetable oil	Chinese light soy sauce for dipping

1. Make a shallow cut lengthwise down the back of each shrimp and wash out vein. Pat shrimp dry with paper towels. Chop shrimp.

2. Wash cilantro and dry. Remove leaves from stems and discard stems. Chop cilantro leaves. (If you prefer, pulse shrimp and cilantro together in food processor.)

3. In a medium bowl, combine shrimp, cilantro, salt, sugar, white pepper, sesame oil, cornstarch, and 1 egg white, mixing well.

4. Cut off corners of wonton skins to form circles. Place 1 teaspoon filling in center of circle. Brush egg white along wonton's edge. Fold over to form a half circle and press edges together. Repeat with remaining wontons and filling, setting aside dumplings as you work and covering with a damp towel to prevent them from drying out. (Dumplings may be frozen at this stage; thaw to room temperature before cooking.)

5. Preheat oven to 200°. Place a large, nonstick frying pan over high heat. Add 1 teaspoon vegetable oil and reduce heat to medium low. Add about 10 dumplings to the pan; do not crowd. Fry and turn 2 or 3 times until both sides are brown. Add 1 tablespoon

water, cover, and cook 1 minute to steam. Remove cover and continue to cook until water is fully absorbed. Remove dumplings from pan and keep warm in the oven until serving. Repeat with remaining dumplings. Serve with soy sauce in dipping bowls or cups for each diner.

Note: Use less cilantro if desired. If you prefer, substitute scallions for the cilantro.

Leeann Chin's Stir-Fry Chicken with Mango

Adapted by ACAI

Serves 6–8

Chicken Marinade:

1/2 teaspoon salt

1/8 teaspoon white pepper

1 teaspoon finely chopped ginger

1 egg white

Sauce:

2 tablespoons white wine

1 teaspoon minced garlic

4 tablespoons ketchup

2 teaspoons red pepper sauce

2 teaspoons sugar

1 teaspoon Chinese light soy sauce

1 large, ripe mango, or substitute papaya or 1 cup canned pineapple chunks

1 green pepper

2 tablespoons flour

2 tablespoons cornstarch

2 teaspoons vegetable oil

steamed rice

1. Trim any fat from the chicken and cut into 2 by 1/2–inch strips. In a bowl mix chicken with salt, white pepper, ginger, and egg white. Cover and refrigerate 20 minutes.

2. In a separate bowl, combine wine, garlic, ketchup, red pepper sauce, sugar, and soy sauce.

3. Peel mango and cut the outside fruit layer into 2 by 1/4–inch strips. Discard the center seed core. Place mango strips in hot water to remove some of the juice and make cooking faster.

4. Remove the seed core and membranes from green pepper and cut pepper into 2 by 2 1/2–inch strips.

5. Mix together flour and cornstarch and coat the marinated chicken to help keep the juices in the chicken during cooking. Set aside.

6. Heat a large nonstick skillet over medium heat. Add vegetable oil to coat the pan. Separate chicken pieces and add to the pan. Stir and separate the chicken pieces, turning the pieces until they turn white and are cooked through. Add green pepper and mix well, then add the sauce mixture. Stir well and bring to a simmer. Cover and cook 1 minute.

7. Drain the mango slices and add them to the chicken mixture. Stir well to heat the mango, but do not cook it. Remove to a heated serving platter. Serve with steamed rice.

David Fong Brings Chinese Food to Bloomington

After World War II, the core cities of Minneapolis and St. Paul became surrounded by rings of suburbs where developers were building small homes especially popular with returning veterans. Richfield, just across the city line from Minneapolis, was one of the first to feel this expansion, followed by Bloomington, the next ring. It was in this suburb that David Fong just happened to build his business.

David Fong had a couple of surprises when he moved to Minneapolis from Canton, China, in 1949. The fourteen-year-old came to live with his family above his father's restaurant, Moy's Café at Broadway and Bryant Avenue in Northeast Minneapolis. The first surprise was his American name, David Fong, when his family name was Moy. (His father changed it to Fong, the name of his American employer.) The second came on David's first

Above: Helen and David Fong at the 2006 awards banquet in Los Angeles, where they received their second Top 100 Chinese Restaurants award.

Three generations of Fongs participate in the "Opening of the Eyes of the New Lion" ceremony before the traditional New Year Lion Dance. Left to right: David, Edward, and Christopher Fong, 2008.

morning in America. When he walked into the restaurant, his father handed him an apron and informed him he was the new dishwasher. Thus began a sixty-three-year career in the restaurant business.

David also continued his education at Franklin Junior High, where one teacher, seeing he needed help with his English, volunteered to work with him daily after school—just one of the many people David found so helpful and encouraging along the way. At the end of ninth grade, the students and faculty voted him the school's "Best All-Around Boy," an honor that came with his photograph in the *Star Tribune* newspaper and a scholarship from the American Legion. He was also elected a class officer and named a member of the National Junior Honor Society.

He wouldn't put the scholarship to use until after finishing high school, serving in the army, and then enrolling in Dunwoody Institute for a career in drafting. After graduation he was offered a position at Honeywell and was about to start his new career when his father became ill and David set aside his own plans to manage the family restaurant. By 1958, David had married Helen Wong and they were raising their first child, Edward. Instead of a career in drafting, David decided to stay in the family business and started looking for a location to launch a new restaurant. When he and Helen heard about a space available in Richfield, they drove out to the suburb but missed a turn and wound up in Bloomington. There they found a vacancy in a small strip mall on Ninety-eighth and Lyndale Avenue South, where they opened Bloomington's first Chinese takeout restaurant.

At the time, Bloomington was still a village, just starting to expand with the housing boom. It did not become a city until two years later, eventually growing to ninety thousand residents. David recalls he and Helen opened the doors to David Fong's Chinese Takeout Restaurant on a Thursday. They had prepared enough chow mein and fried rice to handle their first day, but they sold only one order. Friday was the same, and so were Saturday and Sunday. By the end of the first week, their sales totaled

forty dollars. But soon word spread and slowly customers started to come—and kept coming back. On the restaurant's first anniversary the Fongs were able to donate a thousand dollars to the Bloomington Athletic Association, the first of many local organizations they supported over the years. The *Sun* newspaper ran an article on the Fongs and their restaurant, which helped boost sales—and also attracted eight competitors, who soon opened their own Chinese takeout restaurants in Bloomington.

David and his family continued to support youth activities, business associations, and community organizations. In fact, their restaurant walls are filled with proclamations, newspaper articles, volunteer awards, and contribution acknowledgment plaques, along with hundreds of photos depicting many of the events they have been involved in.

The original takeout menu was limited to chow mein and fried rice, but David wanted to offer more variety. After a few years, he went looking for a larger location and found one not far away, on Ninety-third and Lyndale. Soon David was using his drafting skills to help design the current David Fong's building; he opened the new restaurant in 1966. He offered more Cantonese dishes, added a selection of the American "meat and potato" entrees so popular with suburban families, and kept some of his customers' favorite chow mein, plus he had room to host meetings of community organizations. David Fong's also provides banquet service for everything from company parties to weddings to anniversaries to celebrations of all kinds.

David, his wife, Helen, and their six children were the first Chinese family to live in Bloomington. David became active in several city organizations, and for many years the Bloomington Lion's Club and a local business group chose David Fong's restaurant to hold their regular meetings. In 2005, David Fong was among the first eight people elected to the Minnesota Hospitality Hall of Fame. In 2006, the restaurant received the first of its Top 100 Chinese Restaurant awards from *Chinese Restaurant News*, followed by its second in 2007. The newspaper annually selects top locations from the forty-one thousand Chinese restaurants across the United States.

The Fongs also created an annual tradition of presenting the colorful Lion Dance for diners celebrating the Chinese New Year. Various members of the Fong family don the two-person costume and wind their way through the dinner tables in rhythm to the beating drums—part of their effort to help keep Chinese traditions alive in the heart of the Midwest.

Many of David's children also followed in the restaurant business. Donald and Barbara worked at David Fong's along with Edward, who became president of the Bloomington restaurant. Daughter Cindy and her husband, Leo Le, opened Fong's Restaurant and Bar in Prior Lake. Son David, Jr., and daughter Amy opened D Fong's Chinese Cuisine in Savage. And in 2008, the whole family celebrated the original restaurant's fiftieth anniversary with special events during October's Moon Festival. Edward continues to reach out to the community through his own volunteer activities, including offering cooking classes for high school students. His youngest son, Daniel, is now a manager at David Fong's Chinese Restaurant, continuing the Fong (Moy) family restaurant tradition to the fourth generation.

David credits his success, in part, to the many people who have helped him along the way, from that encouraging junior high school teacher to the loyal staff at the restaurant to his wife, Helen, and his family and the people of Bloomington. David has retired from the day-to-day restaurant operations, but Edward says his dad is still the company's best public relations person. While David kept the Fong name long after he might have changed it back to Moy, he did add "Moy" in Chinese characters right in the center of the restaurant's placemats.

After fifty-four years, the menu at David Fong's continues to be part Cantonese, part American Chinese, and part American. To this day, some of the regular customers never eat the American food, some never try the Chinese food, and at business meetings the menus are still half Chinese and half American. Edward points out, "we prepare Chinese dishes using local food just as they do in all parts of China." In fact, he adds, "some of the recipes come from my grandfather." Here are two of David Fong's Chinese Restaurant's most popular dishes.

Placemat from David Fong's.

Chicken Almond Ding

David Fong's

Serves 4

2 tablespoons vegetable oil

1 teaspoon minced garlic

1 teaspoon salt

1 pound boneless chicken (white or dark meat or both), diced

4 cups diced celery

1/4 cup sliced mushrooms

1/4 cup diced bamboo shoots

1/4 cup diced water chestnuts

1/4 cup dry white wine

2–3 cups chicken broth or stock

1 cup diced pea pods

pinch white pepper

1/4 cup cornstarch mixed with 1/4 cup water

1/4 cup whole skinless roasted almonds

steamed white rice

1. In a wok or large skillet, heat oil over medium-high heat and add garlic and salt. Stir-fry for 10 seconds.

2. Add the chicken and stir-fry until slightly brown. Add celery, mushrooms, bamboo shoots, and water chestnuts and mix together. Add the wine and broth or stock. Bring mixture to a boil and simmer until celery is tender, about 7 minutes.

3. Add pea pods and season with white pepper, then stir to blend. Stir cornstarch mixture to blend and then add to pan and cook a few minutes, stirring, until sauce is no longer cloudy. Garnish with roasted almonds and serve hot with steamed white rice.

David Fong's chow mein is one of the dishes that kept people coming back for more, decade after decade. Even longtime customers who move out of the area continue to order Fong's Chow Mein by phone or fax and have it shipped to them. There are a number of chow mein recipes in this cookbook, each with its own character and flavor. This is the only one that uses both shrimp and chicken.

Fong's Chow Mein

Serves 4

2 tablespoons vegetable oil

1 teaspoon minced garlic

1 teaspoon salt

1/2 pound boneless, skin-less chicken breast, cut into 1/4-inch-wide strips

1/2 pound medium shrimp, peeled and deveined (about 16)

4 cups shredded celery

4 cups bean sprouts

1/2 cup sliced water chestnuts

1/4 cup dry white wine

2–3 cups chicken stock or broth

1 cup shredded pea pods

pinch white pepper

1/4 cup cornstarch mixed with 1/4 cup water

1 (6-ounce) package crispy chow mein noodles

steamed white rice

1. In a wok or large skillet, heat oil over medium-high heat and add garlic and salt. Stir-fry for 10 seconds.

2. Add the chicken and shrimp and stir-fry until slightly brown. Add celery, bean sprouts, and water chestnuts and mix together. Add the wine and broth or stock. Bring mixture to a boil and simmer until celery is tender, about 7 minutes.

3. Add pea pods and season with white pepper. Stir cornstarch mixture to blend and then add to the pan and cook, stirring, a few minutes until sauce is no longer cloudy. Serve hot over noodles with steamed white rice.

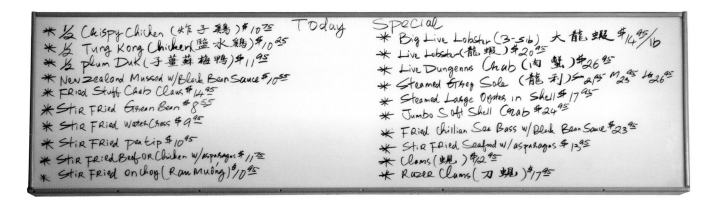

Today	Special
* ½ Crispy Chicken (炸子雞) $10⁷⁵	* Big Live Lobster (3-5lb) 大龍蝦 $14⁹⁵/lb
* ½ Tung Kong Chicken(鹽水雞) $10²⁵	* Live Lobster (龍蝦) $20⁹⁵
* ½ Plum Duk (子薑蘇梅鴨) $11⁹⁵	* Live Dungenns Crab (肉蟹) $26⁹⁵
* New Zealand Mussed w/ Black Bean Sauce $10⁵⁵	* Steamed Grey Sole (龍利) Sm 2⁹⁵ M 23⁹⁵ Lg 26⁹⁵
* Fried Stuff Chab Claws $14⁹⁵	* Steamed Large Oystes in Shell $17⁹⁵
* Stir Fried Green Bean $8⁵⁵	* Jumbo Soft Shell Crab $24⁹⁵
* Stir Fried Watercress $9⁹⁵	* Fried Chillian Sea Bass w/ Black Bean Sauce $23⁹⁵
* Stir Fried Pea tip $10⁹⁵	* Stir Fried Seafood w/ asparagus $13⁹⁵
* Stir Fried Beef OR Chicken w/ asparagus $11⁷⁵	* Clams (蜆) $12⁹⁵
* Stir Fried On Choy (Rau Muống) $10⁹⁵	* Razer Clams (刀蜆) $17⁹⁵

Chinese Menus Expand

The first Chinese restaurants in Minnesota offered an equal balance of chow mein, chop suey, beefsteak, pork chops, potatoes, and gravy. After World War II, as returning servicemen were looking for more "foreign" foods, Chinese restaurants began adding more traditional Chinese dishes. The John's Place menu of the 1950s was one-third "American" dishes, one-third chow mein/chop suey dishes, and one-third classical Chinese dishes. But the restaurants of the twenty-first century were required to expand even further to meet the growing demand for all aspects of Chinese cuisine.

Shuang Cheng, near the University of Minnesota campus in Minneapolis, is a good example of a small Chinese restaurant that created an extensive menu designed to draw diners from across the Twin Cities and its suburbs. Its clientele includes university students and faculty, Chinese families, businesspeople, and a whole host of diners looking for consistently good Chinese food. Its menu of more than three hundred dishes offers Cantonese, Szechuan, barbecue, hot pots, and a wide variety of seafood but does not include "American" entrees.

Shuang Cheng specializes in seafood, including shrimp, scallops, oysters, clams, crab, lobsters, squid, yellow fish, sole, and walleyed pike. One of its most popular dishes is

Deep Fried Walleyed Pike with Hot Meat Sauce—more than 140 served each week. Lobster dishes include Lobster Steamed with Black Bean Sauce, Ginger Sauce, or Five Spice Sauce, with more than 230 orders served each week. The menu board near the ceiling of the main dining room changes constantly to keep up with the fresh fish and vegetables of the day.

Above: Shuang Cheng's daily specials.

Right: Daniel Lam with a few of Shuang Cheng's many awards, including Mpls.St.Paul's *Best of the Twin Cities awards (Best Asian Spice and Best Walleye), City Search's 2003 Best Chinese Food Twin Cities, and 2010 Top 10 Best International.*

Daniel Lam is the driving force behind the restaurant's popularity. A native of Vietnam, Daniel learned about Cantonese cooking from his parents, starting in the restaurant business shortly after coming to the United States in 1979. In 1990 he took over the existing Shuang Cheng and created a restaurant often listed in top readers' choices; with the ever-growing clientele, he has had to expand the space several times.

His twelve-page menu features special luncheon and rice plates that provide a full meal on a limited budget, as well as a three-course Peking duck dinner for people seeking more exotic dining. One of his best appetizers is Fried Crispy Quail, and one of his more interesting hot pots is Oyster and Roast Pig with Ginger and Scallions. A favorite noodle dish is Pan Fried Noodles with Chicken and Vegetables in Black Bean Sauce. Of the hundreds of choices, only forty fall into the category of chow mein/chop suey/egg foo young.

Shuang Cheng's menu.

Dim Sum Comes to Town

Discovered in China about 3000 BCE, tea was supposed to be savored and enjoyed for its own special properties, not to be consumed with food. But teahouse owners decided that in order to encourage their customers to stay longer and spend more money, they would offer a menu of small food items—and dim sum was born.

By the 1970s, restaurants specializing in Chinese dim sum were easy to find in Chicago, New York, and San Francisco but more rare in other areas of the country. As Minnesota's diners were becoming more familiar with Chinese food, however, they were also looking for new and different versions of Chinese cooking. Dim sum was a welcome addition. In 1977, Reiko Weston added a major dim sum operation at her Chinese restaurant, Tiaga (see page 66).

By 1988, a few Chinese restaurants began offering dim sum menus from 10 AM to 2 PM on Saturdays and Sundays, drawing crowds of families and enthusiastic diners. The Yangtze Restaurant at Park Place and Highway 394 in St. Louis Park was one of the first in the Twin Cities to feature a dim sum menu of fifty to sixty different dishes, attracting long lines of diners every weekend. Carts filled with containers of freshly stir-fried, steamed, baked, or cooked dishes were pushed through the dining room, allowing customers to see the offerings and choose the ones they wanted to eat. The bill was based on the number of choices made.

Favorites on Yangtze's dim sum menu included Jiao Zi (dumplings filled with a variety of ingredients), Ha Gau (shrimp dumplings), Fung Zao (chicken feet), and Char Siu (spareribs in black bean sauce); the restaurant served more than a thousand dim sum orders each weekend day. Yangtze's dim sum received *Mpls. St. Paul* magazine's Best Brunch—Dim Sum award, and the restaurant earned City's Best in 2008 and was a City Search winner in 2010.

Yangtze Chinese Restaurant was established in 1982 by Andy Shun. A native of Shanghai, Shun moved to New York when he was twenty-one and worked in the Hunan restaurant in Chinatown. He became friends with the

Yangtze dim sum menu.

chef and moved to Minneapolis when the chef came to open the Empress restaurant in Yorktown shopping mall. A short time later Shun struck out on his own, in 1981 opening the Great Wall at Forty-fifth and France Avenue in Morningside, followed by Yangtze. He sold the Great Wall in 2011 and Yangtze in 2006 to Angela Diong, who is the primary chef.

Mongolian Barbeque Brings Age-Old Fast Food to Minnesota

Mongolian barbeque restaurants became a hit in Taiwan and Japan in the 1970s but did not arrive in Minnesota until 1988. Allegedly based on the method marauding Mongolian warriors used to cook their food on metal shields over a campfire, the four-foot-wide freestanding cast-iron grills (*gors*) offer a very high heat (585,000 BTU) for chefs to quickly stir-fry whatever ingredients the diner has chosen. A buffet filled with raw ingredients allows diners to compose their own entree and give their choices to the grill chef, who deftly stir-fries the selections on the smoking-hot gor, adding sauces and spices as needed. It is part show and part dining at a reasonable price. Similar to the Korean barbecue and the Japanese teppanyaki, the Mongolian barbeque also appeals to fans of the all-you-can-eat style of dining.

The first in Minnesota was Khan's Mongolian Barbeque, opened in 1988 by Mitch and Sherri Law in the Dinkytown area of Minneapolis—an immediate hit with University of Minnesota students and faculty. Sherri remembers the opening well. The first day "we served a hundred dinners," she recalled. At the time she was expecting a baby and working long hours in the restaurant. "I was so tired [at the end of the day] I could hardly make it home," she added. The restaurant became so popular that one hundred dinners turned out to be a slow day.

A graduate of the University of Nevada–Las Vegas hotel and restaurant program, Mitch Law had seen the Mongolian barbeque concept work in Asia and California and felt it would be a good fit for the Twin Cities. He was right. The Laws soon expanded their operation to locations in Roseville, Richfield, and Coon Rapids, closing the one in Dinkytown to concentrate on the suburban markets. By 1994, the Roseville restaurant was serving up to 430 diners in the space of four hours. Truly fast food!

With the assortment of ingredients available on the buffet, diners can create more than thirty different dishes. According to Sherri, some of their regular customers may go through the line three and four times. The first dish may be beef and peppers, the second curried chicken, the third lo mein, and the fourth chow mein. She noted that even people who do not like Chinese food seem to find combinations that appeal to them.

An excellent book on Mongolian cooking by London author Marc Cramer was published in 2001. His *Imperial Mongolian Cooking* tackles the enormous task of explaining the food of the Mongol Empire between the twelfth and sixteenth centuries. The massive empire covered two dozen countries, from China, Korea, and Vietnam on the east to Russia, Turkey, and Poland on the west. Mongolia is a landlocked country bordered by Siberia and China and today has 2.735 million inhabitants.

The grandson of a restaurateur with Russo-Mongolian heritage, Cramer created a collection of recipes that runs the gamut from eggplant caviar and shashlyk to Mongolian hot pots and barbeques. His shashlyk is the Russian adaptation of a basic Mongolian dish that marinates meat, grills it, and then serves it over rice with plum sauce. Cramer indicates this style of cooking was so important that Mongolian hunters would carry the marinade with them until they could find an animal to kill, marinate, and cook over a fire pit.

China

23

Besides grilled Mongolian cooking, another aspect of this cuisine popular with Minnesota diners is the Mongolian Fire Pot, also known as a hot pot. Available on a number of Chinese restaurant menus including Shuang Cheng's, it is basically a fondue with broth. Chicken, beef, or lamb broth is brought to the table in a special fire pot or in a heatproof pot on an electric burner, where it simmers throughout the meal while various ingredients are cooked in it. Starting with paper-thin slices of meat and/or seafood, diners first dip the raw meat into the broth to cook it and then dip it into a sauce before eating. Once the meat is consumed, a variety of vegetables and noodles are added to the simmering broth and then served in bowls with some of the broth. Add steamed rice and the meal is complete. While there are a variety of hot pots with different ingredients, the Mongolian Fire Pot is typically made with lamb and lamb stock.

Mongolian Fire Pot

Florence Lin

Adapted by ACAI

Serves 6

Lamb stock (makes 8 cups):

2 pounds stewing lamb with bones (American spring lamb preferred; see note in Fire Pot ingredients list, below)	1/4 cup dry sherry
	1 scallion
	1 teaspoon salt

Rinse the lamb and bones and then add to a large soup pot and cover with water. Bring water to a boil and blanch the lamb for 5 minutes. Drain, rinse lamb under cold water, and return to the soup pot. Add 3 quarts cold water and bring to a boil. Boil a few minutes to allow the scum to rise to the top, then skim it off. Once the scum is removed, reduce heat to simmer and add the sherry, scallion, and salt. Cover and gently simmer for 5 hours, checking periodically to add water if necessary. Strain out and discard solids, chill broth, and remove fat from the surface.

Fire Pot:

2 pounds boneless leg of American spring lamb (see step 1 below; use bones in stock)	1 (4 by 4 by 1 1/2 inch) piece fresh bean curd, cut into 2-inch by 1-inch pieces
4 ounces cellophane noodles	8 cups lamb stock, heated to boiling
1/2 pound fresh young spinach leaves	1 cup salty dipping sauce (see note)
1/2 pound celery cabbage, slivered	6 cups hot cooked rice

1. Have the butcher remove the bones and tie the lamb as for a roast. Freeze it slightly and then slice paper thin with an electric slicer or cleaver. Divide the slices into six servings and lay the lamb slices overlapping on six serving dishes. Cover each plate with plastic wrap and refrigerate for up to one hour.

2. Fill a medium saucepan half full of water and bring to a boil. Remove from the heat and add the cellophane noodles. Soak the noodles for 20 minutes, drain, and rinse with cold water. Put them in a bowl and cut the noodles into four sections with scissors. Set aside.

3. Rinse the spinach and pat dry with paper towels.

4. Arrange the noodles, spinach, cabbage, and bean curd in separate sections on a serving platter.

5. Place the pot with boiling stock in the center of the table. Give each diner a plate with lamb slices, a rice bowl with 2 tablespoons of dipping sauce in the bottom, and a bowl of hot rice. Provide cooking chopsticks for each diner as well as eating chopsticks. Diners use the cooking chopsticks to select a piece of meat, cook it in the broth, and return it to their plate to eat with their other set of chopsticks. Once the meat is consumed, add the noodles, vegetables, and bean curd to the boiling broth. Serve each diner a portion of the cooked ingredients covered with a little lamb stock.

Note: Traditionally Mongolian Fire Pots are served with a spicy peanut sauce, but you can choose from a number of sauces in this book: Chili with Fish Sauce (page 85), Dipping Sauce for Korean pancakes (page 163), Nuoc Cham (page 144), Peanut Sauce that has been diluted with a little lamb stock (page 149), or even Szechuan Pepper Salt (page 48). The sauce or dip should be salty and complement the lamb.

Chefs Travel from China to Train Hennepin Tech Students

By 1994, the number of Asian restaurants in Minnesota was nearing a thousand (two-thirds of them Chinese), yet opportunities for training culinary students in Asian cooking were limited. As part of the mission of the newly formed Asian Culinary Arts Institutes (ACAI), CEO Phyllis Louise Harris approached Hennepin Technical College to explore the possibility of bringing in two professional chefs from China as instructors. Campus administrator Sharon Grossbach and culinary instructor Chef Donald Wood liked the idea. The primary problem, aside from funding, was getting China's communist government to grant its approval.

To address the issue, Harris recruited assistance from the U.S.–China People's Friendship Association of Minnesota (USCPFA-MN) and attorney Jolie Klapmeier, a specialist in U.S.–China business relations. The Chinese government was so reluctant to grant even temporary travel permits to its citizens, afraid the chefs would not return to China after spending some time in Minnesota, that a year of negotiations was required. After repeated assurances that the chefs would not be staying beyond their four-week visit, the permits were finally approved—the night before the chefs were scheduled to arrive.

Wang Pingxuan and Li Xianghu from Xi'an, China, proved to be talented chefs and patient teachers. Chef Li had twenty-five years' experience in the food business and managed eight restaurants with eighty-five chefs. Chef Wang, one of his top staff members, managed a Szechuan restaurant and was skilled at vegetable carving and noodle pulling. Together they supervised the food service to more than fourteen hundred people in China every day.

Visiting chef demonstrating noodle making at Hennepin Tech.

The chefs spent four weeks giving two classes a day to the college's culinary students, alumni, and faculty. They offered demonstrations to home cooks at Byerly's School of Culinary Arts in St. Louis Park and prepared a banquet for a group of Chinese staff members of the University of Minnesota. Their demonstrations of hand-pulled noodles, seldom seen outside of China, gave Minnesotans a firsthand glimpse of age-old cooking techniques. In all, they performed before more than three hundred people. Their recipes clearly demonstrated the wide variety, rich flavor, and unique qualities of traditional Chinese cooking and, as one student put it, showed "how delicate traditional Chinese cooking can be."

The chefs' brief stay in America gave them experiences they would never forget, including lunch with renowned restaurateur Leeann Chin and a tour of her Union Depot restaurant kitchen in St. Paul; a reception in their honor by members of the USCPFA-MN; shopping trips to various malls; visits to a casino (at their request), the Minnesota Zoo, and the Minneapolis Institute of Arts; being honored guests at a special Asian food event at the Plymouth Library; meeting Executive Chef Steve Mallo and receiving a tour of his Grand Hotel kitchens across from the Mall of America; lunch at Sakura Japanese Restaurant in St. Paul; being guests at a barbecue held by Hennepin Tech culinary staff; and a farewell celebration complete with Chinese food prepared by their students. The chefs were presented with commemorative plaques by both Hennepin Tech and ACAI in thanks for the unique opportunities they provided to the people of Minnesota.

Among the many dishes the chefs prepared, two favorites were boiled dumplings and a garlic dipping sauce.

Dough for Boiled Dumplings

ACAI

Makes 24 large or 30 small dumplings

2 cups flour   3/4 cup water, approximately

1. To a food processor with a metal blade, add the flour and pulse once. Add the water in a slow stream, pulsing the flour as you pour in the water. It takes 20 to 30 pulses to create a dough that holds its shape when you pinch it. You may not need all of the water. If you add too much and the dough is sticky, add flour one tablespoon at a time, pulsing until dough is firm. Place the dough on a lightly floured board and knead several times. Cover the dough with plastic and let it rest at room temperature for 30 minutes. At that point it will be ready to be turned into individual dumplings.

2. Divide the dough in half and keep one half covered. Roll the other half into a cylinder about 1 inch in diameter and 12 inches long. Cut into 12 to 15 pieces, depending on how large you want the dumplings to be. Cover pieces with a damp towel as you work. Repeat with remaining half of the dough.

3. Take one piece of dough at a time and press it down with your palm and fingers to form a small pancake about 3 inches in diameter. Flatten it with a small rolling pin, turning the circle as you roll. Roll from the edges to the center so the edges are thinner than the center. Set aside each dumpling wrapper, covering with a damp towel.

4. Taking one wrapper at a time, add about 1 heaping teaspoon of filling to the center. Fold the wrapper in half to form a half moon. Holding one side still, pinch pleat the other side and press it against the smooth side to form traditional pouches. Put them on a floured tray and cook immediately or cover with a dry cloth and set in the refrigerator up to 2 hours before cooking. They can also be frozen at this stage and cooked later. Do not be disappointed if your dumplings do not look perfect. It takes a lot of practice to get the perfectly formed dumplings served in restaurants.

Boiled Vegetable Dumplings / Su Jiao

ACAI

Makes 24 large or 30 small dumplings

3 cups finely chopped green cabbage

1 cup finely chopped celery

6 tablespoons vegetable oil, divided

12 ounces fresh shiitake or portobello mushrooms, cleaned, each cut into 4 or 5 slices

1 1/2 tablespoons Chinese light soy sauce

1 teaspoon sugar

3 tablespoons dry white wine

2 teaspoons minced ginger

1 teaspoon salt

1/4 teaspoon white pepper

1. Combine the cabbage and celery in a bowl.

2. Heat a wok over medium-high heat and add 2 tablespoons vegetable oil to coat the pan. Add the mushrooms and stir-fry for 1 minute, then add the soy sauce and sugar, stirring well. Add the wine and stir-fry another 4 minutes, until it evaporates. Remove mushrooms from the pan, let cool, and then dice. Set aside.

3. In the same wok set over medium-high heat, add the remaining 4 tablespoons of oil. Add the ginger and stir once, then add the celery and cabbage mixture. Stir-fry for about 4 minutes or until the vegetables are dry. Add the salt and pepper and stir to mix. Add the mushrooms and stir again to mix. Taste and adjust seasonings if necessary. Remove filling to a plate and let cool to room temperature.

4. Fill dumplings as indicated in the dumpling dough recipe at left.

5. When ready to cook, bring 3 quarts of water to a boil in a large pot over high heat. Add 2 teaspoons salt and then the dumplings, stirring gently with a wooden spoon. Return water to boiling and slowly add a cup of cold water. When the water comes to a boil again, add another cup of cold water. Let the water boil and then test the dumplings. The wrapper should be fully cooked and the stuffing hot and flavorful. Remove dumplings with a strainer and serve on a plate with a dipping sauce of your choice.

Xi'an Garlic Sauce

Chef Li Xianghu

Makes about 1 cup

1 whole bulb garlic, cloves
separated and peeled

1/2 cup sesame oil (the
roasted oil used in
Chinese cooking)

1 teaspoon salt

2 tablespoons Maggi sauce
or 1 tablespoon Chinese
light soy sauce

1/4 cup Chinese wine
vinegar (unseasoned)

1. Thoroughly mash the garlic with a mortar and pestle
    or garlic press.

2. Heat sesame oil until it is nearly smoking and im-
    mediately pour over the raw garlic. Mix well.

3. Add the salt, Maggi sauce or soy sauce, and vinegar
    and mix well. Serve at room temperature in small,
    flat dishes for dipping.

A Great Teacher Comes to Minnesota

In 2011, the *New York Times* referred to Florence Lin as
the "the great teacher of Chinese cooking in the United
States"—twenty-one years after she had retired from active
teaching. In the May 9, 2012 edition of the *Washington
Post,* cookbook author Grace Young described Florence as
"America's doyenne of Chinese cuisine. Her books, lectures
and classes long ago established her as one of our most
prominent authorities on Chinese cuisine." The author of
five cookbooks, a contributor to another, and the director
of the China Institute in America's cooking school, Florence was the third daughter of a silk merchant in Ningbo,
near Shanghai. Her interest in cooking began at a young
age as she accompanied her father on his business trips
throughout China, tasting special dishes along the way,
and from watching the family chef prepare everyday meals
or special dishes for her father's clients. When she spent a
year with her grandmother and mother at her aunt's house
in the country, she learned more about the traditions of
wok cooking and about the fine art of embroidery. Here,
too, she learned that the way to be successful at both
endeavors was to "practice, practice, practice," a phrase she
would later use repeatedly with her own students.

At age seventeen, and against her family's wishes, Han Ju
Peng Xia (Florence Shen) joined General Chiang Kai-
shek's national army to defend her country against the
invading Japanese. It was 1937, and the general needed
troops to protect his headquarters in Chunking. After
rigorous training that caused many volunteers to drop
out, Florence became an instructor in rifle use, training
the continuing flow of students volunteering for the fight.
She also studied accounting and nursing while in the
army, and when the war ended, Florence attended Nanjing
University at Chengdu. After graduation she went to work
in an accounting office, where the head of her department was Lin Kuo Yung (K. Y.). They eventually became
engaged, and he moved to New York City, where his uncle
helped him further his career. Finally, in 1949, Florence
agreed to take the long journey to the United States to
marry K. Y. Lin.

Florence Lin stir-frying bell peppers in her California kitchen.

When I met her in 1975, I had no idea that taking a cooking class from the nationally acclaimed Chinese cooking expert Florence Lin would change my career and eventually lead to this book. We were in the teaching kitchen of the China Institute in America in New York City, about to learn the secrets of six-thousand-year-old Chinese cuisine. Facing our class of twenty-five students, this attractive, black-haired, petite woman stood with her arms folded and emphatically stated, "When you finish my class, you will be able to cook Chinese food from whatever is in your refrigerator." I truly doubted it. How wrong I was.

After fourteen years of classes with Florence, after traveling with her through China to meet with and learn from master chefs, and after thirty-seven years as her student and friend, I now know she was right. — PLH

Florence Lin believed she could do anything she set out to do. First she learned English and began cooking for her husband's business clients. Soon she was asked to give cooking classes at the China Institute, and all the while she and K. Y. were raising two daughters, Flora and Kate. She thought living in New York was a temporary arrangement and that they would be returning to China. Instead, she and K. Y. became American citizens and made New York City their home. As K. Y. continued to work in finance, Florence embarked on a career that would last more than fifty years and take her to all parts of the United States. She wrote five cookbooks and created recipes for an additional book, wrote articles for the *New York Times* and national magazines, headed the culinary program at the China Institute for more than twenty-five years, and was made a Lifetime Honorary Member of the New York Association of Cooking Teachers.

In 1995, we asked her to come to Minnesota to take part in the Chinese chefs program at Hennepin Technical College. She acted as interpreter for the chefs who spoke no English, helped explain techniques they were using, provided her own cooking instructions,

answered questions on a call-in show for public radio, and helped Minnesotans gain a better understanding of classic Chinese cooking. At the end of her visit, ACAI presented her with its Lifetime Achievement Award for her outstanding contribution to the understanding and appreciation of Chinese cooking. It was her first and only visit to the state.

Many of the Chinese recipes in this book are selected from hundreds of dishes I first cooked in Florence Lin's classes at the China Institute. They include some of my notes to help the reader re-create this wonderful food. It was difficult to select just a few, but I listened to my friends, relatives, students, and colleagues who have enjoyed my Chinese cooking over the years and have told me again and again which were their favorites. The first twelve recipes show the creative methods Chinese cooks developed for making vegetables more flavorful and fun. — PLH

Vegetarian cooking has been part of China's extensive cuisine for thousands of years. When Confucius and his contemporary Lao-Tse created philosophies of living a peaceful life filled with harmony and happiness, an important element was eating good natural foods from the earth. Buddha expanded on this thinking with the philosophy that no animal should be killed unless it is harmful to human beings. So it is not surprising that Buddhist monks developed creative vegetarian cooking that later spread to restaurants and homes. Even today, some of the most intriguing vegetable dishes come from Buddhist monasteries. The addition of small amounts of sugar helps bring out the natural sweetness of the vegetable.

Green Bean Salad with Mustard Sauce

Florence Lin

Adapted by ACAI

Serves 6–8

1 pound fresh green beans	1 tablespoon finely shredded ginger (start with shavings)
4 cups water	

Sauce:

2 teaspoons mustard powder	1 tablespoon Chinese light soy sauce
1 1/2 teaspoons cold water	1 1/2 tablespoons distilled white vinegar
1 teaspoon salt	
1 teaspoon sugar	1 tablespoon sesame oil

1. Snap off and discard the ends of the green beans. Break beans into 2-inch pieces or leave whole—approximately 4 cups.

2. In a saucepan over medium-high heat, bring 4 cups of water to a boil. Add the beans and return to boiling. Cook for about 5 minutes or until the beans are barely tender. Do not overcook.

3. Drain the beans and plunge them into a bowl of ice water to stop cooking process and enhance color. Drain again and dry with paper towels. Set beans in a large mixing bowl or refrigerator container. Sprinkle shredded ginger over beans and toss lightly.

4. Place the mustard powder in a small bowl and slowly add the water, 1/2 teaspoon at a time, thoroughly mixing with the powder after each addition. This is the real trick to this recipe, as slowly mixing the mustard powder with water will begin the chemical process that gives the mustard its potent flavor. Mixing too quickly prevents this reaction, and the dressing will be bland. If after the third blend with water the mustard does not have a "kick" to it, throw it out and start again. Once the paste has formed and has a very strong aroma, add the salt, sugar, soy sauce, vinegar, and sesame oil, blending well after each addition.

5. Pour sauce over the bean and ginger mixture and toss well. Cover and refrigerate at least 1 hour and up to 4 hours to blend flavors, tossing ingredients 2 or 3 times during chilling. Serve cold.

Braised Eggplant / Hung Shao Ch'ieh Tzu

Florence Lin

Adapted by ACAI

Serves 4–8

1 large (1 1/2-pound) eggplant, or 1 1/2 pounds long, thin Chinese eggplant	3 tablespoons corn oil
	2 tablespoons Chinese light soy sauce
1 green bell pepper	2 teaspoons sugar
1 red bell pepper	1/2 cup chicken broth or water (add salt to taste if you use water)
2 (1-inch) pieces ginger, peeled and crushed	
1 large clove garlic, peeled and crushed	

1. Peel the eggplant. (If it is Chinese eggplant, no need to peel.) Remove and discard the stem and any seeds. Cut the eggplant into 2 by 1 by 4–inch strips. Set aside on a plate.

2. Wash peppers and remove and discard stems, seeds, and membranes. Cut peppers into 2 by 1/4–inch strips and set aside with ginger and garlic.

3. Heat a 3-quart nonstick saucepan over medium heat until hot. Add the oil, and then the ginger, garlic, and peppers. Stir-fry for 1 minute. Add the eggplant one handful at a time. Shake the pot and gently stir to evenly fry. Add soy sauce, sugar, and broth or water and stir well. Cover, bring to a boil, and simmer over medium heat for 8 minutes. Stir or shake pan to redistribute contents. Cover and cook another 7 or 8 minutes, until very little liquid remains in the pan. Remove from heat. Discard the ginger and garlic pieces. Season to taste. Serve hot, cold, or at room temperature.

Asian cooks use every part of the vegetable possible. Broccoli stems are often thrown away after the florets are cut off, but the stems are delicious, crunchy, and useful. Remove the florets to use in other dishes and peel the main stem, usually about one inch in diameter and as long as five inches. To make peeling easier, let the stems come to room temperature and with a paring knife cut away a portion of the outer layer, stripping it off all the way down the stem. It takes just a few minutes, leaving the tender, flavorful center. Stems can be julienned for stir-fries, cut into coin-shaped disks for salads, or chopped for soups.

Broccoli Stem Salad /
Liang Pan Chieh Lan

Florence Lin

Adapted by ACAI

Serves 4–8

about 6 (5-inch-long by 1-inch-diameter) broccoli stems, peeled (see head note)	4 cups water

Dressing:

1/2 teaspoon salt	1 tablespoon Chinese light soy sauce
1/2 teaspoon sugar	1 tablespoon sesame oil

1. Cut the broccoli stems into 1 1/2-inch lengths, 1/2 inch wide and 1/2 inch thick, or into diagonal slices 1/4 inch thick, to yield 2 cups.

2. In a medium saucepan bring 4 cups water to a boil and add the broccoli pieces. Parboil 1 minute. Drain and plunge broccoli into ice water to stop the cooking and brighten the color. Drain broccoli and dry with paper towels. Add broccoli to a medium mixing bowl.

3. Combine dressing ingredients in a separate bowl and add to the broccoli. Mix well, cover, and chill in the refrigerator for 1 hour. Serve cold.

Stir-Fried Asparagus /
Ch'ao Lou Sun

Florence Lin

Adapted by ACAI

Serves 4 with other dishes

1 pound fresh asparagus, any size	1/2 teaspoon sugar
2 tablespoons vegetable oil	1–2 tablespoons water
1 teaspoon salt	

1. For asparagus, on larger spears peel off the lower portion with a potato peeler, leaving the more tender center. Break each spear at the point where it easily breaks clean; discard the lower tough portions. Cut each spear into 2-inch pieces by slicing off the tender top portion on an angle, then give the remaining spear half a roll and angle cut again, continuing until the spear has been completely cut. It takes 2 or 3 turns. Wash thoroughly and soak in water for 15 minutes. Drain the asparagus and pat dry.

2. Heat a wok or large frying pan over high heat until hot. Coat with the oil, add the asparagus, and stir-fry for about 2 minutes. Add the salt, sugar, and 1 tablespoon water and mix well for another 2 minutes. Very thin asparagus will be done at this point; bigger spears will need another tablespoon of water. Cover the wok and let the asparagus simmer for about 1 minute longer or until tender. Remove from the heat and serve hot.

Vegetables can be raw, boiled, steamed, stir-fried, deep-fried, or even smoked. This recipe uses a Chinese batter that becomes crisp with the addition of cornstarch. It is easy to use and holds well in a warm oven or reheats well in a hot oven. The crisp coating on the soft eggplant is delicious.

Deep-Fried Eggplant / Cha Ch'the Tzu

Florence Lin

Adapted by ACAI

Serves 8–10 with other dishes

Sauce:

1/4 cup hoisin sauce	2 teaspoons sugar
2 tablespoons water	1 teaspoon sesame oil

Batter:

3/4 cup all-purpose flour	1 1/2 teaspoons baking powder
1/4 cup cornstarch	
	3/4 cup water
1 medium (1-pound) eggplant	2 cups vegetable oil

1. Combine the sauce ingredients and set aside. Heat the oven to 200°. Set a wire rack on a baking sheet and set aside. Line another baking sheet with paper towels.

2. Combine the flour, cornstarch, and baking powder in a medium bowl. Add the water and stir into a smooth batter with a wire whisk. The batter will be a little runny, but thick enough to coat the eggplant.

3. Wash the eggplant and discard the stem. Do not peel. Cut the eggplant crosswise into 1/4-inch slices. Cut each slice into quarters about 2 inches by 2 inches.

4. Heat the oil in a wok or deep fryer to about 350°. Add 1 tablespoon of the warm oil to the batter and mix well.

5. Dip each piece of eggplant into the batter and carefully drop into the hot oil. Fry about ten pieces at a time until lightly browned and crisp. Remove to paper towel–lined pan to drain excess oil, transfer to the baking sheet with a rack, and keep warm in the oven. Repeat with remaining eggplant.

6. Serve with the sauce or sprinkle with Szechuan Pepper Salt (page 48).

Note: If the eggplant is fried ahead of time, it can be reheated on a rack in a 425° oven until the outside is crisp, about 7 to 8 minutes.

Here is a popular party snack that is easy to prepare ahead of time. The Chinese also use it as a topping for congee. While peanuts are not indigenous to China, after they were introduced by seventeenth-century spice traders the Chinese found myriad ways to use them. Here are just two.

Peanuts with Seaweed / T'ai Tiao Hua Sheng Mi

Florence Lin

Adapted by ACAI

Makes 1 1/2 cups

1 cup peanut or corn oil	1/2 cup green seaweed (green moss) or Japanese aonoriko (see note)
1 cup raw, skinless peanuts	
	1 teaspoon sugar (see note)

1. On the stove away from the heat set a metal strainer on a medium saucepan.

2. Heat a wok over high heat until very hot. Add the oil and heat to about 325°. Add the peanuts and fry for about 4 to 5 minutes, stirring to evenly cook the nuts. Do not overcook. The moment the nuts begin to change color, pour them into the strainer, catching the oil in the pan. Cool the oil and reserve for later use.

3. Add 1 tablespoon of reserved oil back into the wok and stir-fry seaweed over low heat for 3 to 4 minutes, until crispy. Do not brown. Return the fried peanuts to the wok and toss with the seaweed, which will stick to some of the peanuts. Remove mixture to a baking sheet, spread out, and cool completely. Once cooled, sprinkle the mixture with sugar and mix well. Serve as a snack or as a vegetable with other salty dishes.

Note: If the seaweed comes in wads, pull and cut them into very fine, small chips before frying. While the sugar adds a little sweetness, it may be eliminated.

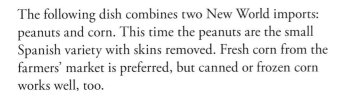

The following dish combines two New World imports: peanuts and corn. This time the peanuts are the small Spanish variety with skins removed. Fresh corn from the farmers' market is preferred, but canned or frozen corn works well, too.

Stir-Fried Corn with Peanuts

Florence Lin

Adapted by ACAI

Serves 4–6

1/4 cup peanut or corn oil	2 cups fresh corn; or 2 cups frozen corn, thawed; or 1 (16-ounce) can whole kernel corn, drained
1/2 cup raw, skinless Spanish peanuts	
1/4 cup diced fresh medium-heat chili	1/2 teaspoon salt, or to taste

1. Heat oil in a wok over medium heat for 2 minutes or until it reaches 350°. Add the peanuts and carefully stir-fry for 4 or 5 minutes, just until they begin to turn pale golden. Turn off the heat. Using a metal strainer, remove the peanuts from the oil and drain them on paper towels.

2. Reduce the oil in the wok to 1 tablespoon and reheat over medium heat. Stir-fry the chili for 1 minute and add the corn. Stir-fry for 2 minutes. (Canned corn may spatter, so be careful.) Add the salt and peanuts. Mix well and remove from heat. Serve at room temperature.

Seaweed is an important ingredient in vegetarian cooking, and this combination of kelp and carrot will be a little salty but very good. The texture of the kelp will be a little like cooked cabbage and the flavor similar to green beans. The dish may be cooked ahead of time and reheated in the microwave.

Braised Sea Kelp with Carrot / Hung Shao Hai Dai

Florence Lin

Adapted by ACAI

Serves 4

2 ounces dry sea kelp (sea girdle)	1 1/2 cups water (see note)
3 tablespoons peanut or corn oil	2 tablespoons Chinese light soy sauce
	1 teaspoon sugar
3 (1-inch) pieces ginger, peeled and cut into 1/2-inch slices	2 carrots, peeled and diagonally sliced into pieces 1/3 inch thick

1. Soak the kelp in warm water for 30 minutes or overnight. Drain and cut into 1 inch by 2 inch pieces, about 2 cups. Soak in clean water until ready to use. (The kelp may be kept in the refrigerator for up to 1 week.) When ready to use, rinse the kelp again, drain, and set aside.

2. Heat a medium saucepan over medium-high heat and add the oil. Stir-fry the ginger about 1 minute to season the oil and then add the kelp, stir-frying for about 3 minutes or until some small bubbles form on the kelp. Add the water, cover, and cook over low heat for 45 minutes.

3. Add the soy sauce and sugar and mix well. Place the carrots on top of the mixture without stirring. Continue cooking, uncovered, for about 20 minutes, until very little liquid remains. If there is too much liquid, cook over high heat a few minutes, until liquid evaporates. Serve hot with other dishes or simply with a bowl of cooked white rice.

Note: For a non-vegetarian dish, the water may be replaced by weak chicken broth for additional flavor.

Preserved vegetables, which add flavor and texture, have long been a part of Chinese cooking. Recipes and the vegetables chosen vary from area to area. Often it is cabbage: Szechuan preserved vegetable (*Szechuan cha ts'ai*) is a popular choice available in most Asian markets. Even after the jar is opened, preserved vegetable will keep indefinitely in the refrigerator.

Here, the preserved vegetables give green beans a salty boost with a little crunchy texture. The beans are twice cooked, another popular Chinese technique, giving them a wrinkled look. A local food writer once complained about the wrinkled beans she was served. Do not despair if yours looked wrinkled: they are supposed to!

Fried Green Beans with Szechuan Preserved Vegetable / Kan Shao Tou Chiao

Florence Lin

Adapted by ACAI

Serves 2 or up to 8 with other dishes

1 pound fresh green beans	1/2 teaspoon sugar
2 cups peanut or corn oil	2 tablespoons water
1/4 cup rinsed and finely chopped Szechuan preserved vegetable (*Szechuan cha ts'ai*)	

1. Remove and discard ends of the green beans by either snapping them off or angle cutting with a cleaver. Wash and drain well. Dry the beans with paper towels. Set aside.

2. On the stove away from the heat place a metal strainer over a medium saucepan.

3. Heat a wok over high heat, then add the oil and bring it to 375°. Carefully add the green beans and fry for about 3 minutes, or until the beans become slightly wrinkled. Gently stir for even frying. Pour the beans and oil into the strainer and reserve the oil for future use.

4. Reheat the wok over high heat and add 1 tablespoon reserved oil. Stir-fry the Szechuan preserved vegetable for 2 minutes. Add the sugar and water and continue stir-frying over high heat for 1 minute. Return the beans to the wok and stir-fry for a few seconds until well mixed. Serve hot or warm.

Another import from the New World, bell peppers react well to the heat of the wok. This dish produces something similar to roasted peppers popular in European cuisines but relies on the extreme heat and flavor of the iron wok to give the peppers their charcoal flavor. Using a nonstick wok will not produce the same result. To give this dish even more spice, add 2 teaspoons wine vinegar and 1/2 teaspoon hot chili oil at the last minute and mix well. This cold dish may be served with others or as a topping for congee.

Charcoal-Flavored Green Peppers / Chiao Pan Ch'ing Chiao

Florence Lin

Adapted by ACAI

Serves 4 with other dishes

4 large green bell peppers (about 1 pound)	1 tablespoon corn oil (see note)
1 teaspoon salt	1 1/2 tablespoons Chinese light soy sauce
1/2 teaspoon sugar	

1. Wash the peppers and dry well. Remove the seeds and carefully slice off the pith and discard. Cut the peppers into pieces 1 1/2 inches long by 1 inch wide, to yield about 4 cups. In a large mixing bowl, place the peppers and sprinkle with salt and sugar. Mix well and let the peppers stand for about 4 hours.

2. Place the peppers in a kitchen towel or cloth bag and squeeze out as much liquid as possible. Set peppers aside.

3. Heat a wok over high heat until hot. Coat the wok with the oil and add the peppers, quickly stir-frying for 4 to 5 minutes. As they start to burn slightly, add the soy sauce and stir-fry for 1 minute more. Remove peppers from the wok, cool, and refrigerate. Serve cold.

Note: Since this dish is served cold, it needs an oil that will look clear when chilled. Corn oil or other vegetable oils will work, but not peanut oil, which takes on a filmy look when chilled.

This vegetarian dish uses flavorful watercress with the lightest of dressings and is mixed just before serving. Fresh water chestnuts add a crunch and flavor that cannot be duplicated with the canned version: if fresh water chestnuts are not available, leave them out. The sesame oil is the roasted variety used in Chinese cooking and available at most Asian markets. The final flavor of the dish will depend on the oil used, so be sure it is fresh. Add the seasonings individually just before serving and thoroughly mix with the watercress. Do not mix them together as a dressing. The dish has a dense texture more like a relish than a leafy salad.

Watercress Salad / Liang Pan Hsi Yang Ts'ai

Florence Lin

Adapted by ACAI

Serves 4 with other dishes

2 bunches watercress

4 fresh water chestnuts, washed, peeled, and finely chopped (see head note)

1 teaspoon salt

1/2 teaspoon sugar

2 teaspoons sesame oil

1. Carefully wash the watercress and remove lower stems.

2. In a medium saucepan bring 2 quarts of water to a boil and add the watercress. Let stand 10 seconds and remove watercress, plunging it into a bowl of ice water. Remove from the water and squeeze out as much liquid from the leaves as possible. Finely chop the watercress to yield about 1 1/2 cups.

3. In a medium mixing bowl, add the watercress and water chestnuts. Toss lightly to loosen and sprinkle on the salt, sugar, and sesame oil. Stir again to mix well. Serve cold as a condiment with other dishes.

Velvet Chicken and Cream of Corn Soup / Fu Rong Yu Mi Tang

Florence Lin

Adapted by ACAI

Serves 8–12

6 ounces boneless, skinless chicken breast

1/2 cup cold water

1/2 tablespoon cornstarch

1 1/2 teaspoons coarse salt

1/2 teaspoon sugar

1 tablespoon dry sherry

3 eggs

1/4 cup water

1 (17-ounce) can creamed corn

4 cups chicken stock

1 (12-ounce) can straw mushrooms, drained and halved

salt and white pepper to taste

1 tablespoon cornstarch combined with 3 tablespoons water

4 tablespoons minced ham and 2 tablespoons blanched, slivered snow peas for garnish (see note)

1. Trim and discard any membrane and tendons from the chicken. Cut the chicken into small pieces and place them in a food processor with a metal blade. Begin processing and gradually add 1/2 cup cold water through the feed tube. Stop the processing action.

2. Add the cornstarch, salt, sugar, and sherry and then process some more, stopping once or twice to scrape the bowl. The chicken mixture should be light and creamy. It can be made ahead of time and refrigerated for several hours or overnight.

3. Set the velvet chicken in a large mixing bowl. In another bowl, beat the eggs with 1/4 cup water until foamy; set aside. Grind the creamed corn in a food processor for 1 minute.

4. To a large soup pot or saucepan, add the corn and chicken stock and bring to a boil. Add the mushrooms, season with salt and pepper, and reduce heat to simmer.

5. Stir the cornstarch and water until well blended and slowly stir into the simmering soup. Ladle about

2 cups of the hot soup into the velvet chicken and fold the mixture together until well blended. Slowly pour the chicken mixture back into the soup and gently stir. Bring to a near boil. Slowly add the beaten eggs and gently stir just once. Remove from the heat. Ladle the soup into individual soup bowls or small cups and garnish with ham and snow peas. Serve hot.

Note: Remove the stems from the pea pods and blanch in boiling water for 1 minute. Drain pea pods and plunge them into ice water, then drain and pat dry. Cut diagonally into julienne slivers.

Wheat gluten is often used in vegetarian cooking for its texture and nutrients as well as the flavor it absorbs from other ingredients. It is available dried or frozen. This dish also incorporates other Chinese favorites for a variety of textures, colors, and flavors. An example of Chinese red cooking (simmering food in soy sauce) it has a licorice/soy sauce/sesame flavor and may be served hot or cold. It is even better if made a day ahead of serving.

Wheat Gluten with Vegetables / K'ao Fu

Florence Lin

Adapted by ACAI

Serves 4

1 bag dried wheat gluten (about 8 pieces, each 2 inches by 1 1/2 inches by 1/2 inch; see note)	1/2 cup sliced bamboo shoots
4 large dried Chinese black mushrooms	1 whole star anise
	2 tablespoons Chinese light soy sauce
30 dried tiger lily buds	2 tablespoons Chinese dark soy sauce
1/4 cup dried tree ears	1 1/2 tablespoons sugar
2 cups peanut or corn oil	2 teaspoons sesame oil

1. Fill a medium saucepan about two-thirds full with water and bring to a boil. Remove from heat and add the wheat gluten to soak for about 10 minutes, or until soft. Drain the water and squeeze as much liquid out of the wheat gluten as possible. Tear each piece into 1 1/2-inch pieces for about 2 cups. Set aside.

2. Wash black mushrooms and soak them in 2 cups warm water for 30 minutes. Remove tough stems, squeeze out excess water, and cut each mushroom into 4 pieces. Retain the soaking liquid for later use.

3. Soak the tiger lily buds and tree ears in 4 cups hot water for 30 minutes, until soft. Pull or cut off and discard the hard ends of each lily bud; cut buds in half and set aside. Clean the tree ears and rinse in water several times. Drain well. Cut the tree ear pieces into strips about 1/4 inch wide. Set aside.

4. Prepare a baking sheet with a layer of newspaper and several layers of paper towels.

5. Heat a wok over high heat and add the oil, heating to 375°. Carefully deep-fry the gluten pieces, which may spatter when put into the oil. Stir as they are cooking, being careful not to burn them. In about 6 minutes they will turn brown and crisp. If they are browning too fast, turn down the heat and continue cooking until crisp. Remove the pieces from the oil and spread out on the paper towels to drain. Save the oil for later use.

6. In a medium saucepan layer all ingredients and seasonings except the tree ears and sesame oil. Add enough water to the reserved mushroom liquid to make 2 cups and add it to the pan. Bring to a boil, lower heat to a simmer, barely cover, and cook for about 45 minutes. Stir ingredients and adjust seasonings if necessary. There should be very little liquid left. If necessary, cook 10 to 15 minutes longer to evaporate the liquid. Add the tree ears and sesame oil and mix well. Cook 5 minutes more and remove from heat. Serve hot or cold.

Note: If using frozen wheat gluten, thaw and tear into pieces. It does not need to be soaked.

Chicken with Chestnuts / Li Tzu Chi

Florence Lin

Adapted by ACAI

Serves 4–8

8 dried Chinese black mushrooms

1 pound fresh chestnuts, peeled (see note), or 2 cups canned or packaged peeled chestnuts

1 (3-pound) frying chicken

2 tablespoons peanut or corn oil

4 quarter-size slices ginger

1 scallion, cut into 2-inch-long sections

1/2 tablespoon sugar

2 tablespoons Chinese light soy sauce

2 tablespoons Chinese dark soy sauce

1 cup chicken broth

steamed white rice

1. Soak mushrooms in warm water until soft, about 20 minutes. Squeeze out water, remove and discard stems, and cut mushrooms into halves by diagonally slicing through the top to the bottom of the cap. Set aside.

2. If using fresh chestnuts, peel (see note) and set aside.

3. Cut the chicken into pieces 2 by 1 1/2 inches including bones and skin. If you prefer, use boneless, skinless chicken and cut into pieces. This will be easier to eat, but will have less flavor than the chicken with bones. Reserve the back, breastbone, wing tips, and neck for soup stock.

4. Heat a heavy saucepan over medium heat until very hot. Add the oil and ginger and stir-fry for a few seconds. Add chicken pieces and stir-fry for 4 or 5 minutes, until they start to brown. Add the scallion pieces and stir-fry for another minute. Add the sugar and soy sauces and stir-fry another 2 minutes, but do not allow mixture to burn. Add the chicken broth and bring to a boil. Cover pan and reduce heat to medium low. Simmer for about 20 minutes.

5. Carefully place the mushrooms and chestnuts over the top of the chicken mixture; cover and simmer for 15 minutes. Shake the pan slightly to mix in the mushrooms and chestnuts. Do not stir as it will break up the chestnuts. Serve hot with steamed white rice.

Notes: This dish keeps well in the refrigerator for several days and reheats easily in the microwave. Do not overcook when reheating. The chestnuts will crumble easily so keep stirring to a minimum. If the mixture gets too dry, add a little chicken broth.

Fresh chestnuts are best. To peel them, cut a slit through the thick outer skin and grill or bake until the nuts start to open. Carefully peel away the outer skin, leaving the whole chestnut. This can be done a day ahead of time. Store peeled chestnuts in a covered container in the refrigerator.

Jellied Lamb / Yang Gao

Florence Lin

Adapted by ACAI

Serves 4–8

1 pound boneless lamb (upper leg)

2 scallions, cut into halves

2 cloves garlic, peeled

1 (1/2-inch) piece ginger, peeled

2 cups lamb or chicken broth

1 whole star anise or 8 pods

2 teaspoons sugar

3 tablespoons Chinese light soy sauce

2 tablespoons dry sherry or rice wine

1 envelope (2 tablespoons) unflavored gelatin soaked in 1/2 cup cold water

cilantro or radishes for garnish

1. Cut the lamb into 8 pieces; place the lamb in a large saucepan, cover with water, and bring to a boil for 2 to 3 minutes. Drain off water and rinse the lamb. Return it to the pan.

2. Add the scallions, garlic, ginger, broth, star anise, sugar, soy sauce, and wine. Bring to a low boil, cover, and simmer over low heat for 1 1/2 hours, until the meat is very tender.

3. Remove the lamb from the broth and cool. Remove any fat and cut meat into small cubes (about 1/2 by 1/4 inches). Distribute the pieces evenly over the bottom of a square or oblong mold just large enough for the lamb and the broth mixture to be about 1 inch deep.

4. Strain the broth through a fine sieve or cloth to remove all pieces. Add water to the broth to make 1 cup of liquid. Pour it back into the pan and add the softened gelatin. Stir over medium heat until the gelatin dissolves. Pour the sauce mixture into the mold to cover the lamb pieces, stirring just enough to distribute the lamb throughout the mold. The broth should completely cover the meat to provide a smooth top. Refrigerate 4 hours or until the liquid jells.

5. Scrape any fat from the top of the mold. Remove the aspic from the mold and slice into 2 inch by 1 inch by 1/4 inch pieces. Arrange on a serving plate and garnish with cilantro leaves or radish flowers. Serve cold.

Steamed Fish with Black Bean Sauce / You Lin Yu

Florence Lin

Adapted by ACAI

Serves 4–6

2 pounds gray sole, fins, head, and tail removed; or substitute any non-oily fish: walleye, sea bass, winter carp

1 tablespoon fermented black beans

1 clove garlic, minced

2 teaspoons minced ginger

1 tablespoon Chinese light soy sauce

1 tablespoon dry sherry or rice wine

1/2 teaspoon sugar

1/4 teaspoon coarse salt

1 tablespoon Hunan chili sauce (see note)

2 tablespoons finely shredded whole scallion

3 tablespoons corn or peanut oil

1. Have the fish store trim off the fins and part of the side fat of the sole. Cut the fish into 4 to 6 pieces through the backbone. Rinse and dry pieces and reassemble into a whole fish on a greased ovensafe platter.

2. Rinse the black beans to remove the salt, then coarsely chop them and place in a small bowl. Mix in the garlic, ginger, soy sauce, wine, sugar, salt, and chili sauce. Spread this paste over the fish.

3. In a steamer (or covered roasting pan) bring water to a boil. Place fish platter on steaming rack (or cup set in center of pan). Cover tightly and steam over medium heat for about 12 minutes, until the fish flakes when tested with a fork. Turn off the heat and carefully remove the lid.

4. Remove the platter and set it on top of a serving platter. Scatter the scallions over the top of the fish. Heat the oil over low heat until hot and carefully pour over the entire fish. (Be careful: the oil hitting the moist fish may spatter.) Serve hot.

Notes: Traditionally the fish is served whole with head and tail intact. If the fish is more than 1/2 inch thick, steam a little longer or until it flakes with a fork. Fish fillets also work well with this recipe: lay one fillet on a platter and top with a second fillet, allowing about 1 inch of the bottom fillet to show. Reduce cooking time by about 5 minutes. Hunan chili sauce is available in Asian markets, or substitute the Hunan Pepper Sauce on page 41.

Cantonese Shrimp in the Shell

Florence Lin

Adapted by ACAI

Serves 6–10

1 1/2 pounds large shrimp in the shell (about 18 per pound)

1 1/2 teaspoons salt, divided

1/2 tablespoon cornstarch

1 teaspoon dry sherry or rice wine

2 cups vegetable or peanut oil

1 tablespoon shredded ginger

1 large scallion, cut into 2-inch lengths and slivered

1/4 cup green pepper julienne slices

1/4 cup chili julienne slices

2 cloves garlic, diced

1/3 teaspoon sugar

1 teaspoon Chinese five-spice powder

dash white pepper

1. Cut the shrimp through the shell down the back and remove vein. Sprinkle on 1/2 teaspoon salt, cornstarch, and wine, tossing the shrimp to distribute seasonings.

2. Preheat oven to 200°. Heat oil in wok until nearly smoking. Add the shrimp in small batches, cooking each for a few minutes to lightly brown and partially cook the shrimp. Remove shrimp from oil, drain on paper towels, and keep in warm oven on a wire rack placed on top of a cookie sheet. Continue until all shrimp have been oil-poached.

3. Remove oil from the wok, reserving 2 tablespoons. Heat wok to high, add reserved oil, and stir-fry the ginger, scallion, pepper, chili, and garlic for a few minutes. (Be careful: the chiles can give off steam that will irritate your eyes.) Add the shrimp, and stir-fry for 2 minutes, until well blended. Sprinkle with 1 teaspoon salt, sugar, five-spice powder, and white pepper and continue to stir-fry for 1 minute. Remove to serving platter and serve hot or warm, with steamed white rice or individually as an appetizer.

Notes: Any leftover shrimp are delicious cold or in a salad. The finished shrimp may be kept warm in a low oven for about an hour. Since they are still in the shell, they do not dry out. Put whole shrimp in your mouth to taste all of the seasonings, then spit out the shell and enjoy the shrimp. Not the most polite way of eating, but tasty!

This dish is a scallop lover's favorite, cooks in less than five minutes, and is very easy to make. It is simply fresh scallops in a light chicken broth sauce with whole fresh button mushrooms. The scallops cook very quickly and the mushrooms will be slightly crunchy when done. This combination can be a last-minute stir-fry to go with other dishes and a nice contrast to deep-fried or more heavily flavored food. Since the egg white coating will easily stick to the side of a hot wok that is not well seasoned, use a nonstick wok or frying pan for easier cooking.

Stir-Fried Scallops and Mushrooms / Ch'ao Kan Pei

Florence Lin

Adapted by ACAI

Serves 4–8

1/2 pound fresh sea scallops, muscles removed, cut into halves to retain their circular shape

1/2 egg white

3/4 teaspoon salt, divided

1 teaspoon cornstarch

12 ounces fresh button mushrooms, about 1 inch in diameter, stems removed

1/4 cup peanut or corn oil

1/2 teaspoon sugar

1/2 cup chicken broth

2 teaspoons cornstarch combined with 2 tablespoons water

1 teaspoon sesame oil

slivered scallion curls for garnish (see note)

1. Place the scallops in a medium bowl and add the egg white and 1/4 teaspoon salt. Mix together with your fingers to coat each scallop, then add the cornstarch and mix again. Cover and refrigerate for at least 1 hour or up to 24 hours. Mix again just before cooking.

2. Wipe the mushrooms or lightly spray them with water and dry them with paper towels. Leave the 1-inch mushrooms whole and cut larger mushrooms down to the smaller size.

3. Heat a nonstick wok or frying pan over medium heat until it is hot. Add the oil to the pan, let it get hot, and then add the marinated scallops. Gently stir-fry until most of the scallops change color and are not quite done, less than 1 minute. With a slotted spoon remove the scallops to a plate, leaving the oil in the pan. Continue to heat the pan over medium heat.

4. Add the mushrooms and stir-fry for just under 1 minute. Carefully add the 1/2 teaspoon salt, sugar, and chicken broth and stir to blend. Stir the cornstarch mixture and slowly pour over the mushrooms while stirring for about 1 minute. Add the scallops and mix together with the mushrooms and sauce. Sprinkle the mixture with sesame oil, mix again, and dish out. Garnish with scallion curls and serve at once.

Note: Sliver the green portion of scallions into long, thin ribbons. Place them in a bowl of cold water, cover, and refrigerate for at least 2 hours or overnight. The thin scallion strips will curl for a decorative and tasty garnish.

Left: Cantonese Shrimp in the Shell.

When I lived in New York City in the 1970s, I read the **New York Times** *restaurant review every Friday. I soon learned if there was a rave review not to visit the restaurant until after the rush died down four or five weeks later. But once I decided to risk the crowds and have dinner at the House of Tu the day after a particularly enthusiastic review. Crowds packed into the small entry and bar, and after more than an hour we got a table. It was well worth the wait. One of the dishes I will never forget was an order of pearl balls. I had never tasted them before and found them so delicious I asked Florence Lin to include them in a cooking class at the China Institute. Here is that recipe, a favorite in our household. Serve them with Hunan Pepper Sauce. — PLH*

Pearl Balls / Zheng Zhu Rou Wan

Florence Lin

Adapted by ACAI

Makes about 20 (1 1/2–inch) balls

1 cup glutinous (sweet) rice (see page 4)	1 teaspoon salt
	1/4 teaspoon sugar
1 pound lean pork, finely ground, or substitute beef plus 2 tablespoons vegetable oil	1 tablespoon Chinese light soy sauce
1 egg	4 fresh water chestnuts, peeled and minced
1 tablespoon cornstarch combined with 1 tablespoon water and 1 tablespoon white wine	1 tablespoon minced scallion, white part only
	vegetable oil
	Hunan Pepper Sauce (recipe follows)

1. Rinse the rice several times and then cover with cold water and soak for at least 1 hour. Drain well and spread out on a clean cloth or paper towels to dry for at least 1 hour.

2. In a large bowl, combine the pork, egg, and cornstarch mixture, mixing well. Add the salt, sugar, and soy sauce and stir in one direction with a chopstick until the meat holds together. The texture will change from ground pieces to little strings of meat all pointed in one direction. Add water chestnuts and scallion and continue to mix. Cover and refrigerate for at least 30 minutes.

3. Set up a wok with racks for steaming. Fill the wok about 1/3 full of water and bring to a boil.

4. Lightly oil the inside base of each rack. Moisten your hands with water and scoop up about 1 1/2 tablespoons of the pork mixture, rolling it into a ball about 1 inch in diameter. Roll the pork ball in the dried rice to completely cover the meat. Set the pearl balls on the steamer rack about 1/2 inch apart. When the rack is filled, place it over boiling water, cover, and steam over medium-high heat for 20 minutes. Remove balls to a serving platter or individual plates and repeat with remaining meat and rice. Serve hot with Hunan Pepper Sauce.

Notes: The pearl balls freeze well and may be reheated. Place the cooked and cooled balls on an oiled cookie sheet and freeze until firm. Store the frozen pearl balls in freezer bags up to 6 weeks. Defrost at room temperature and steam to reheat, approximately 8 minutes.

Minnesotans have become familiar with the fiery flavors of Szechuan cooking, but this spicy sauce is from the neighboring province of Hunan. Peppers are not indigenous to China: they were introduced by the Spanish and Portuguese traders of the seventeenth century when they started bringing "New World" foods to trade for rice, tea, and spices. Hot peppers are now grown in various parts of China.

Right: Pearl Balls with Hunan Pepper Sauce.

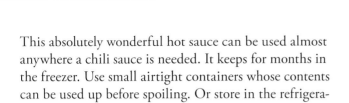

This absolutely wonderful hot sauce can be used almost anywhere a chili sauce is needed. It keeps for months in the freezer. Use small airtight containers whose contents can be used up before spoiling. Or store in the refrigerator for several weeks.

Hunan Pepper Sauce

Florence Lin
Adapted by ACAI
Makes about 1 1/2 cups

30 whole dried Tien Tsin chilies, soaked overnight in 1/2 cup water or more to cover; weigh chilies down with a dish so all peppers are covered

1 pound red peppers, seeded

6 tablespoons corn oil (do not use peanut oil)

2 large cloves garlic, minced

1/4 cup brown bean sauce

1. Drain chilies, reserving liquid. Mince chilies, including seeds, by hand (wear gloves) or in a food processor.

2. Cut peppers by hand into pieces approximately 1/4 inch square, or use a food processor and pulse-chop to minimize loss of liquid. Do not chop too fine.

3. Heat a heavy pot or saucepan at least 12 to 14 inches in diameter over medium-high heat. Add the oil and then the chilies and stir-fry 2 to 3 minutes until brown, being careful not to burn chilies. Add garlic and stir-fry a few seconds. Add sweet peppers and stir-fry for 2 minutes. Add brown bean sauce and 1/2 cup of the soaking water from the chilies. Mix well.

4. Reduce heat to low until mixture is barely bubbling, and cook, uncovered, until liquid is nearly gone, 30 to 45 minutes, stirring occasionally. When a spatula pulled through the sauce leaves a nearly clear path, the sauce is done. It will also have turned from a bright red to a darker red.

5. Store in airtight containers in the refrigerator or freezer. Be sure a film of oil covers the top of the sauce to help prevent spoilage.

Note: This recipe may be doubled, but use a larger pan with more space for the sauce to cook down. More than doubling the recipe does not allow it to cook fast enough for the best flavor.

While Chinese cooking dates back at least six thousand years, many of today's traditional dishes use ingredients that are not indigenous to China. Catsup originated in China as *ke-tsiap*, a pickled fish sauce with no tomatoes, but the introduction of tomatoes by the Spanish traders changed this condiment. Soon a tomato-based catsup was being exported to England, and when the British occupied Hong Kong they brought along their own tomato-based version of the sauce, which became so popular that it was soon added to a variety of Chinese dishes. Here it is the base for a sauce to coat deep-fried ribs. More than 97 percent of U.S. households use catsup (ketchup), but your friends will have a hard time identifying the base of this special sauce.

Ribs in Special Sauce / Ts'u Lu P'ai Ru

Florence Lin

Adapted by ACAI

Serves 8 as a appetizer

1 rack (2 pounds) spareribs, cut across the bones into 1 1/2-inch strips	1 teaspoon salt
	1/2–3/4 cup water
1/2 cup flour	2 cups peanut or vegetable oil
1/2 cup cornstarch	

Sauce:

1/4 cup A-1 steak sauce	2 tablespoons sugar
1/4 cup ketchup	

1. Pull off and discard any skin from the back of the ribs. Cut the ribs into pieces that have one rib and a little meat—about 5 cups.

2. In a large bowl, whisk together the flour, cornstarch, and salt. Stir in 1/2 cup water all at once and mix into a smooth and sticky paste. Add additional water a couple of tablespoons at a time if necessary. Add the ribs to the bowl and stir to coat.

3. Preheat oven to 275°. Heat a wok over medium-high heat, add oil, and bring to 375°. Mix the ribs again and drop them one at a time into the hot oil. Fry in

small batches, 8 to 10 at a time, for 5 to 10 minutes, until ribs are golden brown and crisp and the meat is completely cooked. Drain ribs on a paper towel and place on a wire rack set over a cookie sheet to keep in warm oven. Repeat frying process until all ribs are cooked.

4. Remove the oil from the wok, retaining 2 tablespoons. Heat the wok and add reserved oil. Add the sauce ingredients (A-1 sauce, ketchup, and sugar) and stir, cooking until the sauce thickens, which will happen quickly. Do not let it burn. Turn off the heat and add the hot ribs to the sauce. Stir for a few minutes to coat with sauce. Arrange ribs on a serving platter or on individual plates and serve hot. Or make the dish an hour or two ahead of time and serve at room temperature.

Another Significant Import from China

In 1905, the Minnesota Department of Game and Fish brought in seventy pairs of Chinese ring-necked pheasant. Pheasant had been raised in China for over three thousand years but were not native to Minnesota. The birds were released in suitable rural areas, but none survived. Between 1916 and 1918, the department imported four thousand more pheasant and provided six thousand pheasant eggs to farmers and sportsmen. This time enough birds survived to start a pheasant population that would eventually produce nearly half a million birds annually for harvesting. Today, Minnesota pheasant are also grown commercially and sold around the country. We have adapted the recipe below to work with pheasant as well.

Smoking fowl in a wok is not difficult and is well worth the effort. The smoked poultry can be served hot, cold, or at room temperature and freezes well. Whole chicken, turkey and chicken pieces, Rock Cornish game hens, quail, partridge, and pheasant are all good for smoking. Adjust the steaming time to be sure the meat is very tender before it is smoked. We recommend making the steamed buns (page 44) that perfectly complement this flavorful treat. They also freeze well for later use.

Smoked Duck

Florence Lin
Adapted by ACAI
Serves 4 or up to 10 with other dishes

1 (5-pound) Long Island duckling or equivalent	1/4 cup hickory chips
2 tablespoons coarse salt	1 tablespoon sesame oil
1 (2-inch) piece ginger, smashed	Steamed Buns (page 44)
1 scallion, halved and smashed	Scallion Brushes (below) hoisin sauce

1. Clean the duck by thoroughly rinsing in cold water; dry with paper towels. Sprinkle the salt on the duck inside and out, and then rub evenly with your hand. Cover and store in the refrigerator for 2 to 3 days, changing the position of the duck once a day.

2. Rinse duck again and pat dry. Place duck in a deep dish and rub the outside of the duck with ginger and then scallion. Set ginger and scallion inside duck. Prepare a large pot with 2 to 3 inches of boiling water; set dish containing the duck on a rack inside pot, cover, and steam duck for approximately 1 hour, until very tender when pierced with a fork. Check water level several times and add boiling water as necessary.

3. Remove duck from pan, drain any juices out of cavity, reserving for other uses, and remove and discard scallion and ginger. Place duck on a plate, cover, and cool in the refrigerator.

4. Prepare an iron wok for smoking by lining it with foil, allowing a 3-inch opening in the foil at the base of the wok. Sprinkle hickory flakes in the exposed wok area and insert a wire rack or cross 3 or 4 bamboo chopsticks that have been soaked in water. Place cooked duck on rack, tightly cover wok with foil, and turn heat to high. Smoke for 10 minutes.

5. Turn off heat and let stand 5 minutes before removing cover. Remove duck and rub with sesame oil. Refrigerate for at least 20 minutes.

6. Pull the duck meat away from the bones and cut into 1 by 2–inch pieces. Serve warm, cold, or at room temperature with steamed buns, scallion brushes, and hoisin sauce. Guests take a piece of smoked duck and place it in a steamed bun brushed with hoisin sauce, adding the scallion brush as an extra flavor in this truly Chinese sandwich.

Scallion Brushes

Clean and trim each scallion and rinse thoroughly. Leaving about half an inch of the green portion of the scallion attached to the white end, sliver the white end to form a brush. Place in cold water and refrigerate; the cold will cause the brushes to open and curl. Remove from water and pat dry before serving.

For pheasant:

1. Steam whole breasts in a dish placed in a steamer to catch all the juices (see note page 44). Steam for 60 to 90 minutes, until very tender when pricked with a fork.

2. Remove from steamer and cut breast in half through the breastbone. Lay the pieces meat-side down in a shallow bowl and pour juices over them; for two average-sized pheasants, there will be about a half cup of rich broth. Cover and refrigerate overnight.

3. Remove breasts from broth (reserve broth), wipe with a paper towel, and set up in foil-lined wok as described at left. Smoke over high heat for 8 minutes.

4. Turn off heat and let stand for 5 minutes before removing cover. Remove pheasant from the smoker and place breast-side down in a shallow bowl; cover with reserved broth. Refrigerate for 2 hours or overnight.

5. To serve, bring pheasant to room temperature, remove bones, and slice diagonally. Pour a little broth over the meat and garnish with cilantro leaves. The smoked pheasant may be frozen in plastic bags with broth added.

Smoked Duck on Steamed Buns.

Smoked Pheasant with whole canned cranberry.

Note: If the pheasant has no skin, rub it with a little vegetable or sesame oil before steaming. The very dry meat needs the broth soakings to keep it moist.

Brian Anderson, an avid pheasant hunter for forty years, supplied us with the birds to develop the smoked pheasant recipe. He says wild pheasant have a better flavor and texture than farm-raised birds. In thanks we gave him some smoked pheasant to sample. His wife, Carolyn, a talented hairdresser and creative cook, sliced the room-temperature pheasant breasts into thin slices and topped each one with a dollop of homemade whole cranberry sauce. They served them as appetizers and said their guests were most enthusiastic about this Minnesota-Chinese treat.

Quick Yeast Dough for Steamed Buns / Fa Mian

Florence Lin

Adapted by ACAI

Makes 28 small buns

1 package dry yeast	2 tablespoons peanut or corn oil
approximately 3/4 cup lukewarm water	2 1/2 cups all-purpose flour
2 teaspoons sugar	sesame oil

1. Dissolve the yeast in the warm water and let sit for 1 minute. Add the sugar and peanut or corn oil to the yeast mixture and mix well. Place the flour in a food processor with a metal blade and begin processing. Pour the liquid yeast mixture through the feed tube in a fast stream until the dough forms a ball, about 10 seconds. Continue processing for 1 minute or until the dough is very smooth and not sticky. If dough is dry, add water 1 tablespoon at a time; if dough is sticky, add flour 1 tablespoon at a time.

2. Turn the dough out onto a lightly floured surface and knead a few turns. The dough should be firm and pliable. Divide dough in half and cover one half. Pull and roll the other half into a cylinder about 14 inches long. Cut the roll into 14 (1-inch) pieces, covering pieces with a damp cloth as you work. Quickly roll each piece into a 3-inch circle. Brush half of each circle with sesame oil and cover by folding the other half over the oiled section to form a half circle. Lightly score the bun with a cleaver and set on a small piece of parchment or waxed paper in a steamer tray. Continue until tray is filled, leaving room between the buns for expansion. Set in a warm place and let rise for 30 minutes. Continue process with remaining dough.

3. Set up a wok with boiling water over high heat. Set steamer trays two high over the hot water, cover, and steam over high heat for 15 minutes. Remove buns from the steamers and place on dry towels to absorb some of the moisture. Serve buns hot with smoked duck or barbecued pork slices for delicious sandwiches.

Note: Buns may be refrigerated for a few days or frozen for up to 2 months. Bring to room temperature and reheat in a steamer for 10 minutes.

At the China Institute, I was fortunate to see several demonstrations of Chinese noodle pulling by one of the masters of the art, Chef Kun Jing Mark. Years later I saw him in Las Vegas at the MGM Grand, where he was a chef at the hotel's Chinese restaurant. Every night he would stand in the wide corridor just outside the restaurant entrance, and as a crowd gathered he would stretch, twist, and throw a rope of fresh noodle dough. In a matter of minutes, he would turn it from a wad of dough into two thousand noodles no thicker than a strand of hair. In fact, they are called Dragon Beard Noodles. — PLH

It takes years of practice to perfect this technique, not to mention a high ceiling with room to swing the dough, and very strong arms. While the texture of thrown noodles is chewier than that of rolled noodles, the recipe below will provide wonderful egg noodles that keep well in the freezer and are so much better than dried noodles. While the noodles may be mixed and rolled by hand, we use a food processor and pasta cutter to make the job easier.

Chinese Egg Noodles / Dan Mian

Florence Lin
Adapted by ACAI
Makes 1 1/2 pounds

3 cups all-purpose flour, plus more for dusting	2 teaspoons corn or peanut oil
1 teaspoon salt	approximately 1/2 cup water
2 large eggs	cornstarch for dusting

1. In a food processor with a metal blade add the flour and salt. Put the eggs, oil, and water in a small pitcher; do not mix. Pulse the flour and slowly pour in the eggs, oil, and water through the feed tube, continuing to pulse for gradual absorption of the liquids. The dough should form a ball within a minute or so and cling to the blade. If the dough is too dry, add water 1 tablespoon at a time; if it is too wet and sticky, add flour 1 tablespoon at a time. The dough should form a pliable ball and hold together nicely when you squeeze it with your fingers. Place dough on a lightly floured counter and knead a few times. If the dough is sticky, knead a small amount of flour into the dough until it is smooth and pliable. If the dough is dry, put a little water on your hands and knead it into the dough until it is smooth and pliable. Cover the dough with plastic wrap and let rest for 1 hour.

2. Divide the dough into 4 pieces. Work with one at a time, keeping the rest covered (see note for tips). Flatten the dough with your hand and lightly flour the top. Stretch it into a rectangle about 4 inches wide. Run it through the pasta cutter at the thickest setting; it will begin to stretch. Flour both sides again, fold in thirds, and run it through the pasta machine at the next smaller setting. Continue to do this until you

have run it through the machine 5 times and are now at the next to the lowest setting. If the sheet becomes too long to handle, cut it in half and work with shorter sheets. The dough will be completely smooth and fairly long. Hang the noodle sheet halfway over the edge of the counter on a clean towel to dry slightly before cutting. Repeat with the other 3 pieces of dough.

3. Depending on humidity, the noodle sheets will be dry enough to cut in 10 to 15 minutes. They need to be pliable enough to feed through the cutter but not so dry that they crumble. Working with one sheet at a time, dust each side with cornstarch. Feed the sheet through the pasta cutter and place cut noodles to dry on a wire rack in small nests about 3 inches in diameter.

4. The noodle nests can be boiled after about 10 minutes of drying, or they can be completely dried (about 24 hours) and the noodles stored in plastic bags. The best way is to steam the noodle nests after they have dried for about 10 minutes. Place nests in oiled bamboo steamer trays and steam in a wok for 10 minutes. Place the steamed nests back on the wire racks to completely cool, and then freeze in plastic bags. The frozen noodles will keep for several months. Do not thaw before cooking.

5. To boil, add the fresh, dried, or frozen noodles to boiling water, cook for 3 or 4 minutes until just tender, drain, and toss with a little peanut or corn oil before serving.

Note: The noodle sheets can stretch to six feet or more and become too long to handle. To avoid this, cut the original dough into eight sections and work with one section at a time. The finished noodles will be about five feet long and much more manageable. So that the noodles do not get too dry, work only half of the dough through the cutting process before stretching the remaining dough. As long as it is well covered the raw dough will keep several hours. If the noodle sheets get too dry they will not run through the pasta cutter but will bunch up and tear. If the noodle sheets are too wet they will not separate into noodles after cutting. If the edges of the sheets have dried before cutting but the rest is still pliable, trim away the dried edges with scissors before cutting into noodles. The scraps are still delicious, just not very attractive.

Egg Noodles with Meat Sauce / Cha Chiang Mien

Florence Lin

Adapted by ACAI

Serves 6–8

4 tablespoons peanut or corn oil, divided

1 pound ground pork or beef

1 tablespoon dry sherry or rice wine

2/3 cup brown bean sauce

4 tablespoons hoisin sauce

1/4 teaspoon MSG, optional

1 1/2 cups chicken broth

1/4 cup minced scallions

1 pound fresh or dried egg noodles

garnishes: see Sesame Dressing suggestions, page 47

1. Heat a wok or heavy skillet over medium heat until very hot. Add 3 tablespoons of oil and stir-fry the pork or beef for about 2 minutes, until the meat separates into bits.

2. Splash on the sherry or rice wine and then the bean sauce, hoisin sauce, and MSG (if using). Stir-fry for a few minutes and add the broth. Bring to a boil, reduce heat to medium low, and simmer for about 5 minutes, until the sauce is well cooked, stirring to prevent mixture from sticking.

3. Add the scallions and cook 1 minute. Remove from heat and keep warm. The sauce may be cooled and then reheated in the microwave.

4. Bring a pot of water to boiling, add the noodles, stir with chopsticks or fork, reduce heat to medium, and cook for 2 to 3 minutes or until just barely tender. Drain and add 1 tablespoon oil to the noodles, tossing well to keep them from sticking.

5. Divide noodles into individual rice or soup bowls and top each with 2 tablespoons warm sauce. Add a little garnish for color. Serve additional sauce and garnishes for diners to add as they choose.

Note: Monosodium glutamate (MSG) has traditionally been an important flavor enhancer used especially in China and Japan and is often found in older Asian recipes. In the United States, fewer and fewer restaurants use it because some people experience side effects from it.

Egg Noodles with Meat Sauce, Noodles with Peanut Sesame Dressing, Hunan Pepper Sauce, and assorted toppings.

Several restaurants in the Twin Cities offer sesame noodles, and most often the dish is served warm. This one is served at room temperature with cold garnishes.

Noodles with Peanut Sesame Dressing / Lian Ban Mien

Florence Lin

Adapted by ACAI

Serves 8–10

1 pound fresh egg noodles

2 tablespoons corn oil

Sauce:

1/4 cup creamy peanut butter

2 tablespoons sesame oil

2 tablespoons corn oil

1/2 teaspoon coarse salt

4 teaspoons sugar

1/4 teaspoon MSG, optional (see note page 46)

2 tablespoons Chinese dark soy sauce

2 tablespoons red wine vinegar

2 tablespoons cold water

2 teaspoons Szechuan or Hunan hot chili sauce, including some of the oil

garnish suggestions: slivered scallions, radishes, pea pods, or cucumbers; cooked chicken pieces, ham strips, egg crepes (page 3), or blanched fresh mung bean sprouts

1. Cook noodles in boiling water until barely tender, about 2 to 3 minutes. Drain noodles and plunge into cold water. Drain well and toss with chopsticks for about a minute to remove additional water. Mix with 2 tablespoons corn oil and set aside.

2. Blend together peanut butter, sesame oil, and 2 tablespoons corn oil until very smooth. Stir in salt, sugar, MSG (if using), soy sauce, vinegar, water, and chili sauce, mixing until all ingredients are completely blended. Sauce may be made several days ahead: refrigerate, covered, and bring to room temperature before serving. Stir again.

3. Fill rice or soup bowls with a portion of noodles. Top with two spoonfuls of the sauce, and garnish as desired. Serve additional sauce and garnishes for diners to add as they enjoy the noodles.

Date Wontons / Tsao Ni Hun Tun

Florence Lin

Adapted by ACAI

Makes about 80 wontons

1 (8-ounce) package pitted dates, finely chopped

1/2 cup finely chopped walnuts

2 teaspoons grated orange or lemon rind

1 pound Cantonese egg roll wrappers

2 cups peanut or corn oil

2 tablespoons confectioners' sugar

1. Combine the dates with the walnuts and orange or lemon rind. If mixture is dry, add a little orange juice to help hold it together.

2. Moisten your hands with water and shape the filling into cylinders about 1 inch long and 1/3 inch in diameter. There should be about 80. Set aside.

3. Cut each egg roll wrapper into 9 squares and cover with a damp towel. Place 1 roll of filling at one corner of an egg roll wrapper and roll up, leaving sides open. Use a little water to help seal the edges of the wonton, and then twist the two free ends like a firecracker to enclose the filling. Repeat until all of the filling has been used.

4. In a wok over medium-high heat, heat oil to 250°. Fry a few wontons at a time until they are golden and crisp, about 3 to 4 minutes. Do not overcook: they will continue browning after being removed from oil. Use a slotted spoon to remove wontons from oil; drain on a paper towel and cool to room temperature. Using a small sieve, sprinkle confectioners' sugar over the wontons before serving.

Notes: Finished wontons without the sugar may be stored in an airtight container for up to 2 weeks; sprinkle with sugar before serving. Leftover wonton skins may be cut into strips and deep-fried for wonton chips. Sprinkle with Szechuan Pepper Salt (page 48).

Szechuan Pepper Salt

1/4 cup coarse salt

2 tablespoons Szechuan peppercorns

1 teaspoon whole black peppercorns

In a dry pan over low heat, roast all the ingredients, shaking the pan a few times while roasting, until the peppercorns are fragrant, about 5 minutes. Do not allow to burn. Remove to a dish and cool the mixture. Crush the pepper salt in a spice grinder or with a mortar and pestle or rolling pin. If desired, strain through a fine sieve to remove larger pieces. Store in an airtight jar.

Shopping Malls Bring Chinese Restaurant Chains to Minnesota

Major cities in Minnesota formed on the banks of the largest rivers and on Lake Superior, where steamboats brought settlers and visitors by the thousands. Minneapolis and St. Paul got their start with merchants, warehouses, homes, and stores close to the materials and people coming off the boats. As the population grew the commercial district moved away from the river but was still nearby.

In 1902, George Draper Dayton built Dayton's Dry Goods store at Seventh Street and Nicollet Avenue in Minneapolis, just one mile from the river, and the city's commercial district soon moved to the area around his store. In 1906, John's Place moved to a block away, on Sixth Street off Nicollet, and the Nankin opened a year later just down the street from Dayton's, on Seventh next to the Radisson Hotel.

After World War II, as returning veterans demanded low-cost housing, developers began building homes in the suburbs ringing the major cities. Dayton's management recognized the change in customer needs and in 1956 created the first enclosed shopping mall in the United States. Southdale was built in the affluent suburb of Edina, five miles from downtown Minneapolis. Downtown retailers were shocked by the expansion, worried it would mean the end of downtown shopping.

Because Dayton's kept its primary store in its original location, that fear was partially abated.

Anchored by Dayton's and three other major retailers, Southdale promised high customer traffic with space costs based on sales, resulting in rental rates that many small restaurants and retailers could rarely afford. At the time Joe Bonoff owned the upscale women's fashion store Jackson Graves on Nicollet and Ninth, a block from Dayton's (where Leeann Chin managed the alterations department). While other downtown retailers were afraid of the change, Bonoff could see the value of expanding to the suburbs and took a space in the proposed "Dale." His son Barry became manager of Jackson Graves Southdale and remembers it well. "We started drawing customers from the day we opened," he said, "and by the second year, we were making a profit. At one point our sales were the largest per square foot in the complex for a small store." In fact, Southdale was so successful it was expanded several times to include a major supermarket and eventually a movie theater with additional restaurant space. In this expanded section, P. F. Chang's China Bistro brought its West Coast version of Chinese cooking to Minnesota in 2001. The Southdale restaurant was just one of the chain's sixty-five locations nationwide.

In 1992, the Ghermezian brothers from Canada built the giant Mall of America about five miles south of Southdale in the suburb of Bloomington. It featured several food courts and attracted more restaurant chains, including Panda Express with its Chinese fast food. By 2011 the mall was drawing forty million visitors annually.

As the number of Chinese restaurants in Minnesota grew from one in 1893 to nearly seven hundred in 2009, diners became interested in other cuisines of Asia as well. According to *Asian Restaurant News,* in 2009 Minnesota had 1,091 Asian restaurants including 697 Chinese, 61 Japanese, 97 Thai, 87 Vietnamese, 43 Indian, 7 Korean, and 99 Pan Asian—and the numbers continue to grow. But the Chinese influence was so great that chow mein became synonymous with not only Chinese food but Asian food in general, and the new Asian restaurants sometimes added it to their menus in order to be more accepted by Minnesota diners.

Legend has it that the Chinese kitchen god, Zao Jun, watches over everything in the household and reports to the Jade Emperor a week before the year ends. If the report is good, the year ahead will be filled with good things. If it is not, the family may have an unlucky year. In traditional kitchens a bowl of fruit is positioned below the picture of Zao Jun to ensure a good report.

Philippine Islands

The flavors of...
the Philippine Islands

The more than seven thousand islands of the Philippines originally were inhabited by the natives of the Malayo-Polynesian region of Asia and eventually became home to traders from Malaya, Indonesia, and China. In the sixteenth century, the Spanish conquered the Philippine Islands and ruled them for the next four hundred years. In 1898 the people of the Philippines claimed their independence. During World War II the islands were placed under the protection of the United States before getting their final independence in 1946. Each of the occupying forces left its own influence on Filipino cuisine. One was the introduction of SPAM®, the Minnesota-created ham product from Hormel, brought to the islands by U.S. troops. SPAM® became a favorite of the Filipinos and is still one of the most popular U.S. imports to the islands. In fact, Hormel built a production facility in the Philippines to handle demand for its famous canned pork product.

The first Filipino immigrants to Minnesota came in 1910, when the census showed two were living in the state. More began arriving in the 1920s, primarily students in Minnesota colleges and farm workers recruited from the Philippines. The immigrants of this era became known within the Philippine community as "old-timers," and many of them helped new immigrants adjust to their unfamiliar surroundings. In 1929 Filipino old-timers Filemon and Clara A. Balbuena managed a company restaurant serving Filipino food, the first in Minnesota. In 1949 they opened Balbuena Grocery Store in the Selby-Dale area of St. Paul, operating it

Facing page: Mena-li Canlas's Ube Cake

until 1975. While there have been a number of efforts to open Filipino restaurants in the state, only one has lasted successfully for more than a year.

Today, if you want to experience the food of the Philippines in Minnesota you will need to find a Filipino friend who will cook for you, attend one of several annual Filipino events where food is always part of the celebration, or locate one of the delis or a food truck serving Filipino food. We were very fortunate to find a number of outstanding Filipino cooks willing to share their stories and their food with us. Here are just a few.

A Nursing Career Leads to the Food Business

Yvonne Sanchez's experience with Minnesota began in 1968 at the Mayo Clinic in Rochester, where she participated in a two-year nurses exchange program between the Philippines and St. Mary's Hospital. At the end of the program, she returned to her home in San Jose Camarines Sur. Shortly after that, she married Ely Arcilla and then came back to Minnesota by way of Chicago.

"Ely had a job in Chicago, where we lived for two years," she recalled. "But I really wanted to return to Minnesota, where I had enjoyed living in Rochester." When St. Paul–based 3M had an opening for an engineer in surgical products, Ely applied for the job, and the rest is history.

They moved to Minnesota in 1974 and Yvonne, a registered nurse, went to work for Bethesda Hospital and then St. Paul–Ramsey Hospital. Soon they were raising a family and Yvonne wanted to find a job where she could keep the children with her during the day. Her family in the Philippines had been in the rice business and operated a small market, so she was used to working in the food industry. By 1977 she was ready to launch her own business and with Ely opened Phil.-Oriental Imports on Forest and Maryland avenues in St. Paul. "There were not many Asian markets in the area at that time," she said, "and none that carried ingredients for Filipino cooking."

Phil.-Oriental Imports, located at 789 University Avenue West, St. Paul, since 1988.

Phil.-Oriental Imports initially carried ingredients for Filipino cooking as well as that of India and Indochina. At one point it sold ten varieties of rice, so important to the many cuisines of Asia. After two years on Maryland, Yvonne and Ely moved the store to Lexington and University avenues in St. Paul, where they remained for four years, then to 1046 University Avenue for another four years. In 1988 they bought the building at 789 University Avenue West, where they have operated ever since.

When they took over a space that had been an African market, they soon had customers of the former tenants coming in for items from West Africa. "We found an importer in New Jersey who could supply those items," Yvonne said, "so we began to carry them and found a new source of customers."

The business grew, and Yvonne was indeed able to bring her three children—Eileen, Yvette, and Erik—to work with her, sometimes closing the store for fifteen minutes in the afternoon so she could pick up one or another of the children from school. As they grew up they also worked in the store part time and then went on to other endeavors, including computer science, food science, and mass communications.

Over the years, Yvonne has seen changes in the types of customers and the items they seek. Today, Phil.-Oriental Imports attracts shoppers from the five-state area as well as other retailers for things such as frozen grated ube, red palm oil, mellon seeds, plantains, mango powder, ghee, and agar-agar, to name just a few. In the spring of 2011, they leased out a corner of the store for takeout

Filipino food on Fridays, Saturdays, and Sundays. Operated by Jun Maniago, the deli offers a variety of traditional dishes from the Philippines.

In 2002 the Arcillas celebrated the store's twenty-fifth anniversary with a formal dinner-dance at the Airport Hilton for nearly three hundred customers and friends. While Yvonne says she would rather sell food than cook it, she does have one favorite dish that she shares with us here.

Cassava Cake

Yvonne Arcilla

Serves 12

1 (16-ounce) package grated cassava (a starchy root from the Philippines that is available frozen)	1 cup whole milk
	1 cup granulated white sugar
	2 eggs
1 cup coconut milk, canned or frozen	2 tablespoons melted butter

1. Mix all ingredients together in a large bowl.

2. Pour mixture into a greased 9x13–inch baking pan (see note). Bake at 350° for 1 hour and 15 minutes or until the cake top has turned brown.

3. May be served as is, or cool and top with frosting.

Frosting:

1 cup whole milk	2 tablespoons flour
1 cup coconut milk	2 egg yolks
2 tablespoons sugar	

1. In a saucepan, mix all ingredients together until well blended. Bring to a boil and simmer and stir until thick.

2. Spread the mixture over the top of the cooled cake still in the pan. Return to the oven and bake at 350° until the topping turns brown.

Note: Use a single-layer metal cake pan or Pyrex pan, not a pan with double metal layers.

Ely and Yvonne Arcilla celebrate twenty-five years in business, 2002.

Metallurgist Retires to the Kitchen

Abelando Sioson Malicsi was born in one of the most isolated southern islands of the Philippines but was destined to travel to all parts of the world. First he attended the University of Santo Tomas for a degree in chemical engineering; then he worked in a plywood factory in Taggat, Claveria, Cagayan, the farthest Filipino town north of Manila. Next he worked for the Bureau of Mines as a metallurgist—his friends described his work as making small rocks out of big rocks. In 1962 he was sent to the United States to participate in various metallurgical research projects with the U.S. Bureau of Mines in Oregon, Arizona, and Alabama. He traveled to Europe and then accepted a job with the bureau in its Minneapolis Research Center. After a year he was transferred to the University of Minnesota, where he worked for twenty-five years, until his retirement. There he met Lita Vargas, a U. of M. graduate student in English and theater arts from the Philippines. They married and had a son, Allen, who graduated from St. John's University in Collegeville. Lita taught English and theater at Washburn and Roosevelt high schools in Minneapolis and is now very active in a number of Filipino organizations, often directing theatrical performances at special events.

So what does all this have to do with Filipino food in Minnesota? Everything!

Abe Malicsi with ingredients for vegetable egg rolls.

I met Abe (pronounced AhBay) in 1994 when I was looking for information on Filipino holiday cooking in Minnesota. He and Lita are active in a variety of Filipino organizations, and my editor at Asian Pages *suggested they might be a great source of information. It has been said if you are invited to the Malicsi household you should expect to eat. And each time I visited, eat I did! Wonderful, delicious Filipino food prepared by Abe. He watched his mother cook as he was growing up and eventually started cooking for himself. Now he cooks for the many people who visit the Malicsi home throughout the year. Abe's idea of a snack is a four-course meal. Lunch was nine courses. And each time I visited I learned so much about the wonderful foods of the Philippines. Here are a few of his recipes. — PLH*

Abe's Egg Rolls

Abe Malicsi

Makes 25 egg rolls

1 pound ground pork, fairly lean

1/2 cup coarsely grated rutabaga or butternut squash

1/4 cup finely chopped onion (any color)

1/4 cup finely chopped parsley (flat leaf or curly)

1/2 teaspoon salt (or to taste)

1/4 teaspoon pepper (or to taste)

1 package (25 pieces) spring roll wrappers, thawed and separated (keep wrappers between slightly moist kitchen towels)

1 medium egg, lightly beaten in a small dish

vegetable oil

sweet and sour sauce

1. In a large bowl, mix pork, rutabaga or squash, onion, and parsley very well. Mix in salt and pepper.

2. Take one heaping teaspoon of the filling and place it on one wrapper as shown on the wrapper package. Spread it out into a cylinder in the shape of a thin cigar. Roll the near corner over the filling and tighten to push out any air pockets around the mixture. Brush some of the egg around the three sides of the wrapper and fold in the left and right corners, keeping wrapper tight around the filling. Continue to roll, sealing edges with the egg. Set aside, covered with a damp towel. Repeat with remaining filling and wrappers.

3. Heat at least 3 inches of oil in a deep fryer or deep pan to 350°. Add egg rolls four to six at a time, without crowding pan. Fry until golden brown, turning once or twice, about 6 to 8 minutes. Remove from oil and drain on paper towels. Continue frying egg rolls until finished, adding oil to the pan as necessary. The finished rolls may be kept hot in a 250° oven for up to 1 hour.

4. Serve whole or cut into bite-size pieces, with sweet and sour sauce available from Asian markets.

Abe's Vegetarian Egg Rolls

Abe Malicsi

Makes 25 egg rolls

2 tablespoons vegetable oil, plus more for frying

1 medium onion, finely chopped

1 cup finely shredded green cabbage

1/2 cup coarsely grated carrots

1 cup coarsely grated rutabaga, sweet potato, or butternut squash

1 cup julienned fresh green beans

1 small package fresh bean sprouts

salt and pepper to taste

1 package (25 pieces) spring roll wrappers, thawed and separated (keep wrappers between slightly moist kitchen towels)

1 medium egg, lightly beaten in a small dish

sweet and sour sauce

1. In a wok or large skillet, heat 2 tablespoons oil over medium-high heat and stir-fry the onion for 1 minute. Add the cabbage, carrots, rutabaga, beans, sprouts, salt, and pepper and stir-fry until vegetables are wilted and most of the moisture has evaporated. Remove from heat and pour vegetables into a metal strainer to let the juices drip through. Cool the mixture to room temperature and press slightly with your hand to remove any more moisture.

2. Follow the instructions on page 54 for making the egg rolls, but use 2 tablespoons filling and shape them about 4 inches long and 1 1/2 inches in diameter. Deep-fry and serve hot with sweet and sour sauce.

Chicken with Bean Thread Noodles / Chicken with Sotanghon

Abe Malicsi

Serves 4–6

1/2 cup dried tree ear mushrooms

4 chicken thighs with skin and bones

2 tablespoons vegetable oil

3 cloves garlic, minced

1 small white onion, finely diced

low-sodium chicken broth

1 (2-ounce) package dried bean thread noodles, soaked in water until soft, drained, cut into 2- to 3-inch lengths

salt and pepper to taste

2–3 scallions, diced

1. Soak tree ears in warm water until soft enough to slice. Remove, squeeze out water, and discard any tough parts. Slice into long, thin strips.

2. In a medium saucepan, add the chicken thighs and about 5 cups of water to cover them. Bring to a boil and simmer until fork tender, about 20 to 30 minutes. Remove chicken from pan, reserving broth, and cool on a plate. Remove and discard skin and bones, then pull chicken apart with two forks or by hand.

3. In a heavy saucepan or wok, heat vegetable oil and then stir-fry garlic and onion until brown. Add the chicken and mushrooms and cook for 3 minutes. Add

the reserved broth plus additional low-sodium chicken broth or water to equal 1 cup per serving and bring to a boil. Add bean threads and simmer for 3 minutes. Add salt and pepper to taste.

4. Dish out into individual soup bowls or one large soup tureen and sprinkle scallions over the top. Serve hot.

Puto, the steamed, light bread from the Philippines, goes well with this soup (see page 58).

Breakfast Rice with Scrambled Eggs / Tapa-Sinangag-Itlog

Abe Malicsi

Serves 1

1 tablespoon vegetable oil

1 clove garlic, minced

1 cup leftover cooked rice

salt and pepper to taste

leftover salted beef or pork or ham, thinly sliced, salted overnight, lightly fried, or SPAM® (see note)

scrambled eggs (see page 56)

1. Heat a wok or frying pan, add vegetable oil, and sauté minced garlic.

2. Mash the rice lightly to break up any lumps and add it to the hot oil. Stir-fry to mix with the oil and garlic. Add salt and pepper to taste and continue stir-frying for about 5 minutes.

3. To serve, dish out rice into individual bowls and top with fried thinly sliced leftover salted beef or pork, ham or SPAM®. Serve with scrambled eggs.

Note: Dried fish that has been fried may be substituted for the meat. Sliced sausages or corned beef are also popular substitutes.

Previous page: Abe's meat-filled and vegetable egg rolls.
Left: Finished egg rolls cooling on the stove.

Scrambled Eggs:

1 tablespoon vegetable oil

1 clove garlic, minced

1 tablespoon minced onion

1 tablespoon diced tomatoes

1 teaspoon minced pre-served mustard leaves

1 egg

salt and pepper to taste

Heat a frying pan over medium-high heat and add vege-table oil. Quickly sauté garlic and onion plus tomatoes and preserved mustard leaves. Add egg and scramble. Add salt and pepper to taste. Serve with Breakfast Rice, page 55.

Abe's Flan.

Abe's Flan

Abe Malicsi

Serves 8–10

Caramel sauce:

Place 1/4 cup granulated white sugar in each of two (9x5) aluminum loaf pans. Place one aluminum pan over medium heat and slowly dissolve the sugar, swirling to keep the caramel from burning. Let it cool in the pan before adding the flan. Repeat with the second pan.

Flan:

4 jumbo eggs

2 cans condensed milk

2 cans whole milk (use the empty condensed milk cans to measure)

1 tablespoon vanilla extract

1 tablespoon lemon or orange extract

1 heaping tablespoon cornstarch

1. Place all ingredients in a blender that holds at least 6 cups and blend for 1 minute.

2. Place pans prepared with caramel in another large pan; add flan mixture to each of the prepared pans, fill the larger pan with at least 2 inches of water, and bake for 1 hour at 350°.

3. Remove flan from the oven and from the water bath. Cool the flan and chill before unmolding. Place cooled flan still in the pan in another pan of hot water. Loosen sides of flan away from container. Place a dish upside-down on top of the flan and invert the pan and dish so the flan falls onto the serving dish and the caramel sauce covers the flan. Slice flan and serve.

The "Cake Lady" from the Philippines

After Mena-li Docto Canlas earned her degree in dentistry in the Philippines, she came to Minnesota to pursue graduate studies in children's dentistry. Her husband, Eduard Canlas, also came to the state to earn a graduate degree in accounting. They intended to finish their education and move back to their homeland within five years. Instead they had their first child and Mena-li put her studies on hold. Then, after two more children, they decided to make Minnesota their permanent home. While Eduard pursued his career, Mena-li stayed home to raise the children.

Growing up in the Philippines, Mena-li did not have to help in the kitchen, so when she came to Minnesota she did not know how to cook. Fortunately, her sister Mari-etea Docto was a good cook and became her inspiration. Eventually Mena-li began cooking for potluck suppers within the Filipino community and discovered her favorite food to bring was cake. She soon became known as the "cake lady" and today can be found at many Filipino events selling ube, manlo, and cassava cakes, ensaymadas with cheese, puto, empanadas, and more. In January 2012 she also began offering Pinoy Brunch and Merienda at the Pines Market in Circle Pines, where diners choose from a variety of her favorite foods of the Philippines. She agreed to share three of her favorite recipes with us.

Empanadas

Mena-li Canlas

Makes 32 empanadas

Pastry dough:

4 cups all-purpose white flour	1 cup vegetable shortening (Crisco)
1 teaspoon salt	2 eggs
1/2 cup sugar	1/2 cup ice water

Filling:

1 tablespoon vegetable oil, plus more for frying	1 1/2 cups peas, canned, cooked, or frozen and thawed
3 pounds ground pork	1 1/2 cups raisins
1 medium onion, finely diced	1 1/4 cups soy sauce
1 tablespoon minced garlic	1 tablespoon salt
3 medium potatoes, finely diced	1 tablespoon pepper

Dough:

1. In a medium bowl, whisk flour, salt, and sugar together until well mixed.

2. Blend shortening into flour mixture until it has lumps the size of small peas. Add the eggs and mix well.

3. Using a tablespoon, add ice water to flour mixture one spoonful at a time, stirring quickly into the dough. Use only enough water so the dough comes together and is still crumbly.

4. Wrap the dough with plastic wrap and refrigerate overnight.

Filling:

Heat a skillet or frying pan over medium-high heat and add 1 tablespoon vegetable oil. Sauté the pork, onion, and garlic until the pork is thoroughly cooked. Add the potatoes, peas, and raisins. Stir-fry for a few minutes more and add the soy sauce, salt, and pepper. Stir to mix well, and let mixture cook a few minutes to evaporate liquids. Remove filling from pan and let it come to room temperature on a plate.

Assembly:

1. Make balls of dough about 1 1/4 ounces each. On a floured board, flatten balls into disks and roll out to about 3 inches in diameter. Place 1 tablespoon of filling in center of dough and fold dough in half to form crescent moon shape. Seal edges by pressing down with a fork to form a decorative edge. Repeat with remaining dough and filling.

2. In a deep fryer, wok, or large saucepan, heat vegetable oil about 5 inches deep to 350°. Carefully add four or five empanadas to the hot oil, one at a time. Do not crowd the pan. Fry on one side for a few minutes and then turn over to brown the other side, about 4 minutes per side. Remove to paper towels to drain. Serve warm. May be frozen. Thaw frozen empanadas at room temperature. To reheat empanadas, bake in a 350° oven until hot, about 6 minutes, or microwave for 30 seconds.

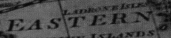

1. Grease 2 (24-count) mini-muffin pans.

2. In a blender container with metal blade inserted, mix together Bisquick, flour, and baking powder. Add milk and water and blend. Add egg whites and blend into a smooth batter.

3. Pour batter into greased mini-muffin tins, filling each cup halfway.

4. In a steamer large enough to hold the muffin pans, steam putos for 15 minutes. Let cool slightly, and then remove putos from tins. Serve with desserts, soups, or stews.

Ube Cake

Mena-li Canlas

Serves 16

Cake:

2 1/2 cups all-purpose white flour	8 eggs, yolks and whites divided
3 tablespoons baking powder	1/2 cup vegetable oil
1 teaspoon salt	1 teaspoon cream of tartar
1 cup grated ube	2 cups granulated white sugar
3/4 cup milk	10 drops violet food coloring
1 teaspoon vanilla extract	
1/2 cup corn syrup	

Icing:

1 cup evaporated milk	1 cup (2 sticks) butter, softened
3/4 cup granulated white sugar	

1. Preheat oven to 325°. Grease 3 (9-inch) round cake pans.

2. In a large bowl, mix flour, baking powder, and salt together.

3. In a separate bowl, add the ube and mix in the milk and vanilla extract until well blended. Mix in the corn syrup, egg yolks, and oil. Add the ube mixture to the flour mixture and blend until smooth.

Mena-li Canlas creates some of her famous empanadas.

Putos are traditional steamed breads that can be made into small cupcakes or a large, round biscuit that is cut into triangles. They are served with soups and dishes with sauce or as a dessert. Either way they are delicious and very easy to make.

Puto

Mena-li Canlas

Makes 48 small breads

2 cups Bisquick	2 cups milk
1 cup all-purpose white flour	1/4 cup water
3 tablespoons baking powder	4 egg whites

4. Using a mixer, beat the egg whites with the cream of tartar and gradually add in the 2 cups sugar, beating until the mixture forms stiff peaks.

5. Fold one-third of the beaten egg whites into the flour batter to lighten it, then fold in the remaining egg whites and blend in the food coloring. Gently mix to blend the color.

6. Pour one-third of the batter into each of the cake pans and bake for 30 to 35 minutes, until done. Cool cakes upside down on wire racks.

7. For frosting, in a small bowl, combine the evaporated milk with 3/4 cup sugar. In another bowl, cream the butter until fluffy and then gradually add the sugar mixture, mixing until well blended.

8. Cover the top of one cooled cake layer with icing, place another layer on top and ice the top of it, then add the third layer. Cover the whole cake with icing.

A Visit to Minnesota Turns Permanent

When Cora Cayetano and her husband came to Minnesota to visit his family, she thought it was just that, a visit, and they would soon be moving on to someplace warmer. Instead, they made the state their permanent home.

It wasn't long before she was in the food business, for that was her background in the Philippines. In 1974 she had begun operating a food stand on the Plaza. "We were open twenty-four hours a day," she recalled. "We would take turns sleeping in the back of the store and go home to shower and start again." Considering temperatures in the Philippines can top 110 degrees, it was long, hot work. But Cora likes warm weather, so it came as somewhat of a surprise that she was now living in the cold north.

In 1986 she opened the Wonton House in St. Paul, selling it to Taco Rico, which became Juanita's. In 1988 she opened Cora Cayetano's Filipino Fast Foods at 168 Concord Street in St. Paul and offered a small menu of dishes to eat in the store or take out. By 1994 she was also appearing at food festivals with her Filipino specialties, including lumpia (the Philippine version of spring rolls), adobo (chicken or pork simmered in a vinegar-flavored sauce), beef kabobs, and chicken wings. At the store she also featured pancit and mami siopao plus a variety of ingredients for Filipino cooking.

After several years Cora closed the diner/market and opened two chicken wing stores, Cora's Best Chicken Wings at 168 Cesar Chavez Street and 1143 Payne Avenue in St. Paul. Here she offers her special variety of chicken wings that continue to draw fans.

A two-layer version of Mena-li Canlas's Ube Cake.

Filipino Food Takes on a New Twist at Subo

Minnesota has had fewer than half a dozen Filipino restaurants from the 1920s through today. The few that opened did not last long. One example is Subo, which launched in 2009 at 89 South Tenth Street in Minneapolis. The chef was Filipino American Neil Guillen, originally from Michigan by way of New York. He attended the Culinary Institute of America and worked in California before joining the staff at the Kuma Inn in New York City. He was invited to come to Minneapolis to open Subo and use his Filipino background to combine the flavors of the Philippines with his classic French culinary training. The result was an interesting menu of lumpia, mustard dumplings, adobo chicken wings, and other offerings touched with Filipino flavors. Pancit, a Filipino favorite, was wok-fried with house-made sausage and vegetables. Roasted pork candy also was a hit with diners, who enjoyed the slightly sweet sausage. While the restaurant received rave reviews from critics and always seemed busy, Subo closed in 2010.

Filipino Food Truck Continues to Offer the Elusive Cuisine

The sous chef at Subo also had a Filipino background and did not want his favorite food to die with the restaurant. So in August 2011, Geoff King opened Scratch, one of the growing number of food trucks in the Twin Cities offering a variety of street food. Trained in classic cooking at the New England Culinary Institute in Vermont, Geoff wanted to find a way to offer Minnesotans some of the wonderful food he grew up with—his mom's home cooking. He and wife Aimee developed a small menu of lunch items drawing on Filipino classics and incorporating some of the ingredients from the islands. Pork egg rolls, tofu lettuce wraps, coconut braised chicken, pork and shrimp sandwiches, and sesame beef sandwiches fill the short menu with foods that celebrate the islands and offer just a taste of Geoff's favorite cooking. The tofu lettuce wraps won Geoff an award for best Food Truck Food in 2011, even though his was the newest food truck in the competition.

Chicken Adobo with Putos (page 58).

Scratch food truck, with owners Geoff and Aimee King.

Geoff looks forward to adding new dishes to the menu and to finding a way to feature Filipino food year-round. Here is a sampling of his favorite food.

Chicken Adobo / Adobong Manok

Geoff King

Serves 4–6

Marinade:

1 1/2 cups sugar cane vinegar

1 cup coconut milk

1/2 cup soy sauce

10 cloves garlic, peeled

3 bay leaves

1 1/2 teaspoons peppercorns or coarsely ground black pepper

1/2 cup brown sugar

2 whole star anise

1 (3 1/2-pound) whole chicken, quartered and cut into pieces

cooked rice

1. In a large bowl, combine all of the marinade ingredients. Add the chicken pieces, cover, and marinate in the refrigerator for 1 hour or overnight.

2. In a heavy-bottomed pot, heat the chicken and marinade over high heat. Bring to a boil, reduce the heat, and simmer on low until the chicken is tender and sauce is reduced by about half, 40 to 45 minutes.

3. Remove the bay leaves and star anise, and serve hot with rice.

Noodles with Chicken and Shrimp / Pancit Canton

Geoff King

Serves 4–6

1 whole, bone-in chicken breast

2 teaspoons salt

1/3 cup canola oil

1 large onion, diced

1 tablespoon minced garlic

1/2 pound medium shrimp, shelled and deveined

1 large carrot, julienned

2 tablespoons soy sauce

2 teaspoons fish sauce

1/4 teaspoon coarsely ground black pepper

1 (8-ounce) package pancit canton noodles (Excellent brand preferred)

1 cup coarsely shredded cabbage

1 bunch scallions, sliced

1. Place chicken breast in a large pot and cover with water and the 2 teaspoons of salt. Bring to a boil over high heat, then reduce heat and simmer until the chicken is cooked through, 15 to 20 minutes. Reserving broth, transfer the chicken to a plate to cool. When cooled, shred it into bite-size pieces and set aside.

2. Heat the oil in a wok or large saucepan over medium-high heat. Add the onion and garlic and sauté until lightly browned. Add the shrimp and continue to cook until the shrimp have begun to turn pink.

3. Add the carrots and 1/2 cup of the reserved broth and cook until the carrots are softened but still crisp, about 2 minutes.

4. Add the shredded chicken, soy sauce, fish sauce, and black pepper and cook just to warm through. Once all the ingredients are cooked and seasoned, add the pancit canton noodles. Increase the heat and continually add the reserved broth, 1/2 cup at a time, until the noodles are steamed through and tender. Add the cabbage and half of the scallions, and gently toss until well mixed. Serve hot and garnish with remaining scallions.

This recipe is a favorite of Geoff's because his grandfather used to cook it for him each time he visited.

Red Snapper with Pepper Sauce / Escabèche

Geoff King

Serves 4

Sauce:

4 tablespoons canola oil, divided

4 cloves garlic, thinly sliced

1 (1-inch) piece ginger, peeled and julienned

1 large onion, thinly sliced

1 red bell pepper, cored and julienned

1 green bell pepper, cored and julienned

1 cup water

1/2 cup sugar cane vinegar

2 tablespoons granulated white sugar

Fish:

1 (4-pound) whole red snapper, scaled and gutted

1 tablespoon salt

1 teaspoon coarsely ground black pepper

flour

1. In a large saucepan over medium-high heat, warm 2 tablespoons of the oil. Add the garlic, ginger, onion, and peppers and sauté until softened, about 3 minutes. Add the water, vinegar, and sugar. Increase the heat and bring to a boil. Reduce the heat and simmer for 5 minutes longer.

2. While reducing the sauce, season the fish with salt and pepper and dredge in enough flour to evenly coat both sides.

3. Add the remaining 2 tablespoons oil to a large sauté pan and heat over medium-high heat. When the oil is hot, add the fish and fry. Carefully turn the fish once and cook about 5 minutes on each side, until crisp and tender.

4. Transfer the fish to a serving plate, pour over the sauce with its vegetables to cover the surface of the fish, and serve.

Geoff suggests the following vegetable dishes for a traditional taste of the Philippines. In the *Pinakbet* recipe, fish sauce adds a distinctive flavor but water may be substituted to make it a vegan dish.

Stewed Vegetables / Pinakbet

Geoff King

Serves 6–8

1/2 kabocha squash, peeled, seeded, cut into 2-inch chunks

1/4 cup fish sauce or water

2 large tomatoes, peeled and chopped

1 large red onion, julienned

2 medium bitter melons, halved, seeded, cut into 1-inch slices

3 Chinese eggplants, halved lengthwise, cut into 2-inch pieces

10 okra, trimmed

15 long beans, cut into 2-inch pieces

1 yellow summer squash, cut into 2-inch slices

1 zucchini, cut into 2-inch slices

3 cloves garlic, minced

1 tablespoon sea salt

cooked rice

1. In a large saucepan, spread the kabocha squash over the bottom of the pan. Add the water or fish sauce and the remaining ingredients except rice. Place the pot over medium-high heat, cover, and simmer without stirring until the vegetables start to soften, 10 to 15 minutes.

2. Remove the cover and simmer without stirring until the vegetables are cooked through but still al dente, about 5 minutes. Serve as a side dish with rice.

Mung Beans / Mongo Guisado

Geoff King

Serves 4–6

1 cup dried mung beans

1 1/2 cups water

1 teaspoon salt

1 tablespoon vegetable oil

1 medium onion, diced

3 cloves garlic, minced

2 medium roma tomatoes, peeled and chopped

2 cups spinach leaves, washed

cooked rice

1. In a medium saucepan add the mung beans, water, and salt and bring to a boil over medium-high heat. Reduce the heat and simmer, uncovered, for 30 to 40 minutes, or until the mung beans begin to split.

2. In a larger saucepan add the oil and sauté the onion and garlic over medium-high heat until softened, about 5 minutes. Add the tomatoes and spinach; stir and cook for 1 minute. Add the mung beans and continue to cook for another 10 minutes to blend flavors. Serve hot with cooked rice.

Today the opportunities for enjoying the food of the Philippines may be limited, but well worth finding. In addition to the deli at Phil.-Oriental Imports, Mena-li's Sunday Pinoy Brunch and Merienda at the Pines Market in Circle Pines, and Scratch food truck, Filipino food is available at a number of annual events celebrating the culture of the Philippines. One of the largest is Philippine Day at St. Paul's Landmark Center, held each year in March or April. Sponsored by the Cultural Society of Filipino Americans, the event features dozens of Filipino dishes from barbecued pork kabobs to bowls of goto, to empanadas and a variety of desserts. It also showcases Filipino music and dance as well as products from the islands. For information about CSFA and its events go to csfamn.org. Better yet, try any of the recipes above and learn why Filipino food has found so many fans in Minnesota.

The flavors of...

Japan

After World War II, Chinese restaurants continued to dominate the "foreign" food picture in Minnesota, with several hundred operating around the state. A Filipino restaurant had survived for a few years, and Italian restaurants were beginning to take hold, but Chinese was clearly the favorite. Reiko Weston entered this atmosphere when she left her native Tokyo and moved to Minnesota in 1953 with her husband, Norman. By 1959, the lack of even a single Japanese restaurant intrigued her so much that she decided to interrupt her studies in mathematics at the University of Minnesota and open one herself. She intended the restaurant to be operated by her father, a former admiral in the Japanese navy, and her mother, who was an excellent cook. As it turned out, it became Reiko's career.

To get a better idea of what Americans liked about Japanese food, she visited more than fifty Japanese restaurants around the country before opening Fuji Ya at 814 LaSalle Avenue, just half a block from Dayton's. In the small space of a former tea leaf–reading room, Fuji Ya became an instant attraction as much for its décor as for its food. It was the state's first Japanese restaurant.

Before I knew anything about the food at Fuji Ya, friends had told me that customers had to remove their shoes and sit on the floor to dine. They heard that the food was cooked right at the table by kimono-clad servers and everyone ate with chopsticks. It sounded more like an adventure than a meal. Food critics of the time were even warning women not to wear tight skirts that would make it difficult to sit on the floor. So one night, wearing full skirts and clean socks without holes in the toes, four of us arrived to be seated on the tatami-covered floor of our own private bamboo and rice paper–walled dining area

Facing page: Sakura's Futomaki.
Right: Reiko Weston offers Japanese-style dining at Fuji Ya, 1984.

called a zashiki. We ordered sukiyaki, the only thing that seemed remotely familiar, cooked at our table with the wonderful aromas permeating the hushed air around us. It was delicious, and we did indeed survive dinner without our shoes.

Fuji Ya was an intriguing change from the usual restaurant experience. Each of the zashikis offered a private dining area, quiet and removed from the busy city streets just outside the door. Servers moved quietly and gracefully and spoke in hushed tones. The food was fresh and new to us and offered flavors that were most appealing. It was truly an experience, not a quick bite or order-ahead takeout, but slow, leisurely dining that was tasty and fun. — PLH

While Fuji Ya operated on LaSalle for ten years, Reiko was looking for another location where she could expand the space and the menu. In 1961 she found the abandoned Columbia Mill and Bassett Sawmill Engine House at 420 South First Street, on the banks of the Mississippi River overlooking the Corps of Engineers locks and the Third Avenue Bridge. She bought the property for twenty thousand dollars and was one of the first business owners to participate in the city's Mississippi Riverbank Renewal project. The land included space for a hundred-car parking lot. Over the next eight years Reiko completely revamped the mill into a 250-seat Japanese-style restaurant occupying two floors. Here the zashikis included huge picture windows overlooking St. Anthony Falls and the river below. In 1975, after a $250,000 expansion project, she added a *teppanyaki* room on a lower floor and introduced Minnesota to the Japanese style of special chefs slicing, dicing, and grilling food at the table (the method later used at Ichiban in 1979 and in the Benihana restaurant chain). In 1981 she opened the first *sushi* bar in the state. Year after year the restaurant was listed as a favorite in reader polls as Best Japanese, Best Sushi, Best Takeout, and so on.

But the Minneapolis Fuji Ya was just the beginning. In 1960 Reiko opened a second Fuji Ya on Alley 29 in downtown St. Paul. Despite her success at this location, she had to close the restaurant after one year to make way for the new World Trade Center building. In 1970 she established Fuji International of Japan, an import-export business that she intended would include Japanese fast-food restaurants throughout the country. As a test of that concept in 1972, Reiko opened Fuji International, a Japanese-style cafeteria at 408 Cedar Avenue on the University of Minnesota's west bank. A self-service restaurant, Fuji International was able to offer freshly cooked Japanese food for $0.95 to $1.95, a bargain for nearby students.

Fulfilling her desire to bring traditional Asian cooking to the Twin Cities, in 1977 Reiko opened Tiaga, a Chinese restaurant in St. Anthony Main just across the river from Fuji Ya. She was among the first in the area to feature *dim sum* but wanted the concept to go beyond the restaurant. She imported special equipment and five dim sum chefs from Hong Kong to make twenty different kinds of dim sum every day. At Tiaga the chefs were turning out four thousand dim sum wrappers daily: enough to sell to

After twenty-three years the boarded-up Fuji Ya building still stands high above St. Anthony Falls as a silent tribute to Reiko Weston and the decades she spent bringing the food and culture of Japan to Minnesota.

other restaurants and food stores locally and nationally. In 1984 Reiko opened Fuji Express in the skyway near Seventh and Marquette in Minneapolis, a location that worked well for about a year.

Reiko Weston's success earned her a variety of awards, including Small Business Person of the Year in 1979, and in 1980 she became the second woman to be elected to the Minnesota Hall of Fame. Even though Reiko had a stroke in 1978, with the help of her daughter, Carol, she continued to operate Fuji Ya and Tiaga until her death in 1988.

In 1987 the Minneapolis Park Board took Fuji Ya's parking lot by eminent domain for the development of West River Parkway, something Reiko had tried to fight. After ongoing legal battles that lasted a year following Reiko's death, the Park Board bought the entire property, including building and contents, for $3.5 million and required the restaurant to close in May 1990. While Carol had been running the business along with her mother, she was unsure about continuing Fuji Ya at another location. In September 1989 Carol held a party for the press and longtime patrons to talk about the future of Fuji Ya. It was also a celebration of the restaurant's thirtieth anniversary and a tribute to her mother.

Carol Weston Hanson and her husband, Thomas Hanson, did move Fuji Ya, to 2640 Lyndale Avenue South in Minneapolis and then to its current location on Lake Street just off Lyndale. In 2004 they opened a second Fuji Ya in St. Paul at Seventh and Wabasha.

I talked with Carol Weston Hanson in December 2011 to learn more about her amazing mother and her own success with Fuji Ya. "Mother did so many things well," Carol recalled, "including playing the piano." Reiko also played the koto and harpsichord, sang, and had ballet training. While Reiko was a quiet, even shy person, she had amazing strength and was determined to see the business succeed. "I grew up in the restaurant business," Carol added, "and began working at Fuji Ya at a young age," not unlike many children of restaurant owners. By the time Carol was in high school and then college, the restaurant was part of her life. Her brother, Michael, also worked in the family business, sometimes as a cook. Carol would host or wait tables or wash dishes—whatever needed doing. At one point Reiko planned to send Carol for sushi training in Japan, but she was told the school did not accept females because their hands were too warm. In 1978, when Reiko suffered a stroke, Carol cut her class schedule to a minimum to help manage the business full time; she eventually did complete her college degree. — PLH

Carol's management of the restaurant shaped her life and even led to her marriage. After Reiko's death, Tom became Carol's business partner as well. As their children—Melissa Nobuko, Benjamin Kaoru, and Sena Reiko—arrived, Tom took over more of the restaurant's management and Carol retired from the day-to-day operations to raise the children at home. While Carol and Tom are not pushing any of their children into the business, Benjamin has shown a flair for cooking, even winning a cook-off at scout camp.

Fuji Ya not only introduced Japanese food to Minnesota; it also provided a springboard for other Japanese restaurants. Miyoko Omori, a friend of Reiko's from Japan, worked at Fuji Ya before opening Kikagawa with John Omori and then Sakura on her own. Reiko brought in the state's first sushi chef, Nobuya, from Japan, and she would later hire Kiminobu Ichikawa, who became the well-known sushi chef Ichi and went on to open the Origami restaurants in Minneapolis and Minnetonka. Carol hired Teng "Tengo" Taho as the sushi chef at the Lyndale Avenue Fuji Ya: he would later open Sushi Tango at Calhoun Square in Minneapolis and in Woodbury.

I met Reiko Weston in 1971 when I was compiling a cookbook featuring local restaurant chefs. We wanted to devote one chapter to her food and her story. She was most gracious and generous with her time and shared a number of her recipes with me. In fact, I became popular among my friends for my rendition of sukiyaki cooked at the table and based on her recipe. We are able to bring you a variety of her recipes for dishes still popular in Japanese restaurants today. By the way, sukiyaki is no longer cooked at the table in Fuji Ya due to the expensive airflow systems now required. — PLH

Sukiyaki

Reiko Weston

Adapted by ACAI

Serves 4–6

1 cup Japanese dark soy sauce	1 tablespoon vegetable oil
1 1/2 cups water or dashi stock (page 68)	1 small can yam noodles (Shirataki)
1/4 cup saké	1 small can bamboo shoots
3 tablespoons sugar	1 cup sliced fresh mushrooms
dash MSG, optional (see note page 46)	1 medium onion, sliced
1–1 1/2 pounds prime rib eye steak, thinly sliced; meat should have some fat marbling for flavor	1 square bean curd (tofu), cut into 8 pieces
	1 bunch scallions, cut into 2-inch pieces
	steamed rice

1. Combine soy sauce, water or dashi, saké, sugar, and MSG (if using) for sauce.

2. Quickly sauté beef slices in lightly oiled hot, heavy frying pan or electric frying pan until just seared. Add the remaining ingredients (except rice) one at a time, being careful not to stir them together. Add enough sauce to half cover everything in the pan. Simmer, uncovered, until meat is nearly done and the flavors meld together, about 5 minutes. Dish out a little of each item into individual serving bowls, adding a little of the broth to each one. Serve hot with steamed white rice.

Japanese White Rice

Serves 3–4

Japanese rice is a shorter and stickier variety than Chinese long-grain white rice. The cooking technique is the same, but the rice-to-water balance is slightly different.

Wash the rice in cold water until the water runs clear. Strain the rice, then add it to a heavy pot or saucepan and add water. For every cup of short-grain Japanese white rice, use 1 1/4 cups of water. Quickly bring the mixture to a boil, cover, and lower heat to simmer until the water is absorbed by the rice, approximately 10 minutes. Turn off heat and leave covered for another 10 minutes. Remove lid and fluff rice with a fork. Serve hot.

Dashi *is a fish-flavored soup stock and sauce base used in Japanese kitchens. It is steeped from dried katsuo (bonito) and can have a very strong fish flavor and odor or be very subtle. When I first began cooking Reiko Weston's sukiyaki, I could not find dashi in Twin Cities markets. I substituted chicken broth, and my friends seemed to like the dish. When I moved to Manhattan with its multitude of Asian markets, in Chinatown I found powdered dashi packaged in tea bags, ready, I supposed, for turning into broth. The instructions were written in Japanese, so when I got home I had no idea what to do with them. I started boiling a few dashi bags in water, and the longer I cooked them, the stronger the odor. I added a few more bags to the boiling water, and the odor became even stronger. Finally, when I made the sukiyaki, I used the very potent dashi—and we could not eat it. It was simply too overpowering. — PLH*

Here is a recipe for making dashi that will be flavorful and not overpowering. And if the flavor is too strong, dilute with water or use plain water instead of the dashi.

Ichiban Dashi

Makes 5 cups

1 piece (about 6 inches) dried kombu, wiped clean	2 (0.175-ounce) packets dried bonito flakes

1. In a large saucepan, add kombu to 5 cups cold water and heat slowly over medium heat, about 5 minutes. Skim off any scum that forms on the surface. Just prior to the boiling point, remove and discard kombu.

2. Increase heat and, just as water begins to boil, add bonito flakes. Bring to a full boil, and then remove from heat. Allow the flakes to settle. Strain through fine sieve or muslin; do not squeeze. Set dashi aside for use as directed in recipes. Use dashi the day it is made.

Sunomono Salad

Reiko Weston

Serves 4

1 cup Japanese unseasoned rice vinegar (see note)	dash MSG (see note page 46)
2 tablespoons sugar or sugar substitute	mixed greens
2 teaspoons salt	cooked crabmeat or shrimp
2 teaspoons fresh lime or lemon juice	

1. Combine vinegar, sugar, salt, lime or lemon juice, and MSG in a small bowl.

2. Clean greens and break into bite-size pieces. Place in a larger bowl.

3. Pour dressing over greens and toss.

4. Serve salad in individual bowls and garnish with cooked or canned crab or shrimp.

Note: Japanese rice vinegar comes in two varieties: seasoned with soy sauce and sugar, which has a pale caramel color, or unseasoned, a clear liquid. Use the unseasoned variety for this recipe.

Teriyaki Sauce

Reiko Weston

Adapted by ACAI

Makes about 1 cup

1 cup Japanese dark soy
  sauce

1/4 cup sugar

2 tablespoons mirin
  (sweet rice wine)

dash red pepper (cayenne)

dash MSG, optional
  (see note page 46)

1 teaspoon grated
  ginger

1. Mix ingredients together in a saucepan and cook over low heat until mixture thickens, stirring occasionally. Remove from heat and set aside or store in refrigerator.

2. Use sauce to baste meat or fish as it is broiled or grilled. Lightly brush the meat or fish with vegetable oil before adding to the hot grill or before putting under the hot broiler. After a few minutes, start brushing the meat or fish with the sauce, turning and basting several times, until done. Do not use the sauce as a marinade: it will burn very quickly.

Tempura is a very light batter that takes some practice to make properly. Don't be discouraged if your first attempt is not quite what you would like. Try it several times until you develop the technique to your liking. Your tempura "failures" are good to eat, even if they don't look as you had hoped they would. For an appetizer, allow four pieces per person. As a main course, double the amount.

Tempura

Reiko Weston

Serves 4

raw shrimp, scallops, etc.

1 egg

1 1/2 cups ice-cold water

3 cups sifted flour

raw vegetables such as
  onion, green pepper,
  parsley, asparagus,
  squash, mum leaves

2 cups vegetable or corn oil

Tempura Sauce
  (recipe follows)

1. Wash, shell, and devein shrimp. Slit underside in two or three places to prevent curling. Cut large scallops into bite-size servings. Clean and cut any other raw fish into bite-size pieces.

2. Clean vegetables and mum leaves. Leave mum leaves whole. Cut onions and green peppers into rings. Slice squash into bite-size pieces. Break parsley into bite-size pieces. Use just the tender portion of the asparagus, and cut into bite-size pieces.

3. Beat egg slightly. Add ice water and mix. Add sifted flour. Mix lightly, leaving small lumps; batter should be thin.

4. Preheat the oil to 350°. Starting with the vegetables, dip pieces into batter, shake off excess, and fry to golden brown. Drain on paper towels. Continue deep-frying shrimp, scallops, and so on, keeping cooked tempura in a warm oven until serving. Serve hot with Tempura Sauce.

Tempura Sauce

Reiko Weston

Serves 4

1 cup dashi stock
  (see page 68)

3 tablespoons Japanese
  dark soy sauce

1 tablespoon sugar

1 tablespoon mirin (sweet
  rice wine) or sherry

pinch MSG
  (see note page 46)

Combine all ingredients in a saucepan and bring mixture to a boil. Remove from heat and serve warm in individual bowls.

Reiko Weston wrote the book *Cooking the Japanese Way* for Minneapolis-based Lerner Publications in 1984, part of a series of ethnic cookbooks for young cooks. No longer in print, it is available in many library collections throughout the state.

And Then There Were More Japanese Restaurants

Growing up in Saitama, Japan, Miyoko Omori always knew she wanted to own a restaurant. When she moved to Minnesota in 1970, she signed on with one of the most popular restaurants in the area, Fuji Ya. She once said that working with owner Reiko Weston was a great training ground. After nine years, Miyoko moved on to help her husband, John Omori, open Kikagawa in the Pillsbury Building in downtown Minneapolis. He would eventually relocate the restaurant to Riverplace on

St. Anthony Main, but by 1990 she was on her own and ready to start her own restaurant.

Miyoko says luck and friends helped create the opportunity for her to open Sakura in Galtier Plaza in downtown St. Paul. But it was also due to her talent, drive, and belief that she would succeed.

Sakura, the small restaurant named for cherry blossoms, offered a variety of Japanese dishes and was soon attracting a loyal clientele who were cheerfully greeted by the ever-smiling, ever-friendly Miyoko. As the business grew, so did the need for more space and a larger kitchen to offer a wider menu. In 1995 she found the perfect location at Sixth and St. Peter streets, moving Sakura into a space that was near Ordway Center, Rice Park, Landmark Center, and busy downtown St. Paul. The open dining room had huge windows on two walls and space for a sushi counter; a separate room was available downstairs for private parties. For the next two years she continued to build Sakura into a successful operation. Then, in November 1996, the City of St. Paul condemned the building to tear it down for the proposed Lawson Software headquarters. Suddenly, she had no restaurant.

In just three months Miyoko had to find a new location, negotiate the lease, refurbish the space, secure licenses, move in, retrain staff, and start up the new operation— a process that often takes more than a year. She said it was stressful for the staff, for her customers, and for her, but once again she succeeded, though not without costs. She lost two key staff people, a local reviewer complained about poor service during the first days in the new location, and the move was very expensive. But Sakura, now at 350 St. Peter, was just two blocks from the previous location, had access to the downtown skyways, was across from the St. Paul Hotel, and was adjacent to a parking ramp. The dining room had a wall of windows looking onto St. Peter Street and a balcony for private parties. It also had a sushi bar and zashikis where guests could sit on the floor and enjoy Japanese-style dining. Her customers followed her to the new location, and Sakura continued to grow.

Miyoko Omori at Sakura, 350 St. Peter Street, St. Paul, 2011.

In 2010 Miyoko expanded the restaurant within the building, moving it to the corner with a view toward the Mississippi River. She enlarged the sushi bar, moved the full-service cocktail bar to the front dining area, and kept the balcony for private parties. Her daughter Tina Ramgren worked at Sakura from its beginning and became manager in 2008. Miyoko's grandson Timothy Ramgren and granddaughters Aundrea Garza and Trina Maurstad also work at the restaurant.

Sakura is often listed in annual polls as one of the top five favorite restaurants for Japanese dining and in 1998 was selected as *Mpls.St.Paul* magazine's Restaurant Critics' Choice for Best Japanese Food in the Twin Cities. Sakura also received the magazine's 2001 Best Sushi Restaurant Award. In this section we'll look at a few of Sakura's popular dishes.

This Japanese bento box from Sakura is filled with a variety of fresh and cooked food providing a well-balanced lunch or light dinner. Selections include (upper left) tuna, salmon, squid, and striped bass sashimi; (upper right) shrimp and vegetable tempura; (lower left) salmon shioyaki (salt grilled salmon), and broccoli with sesame sauce. In the center is a small portion of wasabi.

In the summer of 2011, Miyoko and I discussed the changes in the marketplace since she first opened Sakura in 1990. "We used to have a lot of Japanese families come in," she recalled, "because of the large number of Japanese working at 3M." When they went back to Japan, her clientele became more diversified. Now her business is more seasonal, as customers are in town during the fall, winter, and spring months and away during the summer months. There were also fewer Japanese restaurants in the Twin Cities when she started, "less than ten" she estimated. By 2009 there were sixty-one Japanese restaurants in Minnesota, and the number continues to grow. She still serves a variety of Japanese dishes, but as the demand for sushi grew so did the size of her sushi bar. "Fuji Ya offered the first sashimi in Minnesota," she recalled, "but it was frozen. Fuji Ya also brought the first sushi chef from Japan to Minnesota." Today most Japanese restaurants have special chefs who prepare their sashimi and sushi in-house. On page 72, Sakura sushi chef Haruo Minokata offers a glimpse into the process of making sushi. — PLH

The keys to making good sushi are in the cutting, rolling, and ingredient combinations—and everything must be fresh! Here Chef Minokata places the sushi ingredients on the special sushi mat, carefully squeezes them into a roll, and tightly rolls the sushi. He then cuts it into portions and assembles them on a serving plate. The food is first eaten with the eyes, say the Japanese, so it must be attractive and appealing.

Assembling the ingredients for futomaki is an important first step in the process. Chef Minokata begins the process of making a futomaki by placing a sheet of nori on a sushi mat.

He then carefully adds the seasoned rice that makes this a sushi and spreads it in two sections the full width of the nori. He pushes and spreads the rice until it coats the entire nori and forms a complete white cover.

Chef Minokata places a smaller piece of nori in the center and begins to add the various ingredients of the futomaki one at a time in long rows extending to the full width of the nori.

He carefully rolls up the futomaki, making sure the contents are tightly sealed in the nori, and then squeezes the finished roll again with the sushi mat.

The finished futomaki is cut into bite-size pieces and served with a small ball of wasabi and a small mound of pickled ginger slices.

Preparations for the futomaki do take time and will produce enough ingredients for several sushi rolls. Ingredients include shari (seasoned rice), Japanese omelet, shiitake, kampyo, oboro, spinach, cucumber, nori, wasabi, and pickled ginger. Everything is prepared and assembled, then rolled and served as pictured.

Above:

1. *Sakura sushi chef Haruo Minokata.*
2. *Assembling the ingredients, the first step in the process.*
3. *A sheet of nori is placed on a sushi mat.*
4. *The seasoned rice, started in two sections, is pushed and spread carefully until it fills the full width of the nori.*

Left:

5. *A smaller piece of nori is added to the center, supporting the various ingredients in long rows the full width of the nori.*
6. *Carefully rolling up the futomaki.*
7. *Squeezing the finished roll again with the sushi mat.*
8. *The finished futomaki is cut into bite-size pieces.*

Futomaki

Chef Haruo Minokata, Sakura

Serves 3–4

Shari:

2/3 cup short-grain Japanese white rice	2 tablespoons rice vinegar
	1 tablespoon sugar
1 cup water	1/2 tablespoon salt

Wash the rice several times until water runs clear. Place in saucepan and add water. Bring to a boil over medium-high heat until craters form on the surface. Turn down heat to low, cover pan, and cook for 20 minutes. Turn off heat and let the rice steam for 5 minutes. Fluff the rice with a spoon or fork and sprinkle on the seasonings, stirring well to flavor all of the grains of rice. Cover and set aside.

Japanese omelet:

2 eggs	1 teaspoon Japanese soy sauce
1 tablespoon sugar	

Crack eggs into a bowl and stir with chopsticks until well mixed but not frothy. Add sugar and soy sauce. Pour into an omelet pan and cook without stirring over medium heat until egg is set. Turn once, cool, and cut into strips.

Mushroom sauce:

5 dried shiitake mushrooms	1 tablespoon sugar
1/2 cup chicken stock or broth	1 tablespoon mirin (sweet rice wine)
3 tablespoons Japanese soy sauce	

Soak mushrooms in warm water for 20 minutes or until soft. Remove from water, squeeze out excess water, remove and discard stems. Slice fairly thin. Combine sauce ingredients, and simmer mushroom slices in sauce mixture for 15 minutes. Allow to cool. Set aside.

Kampyo:

1 kampyo (dried gourd strips)

Combine the following in a small saucepan:

1 1/2 cups chicken stock or broth	4 tablespoons soy sauce
	2 tablespoons sugar

Soften the kampyo strips by simmering them in the seasoned sauce. Set aside to cool.

Oboro (sweet white fish with pink color):

1 ounce oboro	saké
red food coloring	salt
sugar	

Boil white fish and remove the skin and bones. Squeeze the fish in a kitchen towel to remove moisture. Grind the fish and add a small amount of red food coloring to make it pink. Add a small amount of sugar, saké, and salt in a saucepan, then add the fish and cook over medium heat until all the moisture is gone. Remove from heat and fluff the oboro so it is light and very fluffy. Set aside.

Spinach leaves:

3 large spinach leaves

Cook the leaves in water for 2 minutes. Drain and plunge into ice water. Drain and squeeze the leaves in a paper towel. Separate the leaves and set aside.

Cucumber strips:

1 medium cucumber

Peel cucumber and cut into 1/4-inch by 4-inch strips without seeds. Set aside.

Nori:

2 sheets nori per sushi roll

Wasabi:

2 tablespoons wasabi powder	2 tablespoons water

Mix well and roll into a small ball with your hands.

Pickled ginger shreds

To assemble each futomaki roll:

1. Leaving about 1/2 inch on the right side of the nori, make an even layer of the rice about 3/8 inch deep. Crush the rice grains on the two right corners of the nori.

2. Turn the sheet 90° so the free end of the nori is closest to you. Lay bands of the omelet strips, shiitake, kampyo, oboro, spinach, and cucumber lengthwise across the rice.

3. Carefully roll up the futomaki by starting with the nori end closest to you. Cover the ingredients and continue to compress into a tight roll about 2 inches in diameter. Fasten the corners that were pasted with the crushed rice.

4. Using a bamboo mat to adjust the shape, cover and squeeze the roll so that it is slightly oval. Remove the mat and carefully cut the roll in half with a very sharp, clean knife. Slice each half into 4 equal parts, making sure to clean the knife after each slice. Arrange the 8 slices on a sushi platter and garnish with a small ball of wasabi and a small mound of pickled ginger shreds.

Sakura's Sesame Sauce

For 4 servings

1 tablespoon goma paste

3 tablespoons soy sauce

2 tablespoons sugar

1/2 tablespoon mirin (sweet rice wine)

1/2 tablespoon saké

Mix all ingredients together.

Serving suggestion: Toss Sesame Sauce with 2 cups of boiled broccoli pieces that have been well drained. Sprinkle with toasted sesame seeds.

Tonkatsu / Japanese Pork Cutlets

Sakura

Serves 4

4 boneless pork chops, 1/2 inch thick

2 tablespoons flour

1 egg, beaten

1/2 cup panko (Japanese breadcrumbs)

vegetable oil

1 cup shredded cabbage

tonkatsu sauce (see note)

1. Pound pork chops to 1/4 inch thick.

2. Coat with flour, shaking off the excess. Dip coated chop into beaten egg and then coat with panko.

3. Heat a large skillet over medium heat and add the oil to 1 inch deep. Heat oil to 350° and deep-fry each chop 3 minutes. Turn chop over and fry an additional 3 minutes or until golden brown.

4. Serve chops hot on a bed of shredded cabbage with tonkatsu sauce on the side.

Note: Tonkatsu is a spicy-sweet sauce available in Asian markets.

Donbori

Sakura

Serves 4

1 cup chicken broth

2 tablespoons sugar

4 tablespoons Japanese soy sauce

1 tablespoon mirin (sweet rice wine)

3/4 pound boneless, skinless chicken breast, cut into 1/4-inch strips

1/2 medium yellow onion, sliced

4 eggs

2 scallions, trimmed and cut into strips

hot cooked Japanese rice

The restaurant cooks one portion at a time, as described here.

1. In a small saucepan, combine the chicken broth, sugar, soy sauce, and mirin. Mix well and bring to a boil to dissolve the sugar. Remove from heat.

2. In another small pan or Crockpot pour in one-quarter of the sauce and bring to a simmer. Add one-quarter of the chicken and one-quarter of the onion and simmer until chicken is cooked, about 3 minutes.

3. Break one egg into a bowl and stir with chopsticks until it is thoroughly blended but not frothy. Add to the simmering chicken mixture and cook just until the egg is set, about 2 minutes. Do not stir.

4. Add 1/4 of the scallion strips, cover, and turn off heat.

5. Pour the soup into bowl of hot, cooked Japanese rice, letting the egg and scallion remain on top. Serve hot. Repeat with remaining ingredients.

Nabeyaki Udon

Sakura

Serves 4

4 boneless, skinless chicken thighs

6 cups dashi stock (see page 68; or 6 cups water with 1 teaspoon dashi bonito soup stock)

1/3 cup Japanese soy sauce

4 1/2 tablespoons mirin (sweet rice wine)

1/2 teaspoon salt

1/2 teaspoon sugar

4 servings boiled udon noodles

4 shiitake mushrooms

8 shredded fish cakes (*kamaboko*)

2 cups shredded napa cabbage, cut into 2-inch lengths

1 scallion, cut into 2-inch lengths

4 eggs

1. Cut chicken into 1/2-inch cubes.

2. Mix dashi with soy sauce, mirin, salt, and sugar.

3. Divide broth into 4 individual earthen pots and bring to a boil over medium heat. Divide chicken into the four bowls and simmer for 5 minutes.

4. Add noodles to each pot and simmer for 2 minutes.

5. Divide mushroom, fish cakes, cabbage, and scallions into each of the 4 pots and simmer for 2 minutes.

6. Gently crack an egg into each pot, cover, and turn off heat. Let egg steam for 3 minutes. Remove cover and serve hot.

Japanese Restaurants Expand

As the demand for Japanese food grew in Minnesota, so did the types of restaurants. In 1979 the Ichiban Japanese Steak House opened on Nicollet Avenue and Twelfth Street in Minneapolis, offering the flying-cleaver style of cooking teppanyaki. It expanded its menu to include all-you-can-eat-in-one-hour sushi and a variety of other Japanese dishes. And its sushi bar eventually added a continuous stream of water carrying miniature boats with freshly made sushi for diners to view and select. In Golden Valley, the national Benihana chain opened a restaurant in 1980, featuring their specially trained chefs with their signature slicing and dicing grill-side performances; a second location, in Maple Grove, was added in 2007.

Benihana in Maple Grove.

Tanpopo Noodle Shop, a Bridge Between Cultures

Koshiki Yonemura Smith comes from a family with a long food history. Her aunt and grandmother ran a restaurant, and her father had one in Japan called Tanpopo. After her father died and the family moved to Minnesota from Kyushu, Koshiki worked part time at Origami and Kikagawa Japanese restaurants in Minneapolis. She earned a degree in psychology at the University of Minnesota, but her passion was still food. Despite several jobs in translating and trips back to Japan, Koshiki's desire to cook the food of her childhood lingered on.

So it wasn't surprising that in the spring of 2000 Koshiki and her husband, Benjamin Smith, opened a restaurant in St. Paul that was based on the food of her homeland. Named after her father's restaurant, Tanpopo Noodle Shop on Selby Avenue did not offer the Japanese dishes that had become familiar to Twin Cities diners. Instead, Koshiki built a menu around the comfort food of Japan, including noodle soups, home-style dinners, tofu in various forms, and specials based on locally grown produce. Her concept of a Japanese noodle shop in the heart of Minnesota became so popular that in 2003 she changed the name to Tanpopo Restaurant and moved it to a larger space at 108 Prince Street in Lowertown St. Paul, just a block from the farmers' market. As restaurants go, with room for just forty-nine diners it is still considered small, but here she was able to expand the menu and offer saké, wine, and beer as well.

Koshiki keeps the menu fresh with daily specials created from produce that looked especially good in the market that day. A typical Monday night feature may be ramen broth with ramen-style noodles, marinated pork, fresh spinach, menma, toasted nori, scallions, and egg. She also offers a variety of desserts such as sesame flan, persimmon tart, mocha strawberry mousse, and tempura green tea ice cream.

Tanpopo is still a family affair, with her husband Benjamin as her business partner and her brother Ira Yonemura as a cook. Initially her mother also helped out

Koshiki Yonemura Smith at Tanpopo.

on occasion. In January 2012 Koshiki opened another Tanpopo in the new Delta Airlines concourse at the Minneapolis–St. Paul International Airport.

In 2008 Koshiki was named one of the top twenty-five chefs in the Twin Cities by *Foodservice News. City Pages* selected Tanpopo as the Best Café in St. Paul in 2008 and 2010, and *Minnesota Monthly* named it the Best Japanese Restaurant in 2008. Koshiki has participated in cooking information events at the Minnesota State Fair and continues to offer classes in a variety of venues.

We sat down to talk one gloomy November afternoon about the changes in Asian food in Minnesota and the growing clientele who were finding Tanpopo in its new location. I first met Koshiki in the original Tanpopo that had room for only twenty diners. Often customers would have to wait outside in line for a chance to savor some of the restaurant's Japanese comfort food. But even in that small space Koshiki

was able to offer locally grown foods of the season in traditional Japanese dishes. "I look at my cooking as a bridge between countries," she said. She extends that bridge with cooking classes she gives periodically at Cooks of Crocus Hill in St. Paul. "I am especially interested in providing customers with affordable food that reflects some of the best of Japanese traditions," she explained. It is also her way of helping her customers learn more about Japan. Koshiki wants to continue the emphasis on traditional Japanese food made with local ingredients and is not interested in adding fusion dishes. "Sometimes people come in hesitant about trying something new," she said, "so we talk with them to see what they are comfortable with and offer them a dish that is close to their own tastes but still in the Japanese tradition." Perhaps that is why they keep coming back. — PLH

Here are three of the dishes Koshiki serves at Tanpopo. The sauce, called *goma*, is a sweet contrast to the savory spinach, providing a flavorful vegetable dish.

Spinach with Sesame Sauce.

Spinach with Sesame Sauce

Koshiki Yonemura Smith, Tanpopo

Serves 4

1 cup organic toasted sesame seeds, natural, plus additional for garnish

2 tablespoons plus 2 teaspoons granulated sugar

1 cup mirin (sweet rice wine)

1/2 cup light or thin Japanese soy sauce

1 bunch fresh spinach leaves, stems removed, blanched and drained

1. Using a nut mill, grinder, or mortar and pestle, grind sesame seeds. Add sugar and mix well.

2. In a separate container, combine mirin and light soy sauce.

3. Cut blanched spinach and then squeeze out any excess water.

4. For each portion of cooked spinach, mix together 2 tablespoon of sesame and sugar mixture with 1 to 2 tablespoons of mirin and soy sauce. Toss well with spinach. Garnish with whole toasted sesame seeds and serve.

Hiyashi Chuka is a dish of chilled, ramen-style noodles served with various kinds of toppings and a sauce drizzled on top. At Tanpopo, the cooks use sliced omelet, marinated pork, cucumber, carrots, and scallions for the toppings. Cooked deli ham may be substituted for marinated pork.

Hiyashi Chuka

Koshiki Yonemura Smith, Tanpopo

Serves 4–6

Hiyashi Chuka sauce:

1 tablespoon ground sesame seeds	1/4 cup rice vinegar
1/2 teaspoon sugar	2 tablespoons water
1/4 cup soy sauce	2 tablespoons sesame oil

Mix all ingredients together and set aside.

Tamagoyaki / Japanese omelet:

6 large eggs	1 teaspoon salt
2 tablespoons sugar	vegetable oil

Traditional tamagoyaki is prepared in a square frying pan to make a rectangular shape.

1. Mix omelet ingredients (except oil) in a bowl.
2. Heat frying pan on medium heat. When the pan is hot, lightly grease the pan with oil and then pour one-quarter of the egg mixture into pan and tilt so egg mixture spreads in an even, thin layer over the bottom. Break air bubbles formed in the first few seconds after the egg is poured into pan. When egg is about 75 percent cooked, use chopsticks or a spatula to start rolling egg from farther side of the pan toward you. Once rolled completely, push the rolled egg away to the farther part of the pan, pour in another quarter of egg mixture, and repeat the process. When complete, grease the pan and pour in another quarter of egg mixture.

3. Repeat until all the egg mixture is rolled and cooked. Remove the tamagoyaki from the pan and cool before slicing.

Roasted and Marinated Pork Loin:

salt	1 pound pork loin (end of loin with more marbling preferred)
pepper	
1 teaspoon finely chopped garlic, or substitute garlic powder	

Marinade:

1/2 cup soy sauce	1/2 cup mirin (sweet rice wine)
1/2 cup saké	1/2 lemon, sliced

1. Sprinkle salt, pepper, and chopped garlic or garlic powder over pork loin.
2. Roast in oven at 350° until meat is fully cooked. Remove from oven and cool to room temperature.
3. Combine and stir marinade ingredients.
4. Add roasted pork to the marinade, cover, and place in refrigerator until needed. Pork should marinate for 2 to 3 hours before serving.

Hiyashi Chuka:

ramen noodles (fresh or frozen; not instant)	2–3 green onions, finely chopped
1 roll tamagoyaki, sliced	marinated pork loin, sliced into 1/8-inch strips
1 medium carrot, julienned	Hiyashi Chuka sauce
1 English cucumber, sliced and julienned	karashi mustard

Hiyashi Chuka.

1. Cook ramen noodles according to instructions. Rinse with cold water and drain.

2. Place noodles on serving plate, arrange toppings colorfully around the top with green onions at the center, and drizzle with 2 to 3 tablespoons (as desired) of Hiyashi Chuka sauce. Garnish plate with karashi mustard.

Star Prairie Trout

Koshiki Yonemura Smith, Tanpopo

Serves 4–6

4 whole rainbow trout, cleaned, heads and tails removed	Ponzu Sauce (recipe follows)
soybean oil	2 green onions, finely chopped
flour	1 (1-inch) piece ginger, peeled and julienned

1. Cut the fish down the backbone and remove bone to produce two fillets with skin on one side. Cut each fillet into 2 to 3 pieces. Rinse in cold water and dry with a paper towel.

2. Heat oil 2 to 3 inches deep in large pot to about 360°.

3. Lightly coat each piece of fish in flour and deep-fry until fully cooked, about 5 minutes.

4. Arrange trout pieces skin side down on a serving platter. Pour Ponzu Sauce over fish and garnish with green onions and fresh ginger. Trout may be served on individual plates instead of one platter. Divide the sauce and garnishes for each serving.

Ponzu Sauce:

1 cup soy sauce	1/2 lemon
1 cup rice vinegar	small handful bonito flakes

1. Combine soy sauce and rice vinegar in a small saucepan.

2. Cut lemon into 2 to 3 slices and add to pan.

3. Heat slowly until mixture is just about to boil. Turn off heat and add bonito flakes.

4. Set aside to cool; strain before using. This sauce will keep up to 3 weeks in a covered container in the refrigerator.

Japanese Food Opportunities Continue to Expand

Yet another type of Japanese restaurant opened in the spring of 2011 in Northeast Minneapolis, an area noted more for German and Polish food than Asian. Masu Sushi & Robata has the bright, bustling, colorful look of downtown Tokyo instead of the quiet, subdued traditional atmosphere of tatami mats and bamboo. As its name implies, along with sushi the menu features *robata*—meat, fish, or vegetables grilled over a coal fire, which creates a distinctive charred flavor. The menu also offers traditional *izakaya* (small plates), noodles, and *teishoku* (set meals), but the difference is in the open atmosphere of Masu, with its bright colors and upbeat music.

By 2012 sushi and sashimi were available as in-house, freshly prepared takeout items in major supermarkets around Minnesota. They are also the subjects of a growing number of cooking classes, including year-round sushi classes at Coastal Seafoods in Minneapolis and in community education classes. Less than forty years after their introduction to Minnesota diners, two more "foreign" foods have become accepted to such an extent that they are now available from non-Asian sources throughout the state.

Tanpopo's Star Prairie Trout.

The flavors of...
the Hmong Community

When the U.S.–supported governments in Laos, Cambodia, and Vietnam collapsed in 1975, 1.5 million people fled from their homelands to avoid reprisal from the new regimes. Many had worked with the U.S. military and civilian agencies fighting against the communist takeover of their countries. That same year, Congress enacted the Indochina Migration and Refugee Assistance Act, permitting aid to help about one-third of these refugees relocate to the United States. The rest were sent to other countries. By 1981 Minnesota became home to 21,000 Indochinese refugees who had lost their homes, their businesses, and in many cases, their families. In Minnesota, they would try to build a new life.

Among them were about 9,200 Hmong. As they settled in the state, they began inviting relatives and friends to visit or live. Additional immigrants settled here, and by 2010 there were 66,181 Hmong living in Minnesota, making it the state with the second-largest Hmong community in the United States, behind California. Even though the major portion of the state's Hmong population (about 53,000) lives in the Twin Cities, public opportunities to enjoy Hmong food have been limited. But access to food grown on Hmong-managed farms has not. The number of Hmong farmers bringing their products to local farmers' markets and selling them through major food chains has grown significantly in the past few years.

Facing page: May Yia Lee working on the family farm, Mhonpaj's Garden in Oakdale.

Introducing New Foods and Learning New Farming Methods

As part of a Hmong family of ten in Laos, Mhonpaj Lee says farming was a natural part of life. "So, when we moved to the United States," she recalls, "we continued to farm, primarily growing cucumbers for pickles" along with vegetables and herbs for the family's needs. They called it Mhonpaj's Garden.

Today, Mhonpaj and her family continue this eleven-year-old business with a few new twists. Mhonpaj's Garden now covers five acres in Oakdale, growing more than thirty varieties of vegetables and herbs, including a wide array of traditional Hmong herbs used for medicinal and health purposes. In 2009 Mhonpaj's Garden became part of the growing community-supported agriculture (CSA) movement, through which farmers sell shares in their crops. Shareholders, in return for their investments, receive their own box of organically grown produce each week from June to October. The CSA farms guarantee that everything is locally grown in safe, sustainable, and chemically free conditions, thus providing the community with the most healthful food possible. This effort requires some methods that go beyond traditional Laotian farming.

I interviewed Mhonpaj, her sisters, and her mother in 2009 to learn about the challenges they faced in bringing age-old farming traditions to Minnesota. "In Laos, every part of the animal or vegetable was eaten or used," said Mhonpaj, "so there was no concept of natural composting because there was nothing left to use." But, as a firm believer in organic farming, Mhonpaj is helping the Hmong community understand the value of composting and the benefits of this natural fertilizer. At that time they were "in the first year of becoming certified as a producer of organically grown food." It takes three years to complete the certification.

"It is difficult [to accomplish these goals] when we rent the land to farm," Mhonpaj said, but she hopes to be able to continue farming in the current location for some time to come. In 2011 theirs became the first

Hmong-owned and -operated farm in Minnesota to be certified organic for the CSA program.

Mhonpaj actually came back to farming after leaving it to earn a college degree in political science and health education/health fitness. "Good health and physical fitness all starts with the food we eat," she added, "and I felt it was important to be part of the effort to improve the quality of food available." — PLH

Hmongtown Marketplace on Como Avenue in St. Paul.

As part of its own community support, Mhonpaj's Garden donates unsold fresh produce to Second Harvest Heartland and the Asian Pacific Cultural Center—more than five thousand pounds of food annually.

When Mhonpaj, her mother May Yia Lee, sisters Macy and Kalie, and the rest of the family moved to Minnesota in 2007, they became part of the Minnesota Food Association (MFA) Big River Foods program and began raising a variety of vegetables. Macy manages the farm along with her mother, May, who also staffs their booths at farmers' markets in St. Paul, North St. Paul, and White Bear. May has also presented Hmong cooking demonstrations at the Mill City Farmers Market and appeared with Mhonpaj on local television shows to provide information about Hmong foods. Mhonpaj is currently assembling an information guide to Hmong herbs that she grows in the farm's greenhouse in Mahtomedi.

The family was selected as the University of Minnesota's 2009 Farm Family of the Year for Ramsey County. The twenty-year-old Farm Family Recognition Program honors Minnesota farm families for their contributions to the agricultural industry and their local communities.

Hmong herbs, so important in Hmong cooking as well as for medicinal purposes, are not readily available in Minnesota except to those who grow their own. They are not only hard to find but difficult for people outside the Hmong community to identify. Traditionally every Hmong household grows its own supply of herbs, preserving some for winter use. In Minnesota some herbs are now available in Hmong markets such as Foodsmart on University Avenue in St. Paul.

Hmong Markets Provide Social Gathering Places

Some years ago when I went looking for Hmong food, several people told me to go to the flea market at Como and Marion avenues in St. Paul. While the name suggested it was not quite what I was looking for, one Saturday morning I found myself at the busiest corner in the state. Located in an old lumberyard, the market was advertised by the sign "International Market," and the parking lot was jammed. Making my way in was a little like going to the state fair, with a multitude of people milling about, exchanging greetings and shopping in the two hundred booths, both indoor and open-air shops, a farmers' market, and a number of food vendors. One woman told me her grandmother insists on going to the market every Sunday to meet old friends from Laos and get caught up on the gossip. — PLH

The market was the idea of Toua Xiong, a Hmong immigrant from Laos who wanted to build his own business in this new land. After purchasing a small food market in St. Paul from a friend, he sold it a year later and opened a larger market/restaurant nearby, turning it into a Hmong meeting place. He later moved to the

Como and Marion location, where his market became a major gathering place for the Hmong community. In 2009 he purchased the property, making it the first Hmong-owned and -operated market of its size. Toua renamed it several times but eventually settled on Hmongtown Marketplace. By 2011 the market employed more than six hundred people, most of Hmong ancestry, and attracted thousands of visitors from across the state every week.

Toua Xiong received the 2010 Immigrant of Distinction Award from the Minnesota/Dakotas Chapter of the American Immigration Lawyers Association. In addition to his business, Toua has been active in contributing to community integration, has sponsored Hmong students on field trips to Thailand, and supports cultural exchanges between the United States and Southeast Asia.

Hmong Village Opens Across Town

Yia Vang, another Hmong immigrant, understands the need for places where Hmong can meet and greet, so in the fall of 2010 he expanded on the market/food idea and opened the Hmong Village at 1001 Johnson Parkway in St. Paul. Spending more than three million dollars to upgrade an old warehouse, Yia wanted to create a community space where people were comfortable shopping and where all generations could meet and just visit whatever the season. Completely enclosed, Hmong Village has thirty-five fresh produce booths, seventeen food stands, 230 import shops, and forty offices and offers a number of services as well. In addition to Hmong products and food, Hmong Village features items from Somalia, China, Mexico, Vietnam, Cambodia, and Laos.

The indoor market, filled with fresh produce all year long, is given an outdoor look with massive hand-painted murals depicting outdoor scenes. The food court offers the option of ordering from a variety of menus and then eating at tables nearby or having takeout. There is so much to see at the vendors' booths that one visit is not enough. On weekends, the crowds make a quick tour impossible. Yia's vision of a place to work, meet friends, shop, and get a taste of Asian culture has given Minnesotans even more opportunities to learn about and enjoy these centuries-old traditions.

By 1985 there were a number of Hmong food stores in St. Paul, including Chouleng Asian Foods at 375 University Avenue North, L. H. Oriental Grocery Store at 191 Western Avenue North, M. A. Food Store at 694 Rice Street, Arcade Oriental Market at 828 Hawthorne Avenue, and Mekong Oriental Food Market at 800 University Avenue.

Colorful wall murals bring outside scenes into the year-round enclosed Hmong Village produce market.

My first visit to a Hmong food market was in 2006 when I wandered into Foodsmart at 995 University Avenue West in St. Paul. It had been open more than ten years and included a small restaurant/deli where I could taste a number of Hmong dishes. The chicken with peppers combined pieces of bone-in chicken simmered with red and green bell peppers in a light sauce with a black-peppery flavor. Another dish with house-made Hmong pork sausage was rich and flavorful and reminded me of some of my Iowa grandmother's cooking. Today the market is called Sunrise Market and the deli is the famous Destiny Café. — PLH

There was once a Hmong band named Destiny that made a number of recordings popular in the Hmong community. Their concerts attracted crowds, and their recordings were often played at parties. When the band broke up, keyboardist Chong Souz Vang and wife Doua Yang opened Destiny Café at the Sunrise Market. It is a small deli within a large dining room complete with stage, in case Destiny should reunite. Until then, Destiny Band songs are played through the sound system.

In the café, crisp pork belly, Hmong sausage, and pork ribs are featured along with *fawm kauv*, steamed rice flour rolls filled with pork. Whole fish such as tilapia may be served fried with an herb and tomato sauce or a curry sauce or steamed with limes or herbs. Some reviewers have pointed out that the *pho*, available in a number of combinations, may be the best around. The most popular choice contains pork meatballs, crispy pork, crabmeat, shrimp, and sliced steak. Another contains tripe, meatballs, blood, and beef tendons.

After five years, Destiny Café opened a second location at Maryland and Clarence avenues in St. Paul.

Hmong Home Cooking

Hmong history can be traced back more than five thousand years to China, but there were no written works. Everything was verbally passed down from one generation to the next, leaving us with little more than the most recent memories. In the 1950s several Hmong alphabets were created and now more and more written history is available.

*In 2000 when I went looking for more information on Hmong cooking, I found the **Hmong Recipe Cook Book**, produced in 1985 by the New Citizens' Hmong Garden Projects, sponsored by the First Presbyterian Church of South St. Paul and administered by Sharon Sawyer and Ngia Gao Yang. Only one copy was available to see, and it was at the Hmong Arts, Books, and Crafts store in St. Paul. Storeowner Shoua V. Xiong believes the book truly reflects the traditions of Hmong cooking. She especially recommended the chicken soup, egg salad, and tofu recipes, which her mother had used. — PLH*

The book explained many of the cooking traditions the Hmong followed in Laos. "In Laos sweet potatoes were baked in the ashes of the evening fire after the main meal," it explains. "In cool weather, the baked potatoes were wrapped in large leaves (to retain their heat) and taken to the fields as a lunch. In warm weather, they were cooled and eaten cold during the work day." It goes on to instruct cooks that in order "to receive the plant's energy, Hmong gardeners harvest greens and vegetables early in the day or late in the day. When the sun shines hot, the plant's energy is in the roots; it is not a good time to harvest food."

As part of this project we contacted staff at the First Presbyterian Church of South St. Paul to see if any copies of the cookbook were still available. They were happy to provide a photocopy of the fifty-four-page book and allowed us to reprint some of the recipes here.

Meat Salad

Hmong Recipe Cook Book

Wash 1 head of lettuce, or an equal amount of leaf lettuce. Dry and break into bite size pieces.

Put 1/2 pkg. of 1 lb. rice sticks or cellophane noodles into warm water to soak for 15 minutes.

Sauté 1 lb. ground pork. Salt/pepper/soy or fish sauce.

Drain rice sticks. Chop into 2 inch pieces. Add to meat mixture and cook for 3 minutes.

Cool and toss with lettuce.

We made this tasty, simple recipe with cellophane noodles for one of our food photos. It is a good example of the Hmong preference for noodle-meat-vegetable dishes. While fish sauce would be good in this recipe, we used Thai light soy sauce, which nicely enhanced the pork, noodles, and lettuce without overpowering them. The best way to cut wet noodles is with large kitchen scissors while they are still in the soaking water. Dry cellophane noodles are not easily broken, but soaking allows for easy cutting. Drain off the water before adding the noodles to the cooked meat. The stir-frying step is very short because the noodles will start to stick to the wok as they dry out. Use a wok or large frying pan; even one that is nonstick will work. Be sure to coat the pan with a little vegetable oil before cooking the meat. As the meat fries it will add some of its own juices that the noodles will absorb.

The rest of the samples from the *Hmong Recipe Cook Book* have been adapted to the format used throughout *Asian Flavors*. Many were provided by area Hmong home cooks who worked on the church's New Citizens' Hmong Garden Projects in 1985. We are grateful to them all for continuing the Hmong culinary traditions and for sharing their favorite foods with us.

Hot Dipping Sauce / Kua Txob

Hmong Recipe Cook Book
Adapted by ACAI

Each of the following combinations should be mixed together with a mortar and pestle to create a very spicy condiment. The sauces are added a small amount at a time while eating other dishes.

Chili with Fish Sauce:

1 1/2 tablespoons fish sauce	2–3 red chilies, seeded and finely chopped

Chili with Fish Sauce, Scallions, and Cilantro:

2 tablespoons fish sauce	2 scallions, chopped
2–3 red chilies, seeded and finely chopped	1/2 cup chopped cilantro leaves

Chili with Fish Sauce, Lemon, or Lime:

2 tablespoons fish sauce	2–3 chilies, seeded and finely chopped
1–2 tablespoons lemon or lime juice	

The above quantities will be easy to mix in a mortar and pestle but will not produce very large amounts of sauce. Increasing the measurements will produce more sauce but will be harder to process by hand. Using a blender or food processor will not produce the same results as hand mashing.

Hmong Meat Salad served with noodles.

Egg Salad

Hmong Recipe Cook Book

Adapted by ACAI

Serves 2

4 hardboiled eggs, peeled	2 tablespoons vegetable oil
1/2 head lettuce, broken into bite-size pieces	1/2 teaspoon salt
2 carrots, sliced	1/4 teaspoon freshly ground black pepper
1 cucumber, peeled, seeded, and cubed	1 tablespoon Thai light soy sauce or other light soy sauce
3 tablespoons lemon juice	

1. Separate the egg yolks from the whites and set the yolks aside. Chop the egg whites into small pieces.

2. Fill a mixing bowl with the lettuce pieces. Add the egg white pieces, carrots, and cucumbers.

3. In a separate bowl, mash the egg yolks and mix with the lemon juice, oil, salt, pepper, and soy sauce to create a salad dressing. Adjust seasonings as desired.

4. Pour the dressing over the vegetables and toss together.

Greens are an important part of the Hmong diet. They are grown in gardens, provide season-long food, may be eaten alone or with other ingredients, and can be served raw or stir-fried, boiled or steamed. There is nothing more delicious than freshly picked greens cooked with just a little oil and lightly seasoned.

Steamed Chinese Broccoli

Hmong Recipe Cook Book

Adapted by ACAI

Serves 2

4 cups Chinese broccoli greens, including leaves, tender stems, and flowers, cut into thumb-size pieces	oyster sauce or fish sauce

Put well-washed broccoli pieces in a steamer basket and steam over boiling water for about 30 minutes or until tender. Sprinkle oyster or fish sauce over the cooked greens before serving.

Sautéed Meat and Broccoli Greens

Hmong Recipe Cook Book

Adapted by ACAI

Serves 4–6

2 tablespoons vegetable oil	1 teaspoon salt
1 pound pork or boneless chicken, cubed	1/4 teaspoon black pepper
8 cups broccoli greens, including leaves, tender stems, and flowers, cut into thumb-size pieces	1 tablespoon light soy sauce
	cooked rice
1/2 cup water	

1. Heat a large wok or skillet over high heat. Add oil to coat the surface and stir-fry the meat until barely done, about 3 to 5 minutes.

2. Add the greens and stir-fry 1 minute. Add the water, bring to a boil, and reduce heat to simmer the mixture for 5 minutes. Add salt, pepper, and soy sauce. Adjust seasonings to taste. Serve over rice.

My grandmother on the farm in Indianola, Iowa, used to make boiled pork and cabbage, adding potatoes, onions, and carrots as well. This recipe uses the same method she did. Hmong cooks also make this dish with cabbage: substitute 5 cups of bite-size pieces of cabbage for the mustard greens and increase the broth to 2 cups. — PLH

Boiled Pork and Mustard Greens

Hmong Recipe Cook Book
Adapted by ACAI
Serves 4–6

4–8 cups water, enough to cover the meat

1–2 pounds inexpensive pork (pork hocks, country ribs, etc.); if boneless, use the smaller amount; with bones, use the larger amount

8 cups mustard greens (tender greens and flowers; about 4 pounds), washed thoroughly and cut into thumb-size pieces

1 teaspoon salt

1/4 teaspoon black pepper

cooked rice

1. In a large kettle, bring the water to a boil. Add the pork and bring the water to a boil again. Skim off the scum that forms on the surface of the water until the broth looks clear. Cover, reduce heat to simmer, and cook pork until it is very tender. Remove the meat, discard bones, and cut pork into cubes to yield approximately 2 cups. Cool the broth, remove the fat, and reserve 3/4 cup of broth in the kettle. Refrigerate the remaining broth for soup.

2. Add the pork pieces back to the broth and bring to a simmer. Add the mustard green pieces, mix together, and simmer for about 5 minutes. Sprinkle with salt and pepper. Adjust seasonings to taste. Serve with cooked rice.

The Hmong sausage available at Hmong grocers and delis in Minnesota is usually house-made with flavorings that often include fresh gingerroot and lemongrass. It is very good and distinctly different from pork sausages sold in general supermarkets. If Hmong sausage is not available, substitute any sausage; however, the flavor of the dish will be changed. Pea vines are a favorite of Chinese cooks as well and are only available seasonally. Look for stems of bright green leaves with a little curl on the end of the stem. Their strong pea flavor cannot be duplicated.

Pea Vines and Sausage

Hmong Recipe Cook Book
Adapted by ACAI
Serves 4–6

1 pound Hmong sausage, cut into 1/2-inch slices, or substitute ground sausage meat

5 cups tender pea vines and leaves, washed thoroughly and coarsely chopped

1 teaspoon salt

1/4 teaspoon black pepper

cooked rice

1. In a large skillet, stir-fry the sausage over medium-high heat until it is thoroughly cooked. Remove the grease from the pan.

2. Add the pea vines to the cooked sausage and stir-fry over medium-high heat until the vines are tender but still slightly crunchy. Sprinkle with salt and pepper. Adjust seasonings to taste. Serve with cooked rice.

Yia Moua's Glass Main Dish Noodle Soup

Hmong Recipe Cook Book

Adapted by ACAI

Serves 4

1 (3.5-ounce) package bean thread (cellophane) noodles

2 tablespoons vegetable oil or chicken fat

1/2 cup chopped chicken, raw or cooked

1/4 cup chopped green onions

4 cups water

2 teaspoons fish sauce

1 teaspoon black pepper

1/2 teaspoon MSG, optional (see note page 46)

1 tablespoon sugar

1/4 cup unsweetened coconut milk

1. Soak noodles in warm water until soft, about 15 minutes. With scissors, cut noodles into pieces about 2 inches long. Drain off water and set noodles aside.

2. Heat a 4-quart saucepan or wok over medium heat and coat with oil or fat. If using raw chicken, add pieces and stir-fry 3 to 5 minutes until cooked; add green onions and stir-fry another minute. If using cooked chicken, stir-fry the onions first for about a minute and then add chicken pieces and stir-fry another minute.

3. Add 4 cups water, noodles, fish sauce, black pepper, MSG (if using), and sugar. Bring mixture to a boil and stir to combine flavors. Turn off the heat and add the coconut milk before serving.

This Hmong sweet and sour pork dish is quite different from the Chinese version and similar to the Filipino *adobo*. The addition of hard-boiled eggs sets it apart from them all.

Sy Xiong Vang's Sweet-Sour Pork with Eggs

Hmong Recipe Cook Book

Adapted by ACAI

Serves 8

1 tablespoon lard or chicken fat

3 quarter-size slices ginger

1 clove garlic, peeled and crushed

1 stalk lemongrass, cut into 2-inch pieces (see note page 89)

1/2 cup brown sugar

1 1/2 pounds pork, cut into bite-size pieces

3 tablespoons vinegar

2 tablespoons fish sauce

1 teaspoon salt

1 tablespoon light soy sauce (or to taste)

8 hard-boiled eggs, peeled

cooked rice

1. Heat a large heavy skillet or wok over medium-high heat and coat with lard or chicken fat. Stir-fry ginger, garlic, and lemongrass. Remove from pan and set aside.

2. In the same pan over medium-low heat, melt the brown sugar, being careful not to burn it. Return the ginger, garlic, and lemongrass to the pan and stir. If the mixture is sticking, add several tablespoons of water. Then add the pork pieces and cook, uncovered, for 15 minutes, stirring frequently.

3. Add vinegar, fish sauce, salt, and soy sauce. Stir mixture and cook 5 minutes.

4. Add the hard-boiled eggs and enough water to cover the eggs. Cover and simmer over low heat for 1 hour. Remove lemongrass pieces and discard. Serve with or over cooked rice.

Sweet Potatoes with Pork or Chicken

Hmong Recipe Cook Book

Adapted by ACAI

Serves 2–3

1 tablespoon vegetable oil

1/2 pound raw pork or chicken, cubed (about 1 cup)

2 cups water

1 large or 2 medium sweet potatoes, peeled and cut into bite-size pieces (about 2 cups)

2-inch piece lemongrass, white portion only, finely chopped (see note)

1 teaspoon salt

1/4 teaspoon black pepper

cooked rice

1. Heat a wok or skillet over medium-high heat and coat with oil. Add pork or chicken and stir-fry until nearly done, 3 to 5 minutes.

2. Add water, sweet potato cubes, lemongrass, salt, and pepper. Bring to a boil and turn heat down to simmer. Cook until potatoes are soft, about 10 minutes. Serve with or over cooked rice.

Note: Do not chop lemongrass until just ready to use. Its flavor dissipates when exposed to air.

Sweet Potatoes with Pork.

Home chefs often ask why their version of a dish does not taste like the food in a particular restaurant. Early Chinese restaurants in Minnesota used lard extensively, especially in deep-frying, to impart a particularly pleasant flavor. Chicken fat also added its distinctive essence to dishes such as chow mein. Hmong cooks also use lard and chicken fat because these ingredients were readily available to them from the chickens and pigs they raised. Today's home chef probably uses vegetable oil instead, thereby changing the dish's traditional flavor and in essence creating a fusion dish. Lard and chicken fat are available in the frozen meat sections of many supermarkets. Try it and see the difference in flavor.

Pumpkin soup can be found in a number of Asia Pacific Rim countries. This Hmong version adds only water and sugar to the pumpkin, providing an example of the vegetable water Hmong sometimes drink with their meals.

Pumpkin Soup/Drink

Hmong Recipe Cook Book

Adapted by ACAI

Serves 6–8

4 cups water	2 tablespoons sugar
1 medium pumpkin, peeled, seeded, cut into pieces (about 3 cups)	

In a large soup pot, bring water to a boil over high heat and add pumpkin pieces. Add the sugar and reduce heat to simmer the soup until the pumpkin is dissolved in the water, about an hour. Stir and serve as a soup or drink with the meal.

Perhaps the most important dish in the Hmong collection is chicken broth. This very simple version is used for medicinal purposes or as a basis for other soups, sometimes spooned over meat, vegetables, or rice, and often just sipped as a beverage.

Chicken Broth

Hmong Recipe Cook Book

Adapted by ACAI

Makes about 4 cups

2 pounds chicken pieces (necks, backs, wings, thighs, and drumsticks, including skin and bones), larger pieces halved through the bones so the marrow can flavor the broth	3 scallions 3 quarter-size slices ginger salt to taste

1. In a large soup pot bring 2 to 3 quarts of water to a boil over high heat and add chicken pieces. Bring to a boil again and begin to skim off the scum from the surface of the water. After a few minutes, add 1 cup of cold water, bring soup to a simmer, and continue to skim off the impurities. After 20 minutes, add scallions and ginger. Simmer partially covered for 2 hours. Add water if necessary.

2. Salt to taste and turn off heat. Leave chicken pieces in broth and cool. Remove and discard the solids from the broth and strain. Heat and serve or freeze broth for later use.

A New Hmong Cookbook

When Sheng Yang moved next door to Sami Scripter in Portland, Oregon, they began exchanging favorite family foods. Some years later the two collaborated on the first Hmong cookbook published in hardcover, *Cooking from the Heart: The Hmong Kitchen in America*, which appeared in 2009 from the University of Minnesota Press.

I chatted with the authors in May 2009 when they appeared at the Mill City Farmers Market in Minneapolis to promote their book. Sheng and Sami described Hmong cooking as basically simple, wholesome food prepared from fresh ingredients. They gave the example of Fresh Chicken with Hmong Herbs: a freshly killed chicken boiled in water with salt, pepper, lemongrass, and herbs. So, it seems, chicken soup is everyone's favorite food around the world. — PLH

A Glimpse of Hmong Life at the Science Museum

In 1990 the Science Museum in St. Paul had a house built by area Hmong elders to give viewers a glimpse of the Hmong lifestyle in Laos and Cambodia. The elders used traditional tools and wood harvested from the state's forests to construct a roofed house complete with living and sleeping quarters and open fires for cooking. According to the museum, the house was similar to ones found in 1960s Hmong villages in Southeast Asia. No nails were used in the construction: instead, the building is held together with wooden pegs and ties made from rattan. The roof, made of wooden planks, is open to the outside to let the smoke from cooking fires rise through the loose thatch. There was no refrigeration, so any fish or animals killed for food were divided among the village's families and used immediately. Rice was a staple along with the vegetables the Hmong grew on their farms and in their gardens. Each family had its own herb garden, a tradition many Hmong brought with them to Minnesota.

Today, opportunities to sample Hmong cooking continue to grow with small restaurants and food market delis popping up in the Twin Cities. It is a very satisfying and healthful cuisine that is easy to make. And with rice, vegetables, and herbs as the basis for most meals with just a small amount of meat, it is also inexpensive.

The flavors of...
Cambodia

Cambodian food has strong hints of Vietnamese, Thai, Malaysian, and Indian flavors. By the 1990s Minnesota diners, well acquainted with Chinese and Japanese food, were beginning to appreciate the Vietnamese, Indian, Korean, and Thai restaurants that popped up on a regular basis. But Cambodian food was something new. So in 1997 when Kunrath and Kevin Lam decided to open their Cambodian restaurant, Cheng Heng, in St. Paul, local food reviewers were surprised by the inexpensive, fresh, flavorful dishes offered and a little confused about how to categorize the food. They weren't alone. Diners had trouble pronouncing the names of the dishes and had no idea what they contained.

The Lams, anticipating some of this confusion, created menus complete with descriptions of each item next to a color photo that clearly showed what the finished dish looked like. So while the name *chha mateh* may not have tempted any but Cambodian diners, on the Cheng Heng menu it was described as "Stir-fried bell peppers in a spicy sauce with your choice of beef, pork, chicken, shrimp or vegetarian style. Served with steamed white rice. $7.95" and clearly illustrated by a colorful, appealing photograph. In fact, the menu features more than sixty such illustrated descriptions. Even desserts and beverages are photographed and clearly explained.

The restaurant is run by the Lams with the help of Kunrath's mother, Chhenglay Meas, and a number of other relatives. When the family came to Minnesota from Cambodia in 1983, Kunrath was thinking only of finishing high school and then college. Her parents had purchased the building at 448 University Avenue West in St. Paul, where her mother ran a jewelry store. But after Kunrath met Kevin Lam and they were married, they started talking about opening a Chinese restaurant. After assessing the competition, they realized there were plenty of Chinese restaurants but no Cambodian ones. Kunrath's mother was also a well-known cook, so using her recipes they opened Cheng Heng, which was almost an immediate hit thanks to rave reviews and exceptional food.

Facing page: Summer Salad from Cheng Heng.

Right: Kunrath Lam with her children. Left to right: Ivan, Vincent, and Sarah.

Cheng Heng's menu.

Kevin Lam believes his wife's cooking is the best. "She knows how to make food just the way I like it," he once commented. Evidently others like it too, because this is the food Cheng Heng has been serving to attract diners over the years. Here is one of the dishes Kevin enjoys, a traditional Cambodian soup containing vegetables, fruit, fresh herbs, and seasonings for a combination that is especially satisfying on a cold winter day. It may be made with shrimp, chicken, fish, or tofu.

Winter Soup / Manchu Angkor

Kunrath Lam

Serves 2

1 (2-inch) section lotus root about 2 inches in diameter

2 cups chicken broth or water

1 cup water

4 ounces cooked chicken, fish, or shrimp

1/2 cup chopped m'am, fresh or frozen (see note)

2 teaspoons fish sauce

1 teaspoon tamarind powder

1 1/2 teaspoons sugar

1/2 cup Asian winter squash, peeled and cut into 2 by 1–inch pieces

1/2 cup fresh or frozen pineapple chunks

1/2 cup colantro, roughly chopped (see note)

1 teaspoon chopped garlic, sautéed in 1 teaspoon oil until brown

1/2 cup tomato, cut into 1-inch pieces

1. Stand the lotus root on end and cut down through it into 4 slices. Keeping the slices together, rotate and cut down across the slices four times, making 16 lotus root pieces. Set aside.

2. In a medium saucepan, bring the chicken broth and water to a boil. Add the cooked chicken or seafood. Simmer for 3 minutes and remove any white bubbles that form on the surface. Add the m'am, fish sauce, tamarind, and sugar. Cook for 3 minutes. Add the squash, lotus root, and pineapple. Cook for 1 minute and taste. Adjust seasonings if needed. Add the colantro and garlic. Lower temperature to simmer, add tomato pieces, and cook 1 minute. Serve hot.

Note: M'am is a leafy herb. Colantro is a single-leaf herb that tastes like the leafier cilantro but has a more concentrated flavor. For a vegetarian version, add fried tofu squares and omit the fish sauce.

Make this stir-fry as hot or mild as you wish by adjusting the amount of chilies added. For the spiciest result, include the chili seeds. For a milder rendition, remove the seeds and add only a small amount of chilies. The flavor also comes from the powdered tamarind, garlic, and oyster sauce. Adjust the seasonings to your own taste.

Cambodian Chicken-Vegetable Stir-Fry / Chha Kaim Som

Kunrath Lam

Serves 1–2

1 cup boneless, skinless chicken pieces, 1 inch by 1 inch by 1/4–inch thick

1 egg

1/2 teaspoon garlic powder

1 tablespoon vegetable oil

5 small whole dried chilies

4 teaspoons sugar

1 teaspoon tamarind powder

1 teaspoon oyster sauce

1/4 teaspoon salt

1/4 teaspoon MSG (see note page 46)

1 tablespoon water

1/4 cup broccoli florets

1/4 cup pea pods, stems and strings removed

1/4 cup red bell pepper pieces, cut into 1-inch squares

1/4 cup green bell pepper pieces, cut into 1-inch squares

1 jumbo onion, quartered

1 teaspoon Chinese dark soy sauce

1 tablespoon cornstarch mixed with 1 tablespoon water

1/2 cup sweet basil leaves

steamed white rice

1. Mix the chicken with the egg and garlic powder and marinate for half an hour.

2. Heat a wok over high heat and coat with the oil. Add the chilies, immediately turn heat to medium high, and stir-fry 30 seconds. Add the chicken and stir-fry 1 minute, then add the sugar, tamarind powder, oyster sauce, salt, MSG (if using), and water. Mix together, add the vegetables, and continue stir-frying for 3 minutes. Add the soy sauce and stir-fry until the liquid has nearly evaporated, about 5 minutes. Quickly stir in the cornstarch mixture and stir-fry a few seconds until the sauce turns shiny. Add the sweet basil and stir just once. Serve immediately with steamed white rice.

Salads of Southeast Asia are really a meal in a dish. Here Kunrath lightly bathes fresh vegetables with a spicy lime-based sauce and adds the diner's choice of chicken, shrimp, tofu, or any other protein to make a complete meal. Tossed at the last minute to keep the vegetables fresh and crisp, it is a delicious way to use leftover meat and seafood.

Summer Salad / Nhum Salad

Kunrath Lam

Serves 2

Sauce:

juice of 1 lime

1 tablespoon palm sugar

1 tablespoon fish sauce (see note)

1 clove garlic, minced

1/4 teaspoon chili flakes, or to taste

1 1/2 cups water

Place the lime juice, sugar, fish sauce, garlic, and chili flakes in a mortar and blend together with a pestle. Add the mixture to a small saucepan and add the water. Stir to mix well, and cook over medium heat about 3 minutes to blend the flavors. Taste and adjust the seasonings. Pour into a container and cool to room temperature.

Salad:

- 1 ounce cellophane noodles
- 1 medium dried white mushroom, about 4 inches in diameter
- 1/2 cup cabbage, cut into julienne strips 3 inches long
- 1/2 cup red bell pepper, cut into julienne strips 3 inches long
- 1/2 cup green bell pepper, cut into julienne strips 3 inches long
- 1/2 cup carrot, cut into julienne strips 3 inches long
- 1/2 cup cucumber with peel, cut into julienne strips 3 inches long
- 1/2 cup radishes, cut into thin disks
- 6 small shrimp, blanched and halved through the back
- 3/4 cup cooked chicken (or other protein), shredded into 3-inch lengths
- 1/4 cup roasted peanuts, coarsely chopped
- fresh mint leaves
- 5 rau rum leaves (another type of mint)

1. Fill a medium saucepan half full of water and bring to a boil. Add the noodles and cook for 30 seconds. Drain, plunge noodles in cold water, drain again, and place them in a bowl. Using scissors, cut across the noodles in one direction and then another. Set aside.

2. Soak mushroom in warm water 5 minutes, drain off water, and pull the mushroom apart into small flower-like pieces about 1 inch in diameter. Discard tough center portion.

3. Prepare the vegetables, shrimp, and chicken (or other protein) and set aside on a large platter.

4. For one serving, place half of each of the salad ingredients (except peanuts, mint and rau rum leaves) in a large mixing bowl. Pour 1/3 cup of the sauce over the ingredients and toss just once. Taste and adjust seasonings. Place salad on a serving dish, top with a sprinkling of peanuts, and garnish with mint and rau rum leaves. Serve at once.

Notes: The sauce may be refrigerated in a covered container for up to one month. Tossing this salad too much will result in limp vegetables as the lime juice begins to soften them. The beauty of this salad lies in the contrasts of fresh and cooked, sweet and sour, soft and crunchy. Any combination of ingredients can be used: choosing whatever is in season at the farmers' market will provide a never-ending variety of fresh flavors.

To make recipes containing fish sauce vegetarian, caramelize 2 tablespoons of white granulated sugar in a small saucepan over low heat until it turns light brown. Add 1/4 teaspoon salt and 1 tablespoon lime juice or vinegar. Remove from heat and mix together.

Cambodian donuts and taro sesame buns are two treats from Cambodia that Cheng Heng offers on weekends. Both are made from sticky rice flour and deep-fried. The donut is slightly chewy with a palm sugar glaze. The bun is filled with coconut and mashed taro, then topped with sesame seeds and palm sugar glaze.

The flavors of Cambodia are making an impact on Minnesota diners, for now there are a number of Cambodian restaurants in the Twin Cities. After fifteen years, Cheng Heng continues to draw diners from across the area and around the state. It also attracted the attention of award-winning photographer Wing Young Huie, who captured this image of Kunrath's father, Bunthary Van, in front of the restaurant's painting of the famous Angkor Wat temple, a fitting mural for this taste of Cambodia in Minnesota.

Right: Cheng Heng Restaurant, 2009, University Avenue Project.

The flavors of...
Thailand

The small country of Thailand (formerly Siam), on the Gulf of Thailand, is bordered by Burma, Laos, Cambodia, and Malaysia. It has been attacked but never occupied by an outside force and remains governed by a constitutional monarchy, an unusual state of affairs in the Asia Pacific Rim. Its food reflects centuries-old culinary creations developed within the country but also borrowing from its neighbors. Many dishes are based on Thailand's plentiful supply of fish, coconuts, lemongrass, Thai basil, galangal, chilies, and rice. Curries, often coconut milk–based, are red, green, or yellow. Many dishes are seasoned with fish sauce or chili paste and have very strong fish smells.

Thai Food Introduced at the State Fair

When a student from Thailand moved to Minnesota in 1972 to earn her master's degree in science, she first lived with a family near the University of Minnesota campus. After weeks of eating typically American food with the family, she asked if she could cook some of her own Thai dishes. They gladly agreed—until the very potent Thai-based seasonings began to fill the house. The aromas were so strong that her hosts demanded that she "stop cooking [her] stinky food!"

The student, Supenn Supatanaskinkasem, went on to marry one of her U. of M. classmates, Bruce Harrison, and to introduce Thai cooking to Minnesota. After earning her degree, she worked in a laboratory and began

bringing in some of her homemade Thai egg rolls for her coworkers. They liked them so much, she decided to try to sell them and looked for the best opportunity that did not require a large investment.

She found that opportunity in a food booth at the Minnesota State Fair, and in 1976 Supenn Harrison offered the first commercial Thai food in Minnesota. It was a hot August day and she was expecting her first child in two months. Despite working all day, she was able to sell only two hundred egg rolls. She went home tired and discouraged but went back and tried again. The second day she sold three hundred, and by the third day she lost count. Sales kept increasing, and at the end of the ten-day run, she knew she had a winner. In fact, Sue's Thai Egg Rolls were so popular that the Minnesota State Fair Board kept renewing her license for twenty-four more years.

Facing page: Holy Basil Supreme from Sawatdee.
Right: Supenn Harrison in her Sawatdee Thai Restaurant on Washington Avenue in Minneapolis.

Supenn's Thai Red Beef Curry may have seemed "stinky" to her Minnesota host family in 1972, but it is now a favorite with diners at her restaurant, Sawatdee. While fish sauce is one of the more potent-smelling Thai seasonings, in this recipe it is the Thai red curry paste that may "stink up" the house. Its odor intensifies as it cooks and the idea is to let it get really smelly to achieve maximum flavor. Using less curry paste may curtail the odor but will also cut back on the flavor.

Supenn's Thai Red Beef Curry (1972)

Supenn Harrison

Serves 4–6

2 tablespoons vegetable or peanut oil

2 tablespoons red curry paste

1 pound beef chuck, cut into 1/2-inch cubes

1 cup milk (Supenn did not have coconut milk in Minnesota in 1972 and used regular milk; coconut milk preferred)

1/2 teaspoon salt

1 teaspoon sugar

1 carrot, peeled and cut into 1/3-inch slices

2 cups frozen, fresh, or canned peas

steamed rice

1. Heat a heavy saucepan or skillet to hot but not smoking. Add oil and heat until shimmering. Stir in the curry paste and mix well until the paste has a strong odor. Add the beef and keep stirring until the meat and paste are well mixed. Add the milk, salt, and sugar and stir well. Add vegetables, stir, and simmer for 20 minutes, until all the spices are well mixed with the meat.

2. Serve hot with steamed white rice.

Here is the recipe for the first Thai food sold in Minnesota, Sue's Thai Egg Rolls. They became such favorites that Supenn's daughters, Jennifer and Cynthia, worked in the booth during their teen years and made enough money to help pay for their college degrees. Both graduated from Macalester College in St. Paul.

Sue's Thai Egg Rolls

Supenn Harrison

Makes 15–20 egg rolls

1 pound lean ground beef

2 tablespoons sugar

1/4 teaspoon salt

1/2 teaspoon black pepper

6 tablespoons Thai light soy sauce

1 teaspoon garlic powder

1 head cabbage, about 2 pounds

1 medium onion

1 (20–24 count) package egg roll skins

soybean oil for deep-frying

1. Marinate beef by mixing it with the sugar, salt, pepper, soy sauce, and garlic powder and let it stand 10 or 15 minutes.

2. Slice cabbage and onion in long, thin strips and place in a bowl.

3. Combine the cabbage, onion, and beef mixture, using the soy sauce to moisten the mixture. (Using your hands to mix the ingredients is the easiest way to incorporate everything together.)

4. Put a heaping tablespoonful of the meat mixture on an egg roll skin about 1 inch from the edge coming toward you; roll once. Then fold both the right side and the left side to the center and continue rolling into a tight roll. If desired, you can use water or egg beaten with a little water as "glue" to help seal the roll. Repeat, filling remaining skins.

5. Heat oil in deep fat fryer or deep saucepan to 350–75°. If heat is too high, it will burn the egg roll and the mixture inside will not be thoroughly cooked.

6. Fry egg rolls two, three, or four at a time for 2 to 3 minutes or until golden brown, turning twice. Drain fried rolls on paper towels.

Reprinted with permission from *Awaken to Thai Cooking* (Supenn Harrison, 2009).

When Supenn bought her first restaurant, the Gopher Grill, in 1979, it was a breakfast and lunch café with strictly American food. To retain customers, she continued serving dishes on the existing menu but added chow mein, an Asian dish she knew Americans liked. However, she gave the chow mein a slight Thai twist, and it became a customer favorite. With only one Asian dish on the menu, Supenn would go home each night discouraged that she was not cooking the food of her homeland. Bruce suggested she put a small sign in the window offering Thai food at night. She did, and soon she changed the Gopher Grill to the Siam Café, dropping the American menu and offering only Thai food—except for the chow mein that she kept for her regular customers. It contains no soy sauce and has a very light flavor, with the vegetables still colorful and just barely cooked.

Siam Café Chow Mein

Supenn Harrison
Serves 3–4

8 ounces boneless, skinless chicken, white and/or dark meat	2 sprigs cilantro leaves, coarsely chopped
1 carrot	1/2 teaspoon salt
3 stalks celery	pinch sugar
5 fresh mushrooms	1 tablespoon cornstarch mixed with 1 tablespoon water
1 small onion	
1 tablespoon oil	1 package fried chow mein noodles
pinch minced garlic	
2 cups chicken broth	cooked rice

1. Cut the chicken and vegetables into about 1/3-inch pieces.

2. Heat a large frying pan, sauté pan, or saucepan to medium high, add the oil, and stir-fry the chicken and garlic until well done. Do not burn the garlic.

3. Add the vegetables, chicken broth, cilantro, salt, and sugar, and simmer for about 3 minutes, until flavors combine. Stir in the cornstarch-water mixture and cook for 1 minute more. Remove from heat.

4. Serve a portion of hot chow mein over a pile of crisp noodles and add a scoop of cooked white rice.

Supenn wrote three cookbooks: *Cooking the Thai Way* with Judy Monroe (Minneapolis: Lerner Publications, 1986) and her own *Sawatdee Cookbook* (2003) and *Awaken to Thai Cooking* (2009).

Tom Yum Soup

Supenn Harrison

Serves 4

2 cups chicken stock or broth	3 kaffir lime leaves
1 teaspoon chili paste (*nam prig paw*/chili paste with bean oil; see note)	salt to taste
	chili pepper to taste
	1/4 teaspoon fish sauce
12 ounces beef, chicken, shrimp, or pork, cut fine	juice of 1/2 lemon
8 fresh mushrooms, sliced	1 sprig coriander (cilantro), chopped
1 small onion, chopped	1 stalk green onion, sliced
1 stalk fresh lemongrass, white portion only, finely chopped	cooked rice

1. Heat the broth in a soup kettle; stir in chili paste.

2. Add your choice of meat or shrimp along with mushrooms, onion, lemongrass, and kaffir leaves. Season with salt, chili pepper, fish sauce, freshly squeezed lemon juice, coriander, and green onion. Cook 5 to 10 minutes, until meat and vegetables are done. Serve with cooked rice.

Note: Adjust chili paste to taste. Use 1/3 teaspoon for mild to medium heat, 1/2 teaspoon for medium, and 1 teaspoon for hot—or more if you like it hotter.

Reprinted with permission from *Awaken to Thai Cooking* (Supenn Harrison, 2009).

Pad Thai is often thought of as the national dish of Thailand. *Pad* means "fried," and in this case it is stir-fried rice noodles, shrimp, bean sprouts, and egg. To prepare the bean sprouts, put them in a colander and pour boiling water over them. Plunge them into cold water, drain, and pat dry with paper towels. The black soy sauce in this recipe is Thai black soy sauce, available in Asian markets. The rice noodles tend to stick to a hot metal pan or wok; using a large, nonstick frying pan helps prevent the problem.

Sawatdee Pad Thai

Supenn Harrison

Serves 4

1 (8-ounce) package rice noodles	1 tablespoon paprika
3 tablespoons oil	1 egg, beaten
3 cloves garlic	1 teaspoon Thai sweet black soy sauce
1/4 cup fresh shrimp or prawns, optional	2 green onions, green part only, chopped
1/4 cup Thai fish sauce	1/4 cup ground roasted peanuts
1/4 cup sugar	1 cup bean sprouts (see head note)
2 tablespoons vinegar	

For garnish:

1/2 cup bean sprouts	1/2 lemon, cut into wedges
1/2 cup chopped green onions, green part only	

1. Soak the rice noodles in cold water for 30 minutes or until soft. Drain noodles and set aside.

2. Heat a large skillet or wok (see head note) until hot and then add the oil. Stir-fry the garlic and fresh shrimp (if using). Add the noodles and stir-fry until the noodles are translucent. Reduce the heat if the mixture is cooking too quickly or the noodles stick together.

3. Add the fish sauce, sugar, vinegar, and paprika; stir-fry the mixture until thoroughly combined.

4. Stir in the egg. Turn the heat to high and cook, stirring gently, until the egg sets. Thoroughly combine the mixture and continue cooking over medium-high heat for about 2 minutes, until most of the liquid is reduced.

5. Mix in the soy sauce, green onions, peanuts, and bean sprouts; stir well.

6. Place on a serving dish, arranging the additional bean sprouts and green onions with the lemon wedges in an attractive manner.

Reprinted with permission from *Awaken to Thai Cooking* (Supenn Harrison, 2009).

This Thai chicken stir-fry dish is popular with Sawatdee customers and a Harrison family favorite. It uses the distinctive flavor of holy basil, available fresh in many Asian markets. Lemon basil may be substituted, but the flavor will not be the same.

Holy Basil Supreme

Supenn Harrison

Serves 2

2 tablespoons oil	red chilies to taste
1 skinless, boneless chicken breast, sliced into 1 1/2 by 1 by 1/4–inch slices	1 small onion, sliced
	1 tablespoon fish sauce
1 clove garlic, peeled and crushed	1 tablespoon sugar
	dash salt
1 tablespoon water	3 tablespoons fresh holy basil leaves
4 ounces fresh mushrooms, sliced	cooked rice
3 jalapeño or green chilies, sliced	

1. Heat oil over high heat.

2. Stir-fry chicken with garlic until done.

3. Add water, mushrooms, chilies, onion, fish sauce, sugar, salt, and basil leaves. Continue cooking until flavors mix well.

4. Serve with cooked rice.

Reprinted with permission from *Awaken to Thai Cooking* (Supenn Harrison, 2009).

In 1986, Lerner Publications Company of Minneapolis produced a series of Easy Menu Ethnic Cookbooks for young cooks. Of the twenty-six books in the series, six featured food from the Asia Pacific Rim: China, India, Japan, Korea, Thailand, and Vietnam. Supenn Harrison and Duluth-based Judy Monroe were coauthors of the Thai cookbook, *Cooking the Thai Way*, which is out of print but still available in many local library collections.

Supenn Harrison and her family continued to expand their Thai restaurant business. After four successful years, she sold the Siam Café, and in 1983, with the help of her sister, Gat Jones, Supenn opened the first Sawatdee Thai Restaurant in St. Paul. It became so successful that she opened another Sawatdee on Washington Avenue in Minneapolis and a third in Bloomington. Over the years she added a fourth in St. Cloud and a fifth in Maple Grove, in 2002. She also opened a Sawatdee in the Uptown area of Minneapolis at Twenty-seventh and Hennepin Avenue South with some of her former staff. In 1998 Supenn opened a Sawatdee To Go across from Target headquarters on the Nicollet Mall in downtown Minneapolis. When the building was to be demolished, she moved her restaurant to the skyway and renamed it Sawatdee Express. In 2010 she opened another Sawatdee Express on Lake Street, not far from the location of her original Siam Café. She also opened the Palette Bar and Café in 1993 and added Sushi Sawatdee adjacent to it in the Warehouse District of Minneapolis. Year after year, Sawatdee could be found on the top favorites lists of area diners.

Not everything Supenn tried worked as she had envisioned, but she was not deterred. When a restaurant did not succeed, she closed it or moved it or restructured it. She once said, "Not everything is a success for me. But I never give up."

In 1979, Supenn was named Minnesota Small Business Person of the Year. She attributed much of her success to her husband Bruce, who encouraged her along the way and became her partner in business as well. Their two daughters, Jennifer and Cynthia, also worked in the family business at various times, and in 2009 Jennifer took over day-to-day management of Sawatdee, giving Supenn more time to enjoy her grandchildren.

While Supenn introduced her Thai food at the state fair in 1976 and at the Gopher Café in 1979, other Thai restaurants were beginning to bring their own versions to the area. In 1981, Chavhivan (Bou) Haanpaa opened King and I Thai on the Nicollet Mall in downtown Minneapolis, later moving to LaSalle Avenue. It, too, became popular with Minnesota diners and helped encourage the opening of even more Thai restaurants. By 2009, Minnesota had an estimated ninety-seven Thai restaurants.

Mother's Thai Recipes Launch Another Restaurant

At an early age, Supatra Khommuangpak learned about cooking Thai food from experts. First, she worked in her family's food market in Udon Thani in the Isaan area of northeast Thailand and discovered what it took to operate a successful store. Next, she learned cooking from her mother, whose recipes she still uses. And then she worked in her relatives' restaurant in Bangkok, where she came to understand the restaurant business.

Supatra met her future husband, Randy Johnson, in Thailand, and soon after they were married they moved to Minnesota. While she worked at a variety of jobs, her cooking was primarily for family and friends, along with potluck dinners for some of the Thai Association of Minnesota's New Year's parties and picnics. But she longed to get back to the food business, and in 1999, with Randy as her partner, Supatra opened Jasmine Market in Burnsville. Here she was able to carry many of the foods of her homeland and offer Thai cooking demonstrations. "I wanted my customers to know how Thai food should taste before they tried making it at home," she once said. In addition, she taught Thai cooking to community education students in eighteen different school districts. In 2004 she combined some of her students' and her family's favorite recipes and published *Crying Tiger*, a cookbook with more than one hundred recipes and a wealth of information about Thai food. The recipes she created are true to her home cooking, with changes made only to accommodate ingredient substitutions for things that may be difficult to obtain in Minnesota.

Supatra Johnson at Supatra's Thai Cuisine, 967 West Seventh Street, St. Paul, 2011.

Silver Bean Thread Noodle Salad / Yum Woon Sen

Supatra Johnson

Serves 4

1/4 pound ground pork	1 tablespoon sugar
1/4 pound dried silver bean thread noodles (cellophane noodles)	1 teaspoon soybean paste with chili (*nam prik pao*)
1/2 pound shrimp, peeled and deveined, tails removed	3–4 tablespoons fish sauce (*nam pla*)
2 tablespoons chopped pickled garlic	1/4 cup chopped Chinese celery, or substitute regular celery
1/2 cup thinly sliced purple onion	1/3 cup chopped cilantro
1 tablespoon chopped fresh Thai chili (see head note)	2 tablespoons chopped roasted peanuts
2–3 tablespoons fresh lemon juice	lettuce leaves
	tomato slices

In 2004 the Johnsons purchased the St. Paul Sawatdee location across from the farmers' market and operated it as Supatra's Thai Restaurant. Three years later, Supatra moved the restaurant to 967 West Seventh Street in St. Paul, a spot with both indoor dining for sixty and an outdoor patio. "I wanted a restaurant that my family could comfortably run," she said. Her menu continues to offer many of the dishes she learned to make from her mother.

Supatra serves this salad in her restaurant, where diners have a choice of shrimp or poached chicken with vegetables. If you prefer to add the chicken, poach slices of breast meat in boiling water for 10 minutes, drain, and cool to serve on top of the salad. The fish sauce provides a nice salty balance to the sugar in the salad dressing. To reduce the heat from the Thai chili, remove the seeds before chopping.

1. Fill a saucepan with water and bring to a boil. Add ground pork and cook for 6 to 8 minutes, stirring to break up the pork pieces. Drain and set aside.

2. Fill another saucepan with water and bring to a boil. Add the bean thread noodles and cook for 2 minutes, stirring to break apart the bundles. Add the shrimp and cook for 3 minutes, stirring occasionally. Remove from heat, drain, and rinse in cold water for a few seconds.

3. In a mixing bowl combine cooked pork, bean thread noodles, shrimp, and remaining ingredients except peanuts, lettuce, and tomato, and toss gently to mix. Sprinkle with roasted peanuts and serve with lettuce and tomato slices.

Reprinted with permission from *Crying Tiger* (Supatra Johnson, 2004).

When I met Supatra at the Jasmine Market in 2002, she was demonstrating two Thai soups, a creamy Pumpkin Coconut Soup that was brightened with Thai chilies, galangal, lemongrass, and kaffir lime leaves, and Kuay-tiaw Nua, *a very spicy beef and vegetable soup. Together, these soups offer an excellent example of the wide range of flavors in Thai cooking. — PLH*

Pumpkin Coconut Soup / Fak Tong Gang Ka Ti

Supatra Johnson

Serves 4

2 cups water

1 pound pumpkin squash (also called kabocha or Japanese squash), halved, seeds removed, peeled, and cut into bite-size pieces

1 tablespoon minced galangal

1 tablespoon minced lemongrass

2 tablespoons chopped shallot

1 tablespoon sea salt

2 fresh Thai chilies, minced

5 kaffir lime leaves

1 (13.5-ounce) can coconut milk

3 green onions, cut into 1 1/2-inch lengths

1/2 cup lemon basil (*bai maengluck*; if fresh is not available, substitute dried or frozen)

1. In a soup pot over high heat, bring water to a boil. Add pumpkin, galangal, lemongrass, shallot, salt, Thai chilies, and lime leaves. Cook over high heat until the pumpkin is soft, approximately 5 minutes.

2. Add coconut milk and green onions and let boil for 2 minutes, stirring occasionally. Turn off the heat and stir in lemon basil. Serve hot.

Reprinted with permission from *Crying Tiger* (Supatra Johnson, 2004).

Not all Thai cooking is complex. Here is a very easy recipe that even young cooks can help prepare. Turning the chicken frequently and keeping it away from the hottest coals will help prevent burning.

Grilled Chicken / Gai Yang

Supatra Johnson

Serves 4

1 (2-pound) chicken fryer, cut into breast, drumsticks, thighs, and wings

1/3 cup oyster sauce

6 cloves garlic, minced

1 teaspoon black pepper

1 tablespoon Thai regular soy sauce (Golden Mountain brand preferred)

1 tablespoon sugar

1 teaspoon sea salt

1/4 cup minced lemongrass, optional

chili sauce for chicken

1. Thoroughly wash the chicken and pat dry with a paper towel. Combine oyster sauce, garlic, pepper, soy sauce, sugar, salt, and lemongrass (if using) in a bowl. Mix ingredients together thoroughly and apply as a marinade to the chicken. Refrigerate for at least 15 to 20 minutes.

2. Grill over charcoal at medium-high heat for 30 to 40 minutes, turning occasionally to prevent burning (if charcoal fire is not available, roast in 375° oven for 30 to 40 minutes).

3. Remove from grill and serve with chili sauce for chicken (available at Asian markets).

Reprinted with permission from *Crying Tiger* (Supatra Johnson, 2004).

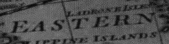

Steamed Walleye with Vegetables / Pla Noong Pak

Supatra Johnson

Serves 4

1 pound walleye fillets

3 tablespoons Thai light soy sauce (see note; Healthy Boy brand preferred)

1 teaspoon sea salt

1 stalk lemongrass, bruised and cut into 2-inch lengths

1/2 medium-sized green pumpkin, washed, peeled, and cut into 2-inch-thick by 4-inch-long pieces

1/4 pound Thai eggplant, halved (see note)

1/4 pound long beans, cut into 4-inch lengths, or substitute green beans

1/2 cup lemon basil (*bai maengluck*)

sticky rice

Nam Prik Noom (recipe follows)

1. Combine the walleye, light soy sauce, salt, and lemongrass in a bowl. Cover with plastic wrap and marinate in the refrigerator for 1 hour.

2. Bring water to a boil in a steamer and place the green pumpkin and the Thai eggplant on the tray. Cover and steam for 10 minutes. Place the long beans, marinated walleye and lemongrass, and lemon basil on top of the pumpkin and eggplant and steam, covered, for 10 more minutes.

3. Using a spatula, carefully lift the fish and vegetables out of the steamer and place on a serving platter. Discard the lemongrass pieces and serve with sticky rice and Nam Prik Noom.

Notes: Thai eggplants are small, round, green vegetables with their own distinctive flavor. Purple eggplants are not a substitute. Thai soy sauce has a different flavor and consistency than Chinese or Japanese soy sauce.

Reprinted with permission from *Crying Tiger* (Supatra Johnson, 2004).

Young Green Pepper Sauce / Nam Prik Noom

Supatra Johnson

Serves 4

10 young green cayenne peppers, or substitute banana peppers

1 bulb garlic, cloves separated and peeled

5 medium-sized shallots, peeled

10 cherry tomatoes

1/2 teaspoon sea salt

2 tablespoons fish sauce

2 tablespoons lime juice

1/3 cup chopped cilantro

1. Preheat oven to 375° and wrap cayenne peppers, garlic, shallots, and tomatoes in aluminum foil. Bake for 15 minutes and allow to cool.

2. In a mortar and pestle, combine peppers, shallots, garlic, and salt and pound until slightly mashed. Add tomatoes and pound several more times. Add fish sauce and lime juice and mix, followed by cilantro. The consistency should be similar to a thick salsa. (If you do not have a mortar and pestle, chop the ingredients into small pieces and combine in a mixing bowl.) Serve with barbecued meats, sticky rice, or steamed fish along with fresh vegetables such as green beans, cucumber, or lettuce.

Reprinted with permission from *Crying Tiger* (Supatra Johnson, 2004).

Left: Supatra's Steamed Walleye with Vegetables.

Below: Nam Prik Noom.

Veggie Combo / Pad Pak Roum

Supatra Johnson

Serves 4

3 tablespoons cooking oil	1/2 teaspoon ground black pepper
2 ounces cauliflower, cut into small pieces	2 teaspoons sugar
4 baby carrots, cut into small pieces	1 teaspoon tapioca starch mixed with 1/2 cup water
2 ounces broccoli, cut into small pieces	1/2 teaspoon salt
2 ounces green beans, cut into small pieces	1/2 teaspoon garlic powder, optional
1/3 cup sliced yellow onion	jasmine rice
2 tablespoons oyster sauce (see note)	

Heat oil in wok over medium-high heat and add the cauliflower and carrots. Stir-fry for 2 minutes. Add the broccoli and stir-fry for 1 minute. Add the rest of the ingredients except rice and stir-fry for 4 minutes. Remove from heat and serve with jasmine rice.

Note: Vegetarian oyster sauce, available in some Asian markets, may be substituted to make this a vegan dish.

Reprinted with permission from *Crying Tiger* (Supatra Johnson, 2004).

Black Sticky Rice Dessert / Kao Niaw Dum Peiuk

Supatra Johnson

Serves 6

1/2 cup coconut cream	1 cup sugar
1 teaspoon salt	5 cups water
1/2 cup sticky rice and 1/2 cup black sticky rice, soaked together in water overnight	

1. Combine coconut cream and salt in a saucepan and cook over medium-high heat for 2 minutes, then set aside.

2. Drain sticky rice and place in a soup pot along with the sugar and water and bring to a boil. Cook for 10 minutes, stirring occasionally. Reduce heat to simmer, and cook for 10 to 15 minutes, or until the rice thickens.

3. To serve, ladle the rice into bowls and top with coconut cream. Serve warm or cold.

Reprinted with permission from *Crying Tiger* (Supatra Johnson, 2004).

The Johnsons' son Tom at age eleven. He now works in the restaurant as a part-time manager while going to school.

The Johnsons' son Tom started cooking when he was seven by watching his mother and grandmother. Scrambled eggs with green onions was his first dish, and it continues to be one of his favorites. The fish sauce provides the salt flavor for the eggs and the added dimension so important to Thai cooking, but if it seems too strong, reduce to 1 teaspoon. This recipe is an easy way to introduce Thai food to young cooks. Serving scrambled eggs with jasmine rice adds to the international dining experience.

Tommy's Scrambled Eggs with Green Onions

Supatra Johnson

Serves 2

3 eggs	2 tablespoons cooking oil
1 stalk green onion, chopped	jasmine rice (recipe follows)
2 teaspoons fish sauce (see head note)	

Combine eggs, green onion, and fish sauce in a bowl and beat until well mixed. In a frying pan (or wok) over medium-high heat, add the oil and heat for 1 minute. Stir in the egg mixture and cook for 2 to 3 minutes, flipping the eggs with a spatula once in a while. Remove from the heat and serve with jasmine rice.

Reprinted with permission from *Crying Tiger* (Supatra Johnson, 2004).

Jasmine Rice / Kao Homm Mali

Supatra Johnson

Serves 2–4

2 cups jasmine rice, rinsed in cold water	1 1/2 cups water

If you have a rice cooker (highly recommended), just add the rice and water and cook. If not, in a saucepan over high heat, add the rice and water and bring to a boil. Cover the pan and cook for 5 minutes. Reduce heat to simmer, and cook for 5 to 10 minutes or until fluffy. Do not stir rice during cooking. Remove from heat and allow to sit for 5 minutes before serving.

Reprinted with permission from *Crying Tiger* (Supatra Johnson, 2004).

Thai dishes often include a variety of seasonings that turn some vegetable-haters into fans. Here are two that are easy to make and very tasty. Water spinach is often available at local farmers' markets and has a different taste and texture than the more commonly used spinach. *Pak Boong Fie Dang*, with its hot, smoky flavor that adds a richness to the spinach, is a favorite dish in Thailand.

Water Spinach with Soyabean Sauce / Pak Boong Fie Dang

Supatra Johnson

Serves 4

1 pound water spinach (see head note), cut into 2-inch lengths	1/2 tablespoon sugar
1 tablespoon soyabean sauce (*tow jiew*)	3 fresh Thai chilies, bruised
2 tablespoons oyster sauce (see note)	2 cloves garlic, minced
	3 tablespoons peanut oil
	rice soup or jasmine rice

1. Place water spinach, soyabean sauce, oyster sauce, sugar, chilies, and garlic in a bowl and set aside. Do not mix the ingredients. They should go into the wok in this order.

2. Heat a wok over high heat and add the peanut oil, swirling to coat the entire surface for 2 to 3 minutes or until it smokes. Using oven mitts to protect your hands from the hot oil, flip the ingredients from the mixing bowl directly into the wok so that the garlic hits the pan first and the spinach last. Cover wok and cook for 2 minutes without stirring. Remove the lid and stir-fry for 2 minutes. Remove from heat and serve with plain rice soup or jasmine rice.

Note: Vegetarian oyster sauce, available in some Asian markets, may be substituted to make this a vegan dish.

Thai Restaurants Lead to Thai Markets

When Xayasack (Cy) Ratsamy's family moved to Minneapolis from Thailand, Thai food was beginning to attract followers in this area. So in 1982, Cy's father, Voun Thont, opened a small food market specializing in Thai ingredients. The New Orient Market, just off Nicollet Avenue and Twenty-sixth Street in Minneapolis, was a family business, and Cy worked in the store while going to school. As the business grew, so did the need for expansion. In 1993, the year Cy graduated from the Carlson School of Management at the University of Minnesota, the family bought a building at Twenty-eighth and First Avenue, just a few blocks away, and moved the New Orient Market to its current location. For the next nineteen years it continued to be a family business, with Cy's cousin Sam Limsithi also working in the store until his death in 2012. New Orient Market handles a wide range of products.

"We were able to add more products and increase our line of fresh fruit, herbs, and vegetables," Cy recalled. Initially, markets were not allowed to import many ingredients essential to Thai cooking, such as kaffir lime leaves, Thai basil, holy basil, and durian. "But the regulations have changed so now we can import many of these items from Thailand," Cy added, "and some of them are now grown in California and Florida as well." Minnesota farmers even cultivate lemongrass and sell it fresh at farmers' markets during the summer.

Cy also carries a wide variety of bottled sauces used by many Southeast Asian countries, including fish sauce. Derived from salted herring, fish sauce is very, very smelly, but adding just a little to soups will give them a dimension that is salty and not at all smelly. It is also used in many stir-fried dishes, dipping sauces, and salad dressings. Fish sauce is to Thai cooking what soy sauce is to Chinese.

New Orient Market added a meat and fish department as well as a takeout deli offering typical Thai dishes such as pork satays, red curries, chicken wings, soups, and more. There are always a variety of snacks available from the kitchen, including taro chips and freshly cooked crisp Thai egg rolls with a very peppery flavor.

One of the nicest things about the New Orient Market is Cy's willingness to answer questions and help with selections. It seems Cy is always on hand, always smiling, always helpful. I have learned as much about Thai food from Cy as from any other source and have developed a fondness for a number of Thai flavors such as lemongrass.

New Orient Market at 2800 First Avenue South in Minneapolis.

Lemongrass.

1. Cut chicken into small serving pieces, chopping through the bones with a sharp cleaver, or use boneless chicken breasts and thighs.

2. Remove outer leaves of the lemongrass and the upper green portion and finely slice the tender white part at the base of the stalks. Mash with a mortar and pestle. Finely slice the spring onions, including the green leaves. Mix the chicken with the salt, pepper, lemongrass, and spring onions and set aside for 30 minutes.

3. Heat wok or large nonstick frying pan, add oil, and when it is hot, add the marinated chicken and stir-fry for 3 minutes. Add chili and stir-fry on medium heat for another 10 minutes, or until the chicken is cooked through. Season with sugar and pepper and add peanuts. Stir well. Add fish sauce and toss to distribute evenly.

4. Serve hot with rice or noodles or cold or room temperature as an appetizer or picnic dish.

Lemongrass, an essential part of Thai cooking, is very easy to use (see note). While it has a citrus flavor, do not substitute lemon or lime zest or juice. This recipe uses lemongrass to its fullest. Be sure to slice and mash it just before adding to the chicken. We suggest using a nonstick frying pan, as the mixture tends to stick to a wok that is not well seasoned. This dish is good hot, at room temperature, cold, and left over—if there is anything left!

Thai Chicken with Lemongrass

ACAI

Serves 4–6

1 small roasting chicken (about 2 pounds, or the equivalent in parts)	2 tablespoons oil
4 stalks lemongrass	1 fresh red chili, seeded and chopped
3 spring onions	1 teaspoon sugar
1 teaspoon salt	1/2 cup roasted peanuts, finely chopped
1/4 teaspoon ground black pepper, plus more to taste	2 tablespoons fish sauce

Note: Lemongrass is an essential flavoring used throughout Southeast Asia. Its mild citrus flavor cannot be replaced by lemon or lime zest or juice even though many recipes suggest that substitution. For cooking, use only the lower white bulb portion. Peel and clean it, then mince it just before adding to other ingredients: cutting it too soon will dissipate the flavor. Or use whole pieces and remove them before serving: they are too tough to chew and digest. The cleaned lemongrass bulbs may be stored for several months in a plastic container in the freezer. Thaw and use them just as you would fresh ones. Fresh lemongrass is locally grown in the summer and available in farmers' markets around the state. Commercially grown lemongrass from Florida and California is available year-round and tends to be somewhat larger than homegrown. Recipes call for the larger version, so make necessary adjustments for smaller-sized lemongrass. Lemongrass leaves are often used to make a soothing tisane.

Thai Food Carving

The art of carving fruits and vegetables in Thailand dates back thousands of years. But to Nuntana Erickson, it is a treasured skill. For the past thirty years she has been teaching this intricate technique to students, first in her native Thailand and then since 1990 in Minnesota and across the globe through her website, creative-carving.com. Currently in garde manger at the Radisson Hotel in Minneapolis, Nuntana also creates ice carvings. In 2009 she produced her first DVD of food carving lessons. Here are just of few examples of the beautiful shapes and colors that can be coaxed from everyday food

.

Top: Carved squash container.

Right: Thai food carver Nuntana Erickson, making a curly scallion garnish, making a leek flower, finished carved mango.

Below: Finished carrot flowers and leaf.

Facing page: Watermelon flower by Nuntana Erickson.

The flavors of...
India

Raghavan Iyer

Historians have said that at one point in history all roads led to India. Some travelers came to buy the country's amazing assortment of spices, some to find a safe home, and others to conquer and rule. So it is not surprising that the flavors of India have been making their way around the world for more than five thousand years. First there were mustard and sesame oils from the Indus Valley in northern India in 3200 BCE. Then valuable black pepper was exported from southwestern India in 2000 BCE. Eventually all of India's amazing spices were sought after by kings and emperors around the globe. Wars were even fought over them. Cardamom, turmeric, coriander, pepper, nutmeg, ginger, and mace were just a few of India's precious commodities bartered for and traded by the spice merchants of Portugal, Spain, France, Britain, Egypt, and Arabia.

Initially giant caravans of thousands of camels carried tons of spices overland to Africa or China. By the fifteenth century, land caravans were augmented or replaced by merchant ships sailing across the world's seas to bring these exotic flavors to their various ports of call. Often their crews consisted of unwilling sailors who had been kidnapped in India and abandoned at the ship's destination. In each port, small Indian communities began to blossom, and the cooking of their homeland made an impression on their new neighbors.

In Great Britain, so many sailors had been left ashore that communities of Indian immigrants began opening curry houses. These early efforts were designed to feed

Facing page: Rice Noodles with Toasted Coconut and Grilled Corn, shown with an antique spice box.
Right: Daljit Sikka.

their fellow countrymen, but soon the aromatic restaurants filled with cheap, fresh, flavorful food were attracting Brits looking for someplace to eat after the pubs closed. The first Indian restaurant opened in London in 1809, and by 1999 that number had grown to eight thousand. Indian food had become so popular in Britain that it outranked fish and chips by two to one.

By the 1800s America's growing population created a demand for India's spices brought by traders sailing to the eastern shores of the United States and then by wagon trains into the heartlands. Over the centuries, as camel caravans and wagon trains were replaced by railroads and trucks and shipping by sea was augmented by jet planes, Indian spices and other ingredients became more readily available throughout the United States. By 2004 an estimated nine thousand Indian food markets were located in the United States. And as the markets grew, so did the restaurants.

Don D. J.—
The Indian Restaurant Kingpin

Known simply as D. J. to many in the restaurant business, Daljit Sikka felt out of sorts on the plane ride to Minnesota during the early days of September 1969. From Chandigarh in Punjab, the breadbasket of India, at the tender age of nineteen he left family and loved ones behind with no aspirations of seeking a career in the restaurant broker business. Instead, he pursued a master's degree in biology from Mankato State University, which led to a PhD from the University of Minnesota in plant physiology.

Still adhering to his religious upbringing as a Sikh, in the years that followed he pioneered a path as a successful restaurant broker for over twenty-five Indian, Sri Lankan, and Nepalese restaurants. To make ends meet, he worked in restaurants and helped with any special events that came his way. In the summer of 1970 he helped serve an Indian meal of tandoori chicken, ground beef–stuffed flatbreads, and spiced garbanzo beans to Minnesotans that came for the Aquatennial celebrations on Nicollet Mall in Minneapolis. He worked in collaboration with Bimla Barar and Chander Mehta, proprietors of the first Indian restaurants: Bimla's on Tenth Street and Nicollet Avenue called Taj Mahal, and Chander's in Fridley called Bombay House.

During his stint at the University of Minnesota, D. J. secured a job as the maître d' at the newly opened Solarium restaurant at the Calhoun Beach Club in 1977. His earnest ways and exotic, turbaned demeanor always drew diners to ask questions about his homeland. Soft-spoken and accomplished, he educated them about all things Indian, including the wonders of tandoori chicken. He returned home in 1980 to get married, and when he came back to Minnesota he dove into the world of restaurant brokerage.

He influenced the opening, in Minneapolis, of Tandoor in 1981 in the St. Anthony Main area and Kebabi Bar and Restaurant in 1986, the latter the first of its kind in the fine-dining arena in the just-opened Riverplace. Now there are over forty restaurants that serve Indian, Pakistani, and Caribbean foods (via their Indian forefathers) all across Minnesota, including in Duluth, Rochester, and St. Cloud.

Tandoori Chicken

Daljit Sikka's
Serves 4

2 cups plain yogurt	1/2 teaspoon ground ginger
1 cup red wine vinegar	
2 teaspoons curry powder	1/2 teaspoon dried thyme
1 teaspoon ground red pepper (cayenne)	3 bay leaves
	1 (3-pound) whole chicken, skin removed, cut into 8 pieces (see note)
1 teaspoon ground coriander	
1 teaspoon salt	1 lemon, cut into wedges

1. Combine the yogurt, vinegar, and all the spices in a medium bowl. Add the chicken pieces to the marinade and make sure the pieces are completely covered. Refrigerate, covered, overnight.

2. When ready to cook, preheat the oven to 350°. Lightly grease a baking sheet or broiler pan with cooking spray. Spread the pieces (including any clinging marinade) on the prepared pan. Reserve the marinade for basting.

3. Bake the chicken, basting the pieces in the first 10 minutes and turning them occasionally until cooked, piercing them in a few places to make sure the juices run clear, 35 to 45 minutes.

4. Serve with lemon wedges for squirting.

Note: Be sure to score the raw chicken pieces in a few places to enable the marinade to soak through.

The Indian Restaurant Pioneer

The same year Daljit Sikka arrived in Minnesota, Chander Mehta did as well, at the age of thirty-two. With ancestral roots from Lahore, Pakistan (before the partition) and then Delhi, armed with an engineering degree, he came to join friends Mahendranath (a successful businessman) and D. J. He too worked the Aquatennial on Nicollet Mall the summer of 1970, selling foods he felt would appeal to the average reveler. Success that summer fueled him to open Minnesota's first Indian restaurant later that year in Fridley: Bombay House, a fast-food concept that seemed ahead of its time. He self-financed the business and put in a rotisserie instead of a tandoor, since a commercial clay oven was not easily secured during those early years.

The menu—lunch and dinner—was a cacophony of dishes incorporating flavors from his corner of the world in northwestern India, with presentation styles similar to those of the neighboring Zapata Mexican Restaurant. The Raja Roll, a taco-like dish with an Indian fried bread called *bhatura* harboring ground beef slow-simmered with assertive spices like cumin, coriander, and ground red pepper, was born. It was his most popular dish, reasonably priced at $0.30, followed by the Bombay Burger, a hamburger patty topped with seasoned ground beef and sandwiched between two pieces of fried bread, all for a whopping $0.50. The menu also included a dal, a curry or two, and tandoori chicken. Plain yogurt shakes were unknown in Minnesota at that time, but he served the popular sweet version called *lassi* to pleased customer responses.

Chander did all the cooking at the restaurant for two years, at which point he grew tired of the operational chores. It was time to close shop, having paved the road for future Indian restaurants in Minnesota. He had arrived in the United States as a Hindu, teaching yoga and meditation, but years later, in 1982, he converted to Christianity with his American wife and now works part time as a pastor at his neighborhood church. He still retains his passion for Indian food and continues to make the delicacies of his homeland and his restaurant in his home kitchen for friends and family.

More often than not, lamb, mutton, or goat meat is used to make *kheema* (minced or ground meat). In many non-Hindu households, beef is also an option. In this country, the quality of beef, especially from grass-fed cows, is quite high. Lean ground meat makes for a lower-fat dish without compromising on its succulence. Serve kheema with a basket of store-bought or homemade *pooris* (page 118) or mounded atop bread for your own version of Chander Mehta's Raja Roll.

Spicy Ground Beef with Chilies / Kheema

Raghavan Iyer

Serves 6

2 tablespoons canola oil

2 teaspoons cumin seeds

1 small red onion, finely chopped

2 tablespoons finely chopped ginger

2–3 fresh green serrano chilies, stems removed, finely chopped (do not remove the seeds)

3 large cloves garlic, finely chopped

1 pound lean ground beef (see head note)

2 teaspoons coriander seeds, ground

1 teaspoon cumin seeds, ground

2 teaspoons coarse kosher or sea salt

1 teaspoon ground turmeric

1/2 cup water

2 tablespoons finely chopped cilantro leaves and tender stems

1. Heat the oil in a medium saucepan over medium-high heat. Add 2 teaspoons cumin seeds and cook until they sizzle, turn reddish brown, and are fragrant, 5 to 10 seconds. Immediately add the onion and stir-fry until limp and light brown, 5 to 10 minutes.

2. Add the ginger, chilies, and garlic. Cook, stirring, until the mixture is caramel brown, 5 minutes.

3. Break up the ground beef and add it to the pan. Cook, stirring occasionally, until the meat browns, 8 to 10 minutes.

4. Sprinkle in the coriander, ground cumin, salt, and turmeric, stirring to coat the meat with the spices. Reduce the heat to medium-low, cover the pan, and simmer, stirring occasionally, for 10 to 12 minutes, to allow the meat to absorb the complex flavors.

5. Stir in water (see note), and add the cilantro. Continue to simmer, covered, stirring occasionally, to allow the flavors to mingle, 5 to 8 minutes. Serve immediately.

Note: You can fold in fresh or frozen green peas along with the water if you wish.

Pooris with Cardamom-Scented Yogurt Cheese (page 120).

A perfect eating utensil, these puffy breads tear easily even with the fingers of one hand to wrap around curries, stir-fries, and stews. Try the combination of cardamom-scented yogurt cheese (page 120) with these breads for an unusual dessert.

Fried Whole-Wheat Bread / Pooris

Raghavan Iyer

Makes about 10 breads, to serve 5

2 cups chapati flour (see note)

1/2 teaspoon coarse kosher or sea salt

2 tablespoons canola oil

about 1/2 cup warm water

canola oil for deep-frying

1. Place flour and salt in a medium bowl. Add the 2 tablespoons oil and rub the flour between the palms of your hands until well mixed.

2. Add the water a little at a time and keep mixing the flour until it comes together as a smooth, pliable dough. Knead the dough for 2 to 3 minutes until smooth. Let it rest, covered, for about 30 minutes. (You can do this even 2 to 3 days ahead and store it, covered, in the refrigerator. Bring it to room temperature before rolling it out.)

3. Break up the dough into rounds approximately 1/2 to 3/4 inch in diameter. Working with one at a time, keeping the remaining ones covered, roll out to a disk approximately 3 inches in diameter. Repeat with the remaining rounds, stacking them between layers of plastic wrap or waxed or parchment paper.

4. Heat 2 to 3 inches oil in a wok or deep 10-inch skillet over medium-high heat until thermometer reads 375°.

5. Line a cookie sheet or plate with two to three paper towels.

6. Gently slide a dough round into the hot oil. With the back of a slotted spoon, gently submerge the dough in oil until it puffs up. Turn once; fry about 30 seconds or until golden brown.

7. Remove from the oil with slotted spoon; drain on the paper towels. Repeat with the remaining dough rounds.

Note: Chapati flour is available in natural-food stores and Indian grocery stores. The flour is ground from a low-protein wheat grain, so it doesn't form the strong gluten that gives commercial yeast breads their structure. If chapati flour is unavailable, use equal amounts of cake flour, pastry flour, and all-purpose flour for each cup of chapati flour.

The Patel Factor: The Indian Store

Bikhalal Patel had no reason to come to the United States, but Idi Amin changed all that. Having settled in Uganda for a number of years with his parents and family, Bikhalal found himself uprooted and country-less in 1972, along with hundreds of thousands of Indians during Amin's tumultuous regime. As part of a refugee quota for entry into the United States, Bikhalal came to New York, where his dislike for the crowded metropolis, much like the cost of living that did not agree with his meager pocketbook, mounted. He requested to be moved to a different city, and Minnesota was the state offered, with the caveat that "it was cold."

"Being young, I did not mind the challenges of winter," Bikhalal says, so he moved to Minneapolis in November 1972, embracing the warmth of the community. He settled into work at the ConAgra wheat factory for five years, but the dusty environment soon aggravated his asthma. He took at position at Minnesota Rubber but then found himself part of the workforce that was laid off in 1982. In between his two jobs, he went to London to marry and returned with his wife, Virbai Patel, to Minnesota.

While Virbai worked at a tie factory, Bikhalal's, thoughts centered around running an Indian grocery store, on the heels of a short-lived place in Dinkytown called Himalayan Imports. Bikhalal opened Reshma International, named after his firstborn daughter, on Tenth and Chicago avenues in the Philips neighborhood in 1982. Within a few months he moved farther south on Chicago, first to Twenty-ninth and then to Thirty-fourth Street, where he ran a two-thousand-square-foot place for the handful of customers who needed groceries to cook the Indian way in a foreign land. He larded his shelves with trips to Chicago, picking up groceries, staples, and produce every few weeks. Soon trucks delivered his goods, leaving him free to focus on expanding his offerings to Minnesota's growing Indian population. Weekends brought traffic from Iowa, Wisconsin, and the Dakotas as well.

His grocery business continued to grow, allowing him to support his wife and three children. A bigger location in northeast Minneapolis, closer to the Hindu Temple by Central Avenue and Eighteenth Street, in 1989 brought greater visibility to his storefront, which soon expanded in a five-thousand-square-foot building, and he changed the store's name to Asia Imports. His wife, children, and relatives chipped in, helping him manage the store seven days a week. In 2004 in a corner of his store he opened Bombay Deli, where daughter Reshma prepared traditional foods from Gujarat, all vegetarian, all simple, all scrumptious.

The growth in stores offering Indian groceries brought competition, and Bikhalal found his profit margins shrinking, especially when the video rental business, an otherwise strong figure in his weekly sales, also took a dive. Hard work, a shrinking economy, and long hours took a toll, and he decided to retire from the million-dollar-a-year business that his children found hard to manage. They all settled into steady jobs with their own families following successful college careers, and Bikhalal and Virbai retired in 2009 after years of pioneering success in the Indian grocery store business.

The state of Gujarat, just north of Mumbai (Bombay), is known for preparing extraordinary vegetarian dishes. Gujarat also grows India's peanuts, in addition to being considered its dairy capital. The common misconception that India's vegetable preparations lack texture due to overcooking is completely debunked in this deliciously crispy cabbage "slaw" that so eloquently balances sweet, hot, and tart.

Gujarati Cabbage Slaw / Bund Gobhi Nu Shaak

Raghavan Iyer

Serves 6

1/4 cup canola oil	3 fresh Thai, serrano, or cayenne chilies, finely chopped
1/4 teaspoon asafetida (*hing*; see note)	
1 cup dry-roasted unsalted peanuts, coarsely chopped	3 tablespoons sugar
	1 teaspoon salt
1 medium (1 1/2–pound) green cabbage, finely chopped (8 cups; see note)	1 teaspoon cumin seeds, ground
	1/2 teaspoon ground turmeric
1/4 cup finely chopped cilantro leaves and tender stems	juice of 1 medium lime (2 tablespoons)

1. Heat oil in wok or deep 12-inch skillet over medium-high heat. Add asafetida and peanuts; sizzle 30 seconds.

2. Add remaining ingredients except lime juice; stir-fry about 5 minutes or until cabbage is hot; remove from heat. Stir in lime juice and serve.

Notes: If asafetida is not at hand, omit from recipe. Chop cabbage with a sharp knife, as opposed to a food processor. Supermarkets often stock finely chopped cabbage for coleslaw, making your job in the kitchen much easier.

Every Gujarati-speaking household serves *shrikhand* on special occasions like family gatherings during holidays and religiously auspicious events like weddings. During the months when mangoes and papayas infiltrate the marketplace, these tropical fruits are essential in this cool, creamy dessert (see note for substitution suggestions). Shrikhand is often served with hot-off-the-fryer *pooris* (page 118).

I have, on many occasions, shown up at my Gujarati friends' doors during mealtimes, hoping to be "invited" in for this sinful combination. Thankfully, they never saw through my transparent ploy! — RI

Cardamom-Scented Yogurt Cheese with Mango and Papaya / Aam-Papaya Nu Shrikhand

Raghavan Iyer

Serves 6

large piece cheesecloth

1 pound plain yogurt

2 teaspoons hot milk

1/4 teaspoon saffron threads

1 cup powdered sugar

1/4 teaspoon cardamom seeds (removed from green or white pods), ground

1 small ripe mango, peeled, seeded, finely chopped (see note)

1 small ripe papaya, peeled, seeded, finely chopped (see note)

1. Line a medium colander with cheesecloth; place in a large bowl. Transfer the yogurt to the cheesecloth; drain for an hour.

2. Refrigerate the lined colander and bowl, loosely covered, 6 to 8 hours, until the texture of the yogurt cheese is smooth and silky.

3. While the yogurt drains, combine the milk and saffron in a small bowl, allowing the threads to steep and release their flavors.

4. Discard the whey and transfer the cheese from the cheesecloth to a medium bowl. Fold in the powdered

sugar, a few tablespoons at a time, until well incorporated; stir in the cardamom and the saffron milk, including the threads.

5. Fold in the mango and papaya; cover and refrigerate about 2 hours, or until chilled. Will keep for up to a week in the refrigerator or up to a month in the freezer.

Notes: Use sweet green and red seedless grapes, halved, instead of mango and papaya. Apples offer a delicious crunch but will discolor quickly, unless you soak them in lime or lemon juice for a few minutes before folding them into the yogurt cheese—although doing so will impart an unwanted tartness to the finished dish. Or substitute Asian pears and sweet ruby red pomegranate seeds when they are their juiciest best.

Southern Comfort

Minnesota's first South Indian restaurant, Udupi Café, opened during the winter of 1998 in the former space of a fast-food restaurant at 5060 Central Avenue Northeast in Minneapolis. It was the sixth restaurant opened by South Indian native Mylappan Nagappan and his wife Meena, following sites in Boston, Atlanta, Pittsburgh, Chicago, and Silver Springs, Maryland. In considering a Twin Cities operation, the Nagappans spent six months looking at other Indian restaurants in the area. Since none were offering South Indian cooking, they decided Udupi would find a ready market here, and so it did.

There were no tandoori dishes on the menu, no lamb curry, naan, or other familiar northern Indian fare. Instead, the menu was filled with the complex and delicate flavors of lentils, rice, tamarind, vegetables, and a vast variety of assertive spices from the south. Steamed lentil cakes called *idlis* ruled the roost in this all-vegetarian restaurant, along with lacy crepes, sourdough-like pancakes, and doughnut-shaped fried lentil fritters—all served with a legume-based stew called *sambhar* and a coconut-cilantro chutney spiked with roasted mustard seeds.

The restaurant's success in that particular location was short lived thanks to a kitchen fire that burned the place down. The Nagappans reopened a block away for a few more years before they sold the restaurant and moved to Phoenix. The new owners operated with the same menu and a different name, NalaPak, until early 2010, at which point they closed shop.

A handful of restaurants around Minnesota offer a few South Indian staples on their menus, but none exclusively delivers foods from southern India.

Rasam has often been called *molaghu tanni* (pepper water). When the first Englishman was served this southern staple, he fell head over heels in love with the thin broth, but his clipped English tongue could not twirl the right way to enunciate the words. What came out sounded more like "mulligatawny," and so it stuck. It landed at the English table many reincarnations later, radically different from the original.

This recipe makes for a simple lunch or dinner when accompanied by bowls of steamed rice. Or serve it as soup for the second course of an elegant multiple-course dinner, to acquaint guests with the true "mulligatawny."

Pepper Soup with Tamarind / Molaghu Rasam

Raghavan Iyer

Serves 6

1/4 cup *toovar dal* (split and skinned pigeon peas; see note), sorted and rinsed

6 cups water, divided

1/4 teaspoon ground turmeric

walnut-size ball dried tamarind pulp or 1 tablespoon tamarind concentrate (see note)

1 medium tomato, cut into 1-inch cubes (see note)

3 tablespoons finely chopped cilantro leaves and tender stems, divided

1 teaspoon coarse kosher or sea salt

1/4 teaspoon ground asafetida (*hing*)

12–15 medium to large fresh curry leaves (see note)

2–3 dried red cayenne chilies (or chile de arbol)

1 teaspoon cumin seeds, ground

1 teaspoon black peppercorns, ground

1 tablespoon ghee or canola oil

1 teaspoon black mustard seeds

1 teaspoon cumin seeds

1. In a 1-quart saucepan, heat toovar dal, 2 cups water, and turmeric to boil over medium-high heat; lower heat and simmer, partially covered, 15 to 20 minutes or until dal is tender; turn off burner and allow dal to cool. Transfer to blender and puree until smooth.

2. In medium bowl soak dried tamarind pulp in remaining 4 cups water. After 5 minutes, loosen pulp with fingertips. Continue soaking an additional 10 to 15 minutes. Using hands, completely squeeze out as much of the pulp as possible and discard it. Strain liquid into a 2-quart saucepan, discarding any residual pulp and fibers. If using tamarind concentrate, dissolve in 4 cups water and transfer to 2-quart saucepan. Stir in remaining ingredients except 1 tablespoon cilantro, ghee, and mustard and cumin seeds.

3. Bring to boil over medium-high heat; lower heat to medium and simmer, uncovered, 30 minutes or until liquid is reduced by almost half.

4. Meanwhile, in a small skillet, heat ghee over medium-high heat; add mustard seeds. Once seeds start to pop, cover with lid until all seeds have popped. Stir in cumin seed and sizzle 10 to 15 seconds. Add to pureed dal.

5. Add pureed dal mixture to reduced tamarind water and reheat to boil. Serve sprinkled with remaining cilantro.

Notes: Use *chana dal* (yellow split peas) as an alternative to toovar dal if you have none in your pantry. Skip the curry leaves if unavailable, since there is no alternative for this recipe. You can substitute 1/2 cup lemon juice for the tamarind for a simple and clear sour flavor. You can eliminate the tomatoes, or, for a sweeter acidic influence, use fresh pineapple instead.

The night's meal in my mother's kitchen had four guarantees: the family ate together, shaadum *(rice) was a must, some type of a* sambhar *(stew) or a* rasam *(soup) made its appearance, and the meal always culminated with yogurt or buttermilk. My favorite was invariably the rasam, watery thin, tart, and nose-tinglingly spicy. I inhaled it as is in a small* katori *(bowl), but more often I consumed it over a mound of perfectly cooked white rice. The fingers of my right hand, moving with the synchronized speed of a factory line worker, emptied the* thali *(platter) in no time, often skipping the buttermilk course for a second helping of comforting rasam. — RI*

Ask any Indian the first thing that comes to mind when thinking of South Indian foods, and the response is instant—*masala dosa*. These lacy crepes grace South Indian kitchens, restaurants, and communal eating places and are often served with pigeon pea stew and coconut chutney. Preparing these crepes can be an art, and professional chefs oftentimes make them as large as two feet in diameter.

Spiced Potato–Stuffed Rice-Lentil Crepes / Masala Dosa

Raghavan Iyer

Serves 10

Batter:

1 cup uncooked long-grain white rice

1 cup uncooked parboiled (converted) rice

1 teaspoon fenugreek seeds

1/2 cup *urad dal* (split and skinned black lentils)

about 2 1/2 cups warm water for grinding

1 tablespoon coarse kosher or sea salt

Filling:

2 tablespoons canola oil, plus more for brushing

1 teaspoon black or yellow mustard seeds

3 tablespoons *chana dal* (dried yellow split peas)

3 tablespoons raw (not roasted) cashew pieces

1/4 teaspoon ground asafetida (*hing*)

1/4 teaspoon ground turmeric

1 cup water

3 medium red potatoes (1 pound), peeled, cooked, coarsely smashed

1 large tomato, cored, cut into 1-inch pieces

1/4 cup finely chopped cilantro leaves and tender stems

2 quarter-size slices fresh ginger

1 teaspoon coarse kosher or sea salt

4 fresh green Thai, serrano, or cayenne chilies, stems removed, halved lengthwise (do not remove the seeds)

10–12 medium to large fresh curry leaves

To make batter:

1. Place the two varieties of rice in a medium bowl; cover with water by about 1 inch. With fingers, gently wash the grains until the water becomes cloudy; drain. Repeat 5 to 6 times until the water in the bowl looks clear. Add the fenugreek seeds to the bowl and cover the rice with warm water by about 2 inches. Soak at room temperature at least 4 to 5 hours or overnight; drain.

2. In separate medium bowl place the urad dal; cover with water by about 1 inch. With fingers, gently wash dal until water becomes cloudy; drain. Repeat 5 to 6 times until water in bowl looks clear. Cover with warm water by about 2 inches and soak at room temperature at least 4 to 5 hours or overnight; drain.

3. In blender place 1/2 cup warm water and half the rice mixture; puree, scraping sides of blender jar, until smooth. Transfer to large bowl; repeat with remaining rice.

4. Puree the dal with 1/4 cup water until smooth; add to rice batter. Fold in salt and additional 1 1/4 cups water or more as needed to make a slightly thin, pancake-consistency batter.

5. In a gas oven with lit pilot light, a slightly warm electric oven, or a proofing unit, keep bowl tightly covered with plastic wrap for 24 hours or until batter ferments, bubbles form, and it acquires a sourdough-like smell.

To make filling:

1. Heat oil in wok or deep 12-inch skillet over medium-high heat. Add mustard seeds. Once seeds begin to pop, cover skillet and wait until popping stops. Add chana dal and cashews; stir-fry about 1 minute or until golden brown.

2. Stir in asafetida and turmeric. Stir in remaining ingredients; reduce heat. Cover and simmer 5 to 7 minutes or until water is absorbed; remove from heat.

To make crepes:

1. Coat and heat a 12-inch nonstick skillet with a teaspoon vegetable oil over medium heat; ladle in 1/2 cup batter and with back of ladle quickly and evenly spread batter to form a paper-thin, unbroken circle roughly 8 inches in diameter. Cook 2 to 3 minutes or until top of crepe is opaque, bottom is golden brown, and it starts to curl up around the edges. Flip crepe and brown other side, about 1 minute.

2. Transfer crepe to serving platter. Place one portion of filling in center and fold crepe to cover filling; serve immediately.

3. Repeat with remaining batter and filling (see note).

Notes: If the pan gets too hot between crepes, the batter will clump up as soon as it's poured, preventing an even spread. Lower the heat or wipe the skillet with a clean paper towel moistened with cold water before continuing.

Leftover batter can be refrigerated for up to a week. When frozen, it can bring you joy even two months later!

A Farmer at Heart

Joginder Pal Cheema left his family farm in Punjab, four hundred miles northwest of Delhi, in 1982 and came to California to work in the fields. He carried the knowledge of growing beets, basmati rice, sugarcane, and wheat as he tilled the fertile California soil. After a year, he moved to New York, where he worked in restaurants within the city, as well as Rochester, where he learned to cook from the owner's wife, and Buffalo, where he stayed for over eight years. He returned to Punjab for an arranged marriage in 1989 and came back to America, wife in tow.

Via Chicago, where he opened and sold two restaurants, he came to Minnesota in 1993, met D. J. Sikka, and found a spot in Maplewood at a freestanding former fast-food restaurant. What set his restaurant, with its standard northern Indian menu, apart was the introduction of a lunch buffet, partly to cut the labor costs of having a full-service staff and partly to help Pal (who also goes by Paul) cook and serve massive amounts of food at once. His establishment proved successful, serving six to seven hundred diners a day, with sales averaging eighty thousand dollars a month.

Over the next few years he opened and closed (or sold) ten restaurants all over the Twin Cities, peppering each location with his array of tandoori chicken, naans, curries, kebabs, and biryanis. He will soon open Raj Darbar, adding to the two locations he currently owns and operates, and plans to serve thali-style lunches and dinners from both northern and southern India.

He enjoys cooking in his restaurant kitchens when he can and still gets a longing spark in his eyes when he talks about farming. Ironically, he lives in America's heartland but does not have the time to get his hands dirty again. Lamb curry is a favorite of his, incorporating the flavors of the north with the assertive, gamey flavors of lamb.

When students request a "basic lamb curry," this recipe, honed in the restaurant kitchen where Raghavan slaved during the early years of his career, is the place to start. The flavors are typical of versions found in many a North Indian, particularly Punjabi, restaurant—the type that seems to dominate the American and European Indian restaurant scene. In restaurants, this curry is usually served with baskets of hot buttered naan and white basmati rice. The Indian customer always requests slices of raw onion, fresh green chilies, and wedges of lime to eat alongside the meal, and you may choose to do the same.

Lamb Curry / Tamatar Gosht

Raghavan Iyer

Serves 4

2 teaspoons coriander seeds, ground

1 teaspoon cumin seeds, ground

1 teaspoon sweet paprika

1 teaspoon coarse kosher or sea salt

1/2 teaspoon ground red pepper (cayenne)

1/2 teaspoon ground turmeric

4 (2-inch by 1-inch by 1/8-inch) slices ginger, finely chopped

4 medium cloves garlic, finely chopped

1 1/4 pounds boneless leg of lamb, fat trimmed and discarded, meat cut into 1-inch cubes

2 tablespoons vegetable oil

4 black cardamom pods (see note)

2 fresh or dried bay leaves

1 small onion, finely chopped

1 cup canned tomato sauce (see note)

2 tablespoons finely chopped cilantro leaves and tender stems

1. Combine the coriander, cumin, paprika, salt, cayenne, turmeric, ginger, and garlic in a medium bowl. Add the lamb and toss to coat it with the spices. Refrigerate, covered, for about 30 minutes, to allow the flavors to mingle a bit.

2. Heat the oil in a medium saucepan over medium-high heat. Add the cardamom pods and bay leaves, and allow the leaves to sizzle and the pods to swell slightly, about 30 seconds. Add the onion and stir-fry until it is dark brown, 5 to 8 minutes. Add the lamb and stir-fry to sear it and cook the spices without burning them, 5 to 8 minutes. The juices from the meat will release the stuck-on spices that coat the bottom of the pan.

3. Stir in the tomato sauce and cilantro. Once the curry comes to a boil, reduce the heat to medium-low, cover the pan, and simmer, stirring occasionally, until the meat is fork tender, about 45 minutes. Remove cardamom pods and bay leaves; serve.

Notes: Black cardamom injects smoky undertones into the sauce, but green or white cardamom pods are perfectly all right as an alternative. If you use unsalted tomato sauce, add an extra 1/2 teaspoon salt to the recipe to bring alive the spices and their incredible flavors.

Adapted with permission from *660 Curries* by Raghavan Iyer, Workman Publishing.

Mumbai to Marshall, Minnesota: My Spiced Life

Panic washed over me as the white station wagon approached the small town of Marshall, Minnesota, and the four-story buildings of the university campus towering above the flat fields. It was my second day in the United States, and my wispy, one hundred-pound, brown-skinned Indian body felt like a swirling leaf on this vast, open field. What was I doing here? More importantly: what was I going to eat?

When I think of my freshman year, it's not football games nor the whiff of burning leaves I recall but rather the odor of pig farms on a dark night and all those broad, blond, milk-fed students consuming thick cuts of meat and mountainous piles of mashed potatoes. While I majored in hotel, restaurant, and institutional management, I learned more about braising and seasonings than I did about world literature, rural history, and composition that first year. And I daresay that my college struggles provided me a glorious career. In that tiny dorm room I learned to conjure the flavors of my homeland, transforming American ingredients into a comforting and satisfying, if not authentic, home meal. I did not replicate the foods of my country; rather, I adapted my food as well as my palate to cross-cultural creations. I was determined to make this place my home, especially in the kitchen.

Left: Lamb Curry with assorted spices.
Above: Raghavan Iyer.

In the neighborhood's supermarket, catering to a town of ten thousand locals and a transient student population of two thousand, I found no traces of black mustard seeds, split and skinned black lentils, Thai chilies, and bunches of fresh coriander leaves (called cilantro in this country, I later learned)—indispensable ingredients in many of my childhood recipes. Potatoes, onions, tomatoes, and corn were abundant, and so were yellow mustard seeds (used in ground form, along with turmeric, in manufacturing prepared mustard), green and yellow split peas (to make split pea soup with ham hocks), ground red (cayenne) pepper (used in minimal quantities to spike deviled eggs), and parsley (the quintessential herb providing a sprig of spring green to umpteen plates as garnish).

So unbeknownst to me, I was learning to use spicing techniques and ingredients to bring the flavors of India into my new midwestern American home kitchen. The enlightened Indian was alive and well, growing within me as my education and expertise in the culinary field flourished. Each time I sampled an American classic, I quickly learned to re-create it by integrating the herbs, spices, and legumes of my upbringing. Over the years I mastered the techniques that refashioned the flavors of my mother's and grandmother's recipes, comforting me with the South Indian classics from my childhood.

India
125

A return to Minnesota, armed with a degree in hotel and restaurant management from Michigan State University, found me working at Kebabi in Riverplace in 1987 and then its sister café on Nicollet and Fifteenth Street in downtown Minneapolis until 1991. Here I learned to cook, in a commercial kitchen, the dishes from northern India, sweltering over a hot, clay-lined tandoor that could reach 700°. Slapping the now-familiar naan breads into the cauldron became second nature, as did stirring the steadfast tandoori chicken, kebabs, and seafood that simmered in sauces redolent of warm spices like cumin, coriander, cinnamon, cloves, and bay leaves.

The restaurant stint ended and my career as a cooking teacher began in late 1991, as I turned to educating Minnesotans in the ways of regional Indian home cooking. This shift gave birth to my successful in-home catering business, the Essence of Thyme, that took the flavors of my birthland and peppered the palates of thousands. I joined Phyllis Harris in starting the Asian Culinary Arts Institutes in 1995, training professionals and students in classic Asian cooking in Minnesota and all across the United States. Soon my flavors drew the attention of the iconic Betty Crocker and General Mills, Inc., and I penned my first book, Betty Crocker's Indian Home Cooking, in 2001, a classic and beautiful work that remains in print more than a decade later. Subsequent titles followed: The Turmeric Trail: Recipes and Memories from an Indian Childhood (St. Martin's Press, 2002), which garnered a James Beard recognition for Best International Cookbook, and the tome 660 Curries (Workman, 2008), which set the bar for the world of curries from the Indian subcontinent. The book was recognized in the "best of" lists compiled by the New York Times, National Public Radio, the Boston Globe, Food and Wine, Barnes and Noble, and Publishers Weekly, among many others. My teaching abilities were honored by the International Association of Culinary Professionals when I received the Julia Child Award of Excellence for Teacher of the Year in 2004. Sub-

sequently I consulted for corporations like General Mills, Target, Bon Appétit Management Company, and Canola.

In 2009, I was brought in as the culinary consultant for OM, the first upscale Indian restaurant in the plush Warehouse District in downtown Minneapolis. The food reviews among the local media were all very positive for this unusual—for Minnesotans—look at the flavors of India: traditional regional flavors served in a contemporary fashion. Some diners shelved OM under the category of fusion, but I always maintained the integrity of the region's classic flavor profiles. I left the restaurant within a year to continue expanding my portfolio.

Now I have a product line, the Turmeric Trail, of roasted spice blends, handcrafted in small batches at the Midtown Global Market's Kitchen in the Market, housed in the historic Sears building on Lake Street in Minneapolis. The blends are sold online and slated to appear in retail outlets in Minnesota and across the United States as well. My iPad app, "Raghavan's Indian Flavors," brings the flavors of India to the world through twenty-five recipes and over seventy-five embedded videos. My fourth book, Indian Cooking Unfolded (Workman, 2013), will teach novice cooks ways to re-create the flavors of India in their everyday kitchens using ten or fewer ingredients without having to stop and shop at an Indian grocery store. — RI

Raghavan's first two cooking teachers, his mother Ganga and sister Lalitha, attend one of his classes in St. Louis Park.

The Mumbai Connection: My Street Food Memories

Though many Westerners still call the city Bombay, *Mumbai reclaimed her Indian name on the fiftieth year of Independence, August 15, 1997. It is a city for the senses. Locals and tourists alike make their way up to the Hanging Gardens at night to see the coastline against the moonlit sky. The jeweled buildings studding the shores of the Arabian Sea bear a strong resemblance to Queen Victoria's legendary diamond necklace. In this bustling metropolis, legacies of the British Raj linger in the majestic Gateway of India and the sprawling Victoria Terminus, while the aromas of* ragada patties *(golden fried potatoes with hot and sweet sauce) and spicy chai are pure India.*

Just saying the name Mumbai, *I think of forbidden dishes on street corners, of the smell of frying onions and cumin seeds, of ginger, garlic, and chilies. I can hear my sister, the ever-cautious medic, admonishing me, "Don't eat the foods on the streets. You have no idea under what hygienic conditions they were all prepared." Still, I'd sneak out to see the* budhiya mai *(old woman), her cotton saree, jade green with a red border, draped over her head to protect her from the searing rays of the sun. She resembled my grandmother, stacking her guavas just so. I'd reach into my pocket for a* char anna *(barely a penny), and she would pluck a light green ripe guava and, with her shiny penknife, slice off the end and cut the fruit three-fourths of the way in four quarters, then smother it with salt and potent cayenne pepper to elevate its intensity.*

In the sweltering heat of the early afternoon sun, vendors, men wearing white half-sleeved vests with dhotis wrapped around their waists, set up their folding tables and kerosene stoves that support a heavy kadhai *(wok). By late afternoon, the scent of frying and spices thickens the dusky air, tempting office workers heading home to briefly sate their appetites until their late suppers at 9 PM.*

No one uses silverware on the streets. It's impractical; it's unnecessary. Eating with silverware is akin to making love through an interpreter. Far better to hold this food in your hands or eat it from the bowls fashioned from leaves held together with toothpicks. Once emptied, these "bowls" are fed to the wild dogs, cows, and monkeys that roam Mumbai's streets.

Mumbai draws people from all corners of India, and its street food reflects a mosaic of cultures. One vendor from Old Delhi sells chana bhatura, *garbanzos simmered in a tart mango sauce with puffy fried breads; the next, a hawker from Madras, is selling* vadaa sambhar, *split black lentil fritters bathed in a sweet yellow lentil stew sweetened with coconut and spiked with red chilies. Here you'll find* vadaa paav, *garlic potatoes spiked with green chilies and cilantro, served in a soft bun with garlic and red pepper chutney, or chili-stuffed vadaas. With your mouth on fire, find the toothless sixty-year-old man garbed similarly to Gandhi, ready to offer a cup of freshly brewed* chai, *Darjeeling tea steeped in whole milk and many spices.*

Near the train depot in Andheri, a suburb of Mumbai, vendors sell everything from used books to soaps and perfumes imported from the West on makeshift tables or in permanent stalls like the newsstands of Manhattan. A distinguished older Muslim man looms above the rest with a traditional white turban wrapped carefully around his head of shocking white hair. He sells seekh kebabs along with a salad of fresh mint, raw red onions, cilantro, and wedges of plump limes. He squats on the sidewalk over a grill he's fashioned of a broken grate set on four large stones. His twelve-year-old son fans the coals to keep them burning, learning his father's trade. The father purses his lips, barely visible through his majestic beard and mustache, yellowed with age hastened by fatigue, and draws on his long hookah, making a childish bubbling sound while inhaling the intoxicating tumbaako *(raw tobacco). Long* seekhs *(metal skewers) of compressed ground mutton lie across the grease-spitting grates, and the wafting aroma makes even a Brahmin vegetarian like me hungry. — RI*

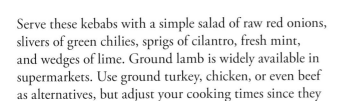

Serve these kebabs with a simple salad of raw red onions, slivers of green chilies, sprigs of cilantro, fresh mint, and wedges of lime. Ground lamb is widely available in supermarkets. Use ground turkey, chicken, or even beef as alternatives, but adjust your cooking times since they vary for each of these meats.

Skewered Lamb Kebabs / Seekh Kebabs

Raghavan Iyer

Serves 6

12 (6- to 8-inch) bamboo skewers	1 tablespoon finely chopped garlic
1 pound ground lamb	1 tablespoon garam masala
1/2 cup finely chopped red onion	1 teaspoon coarse kosher or sea salt
2 tablespoons finely chopped cilantro leaves and tender stems	

1. Soak the skewers in water for about 1/2 hour.

2. In a medium bowl combine the remaining ingredients. Divide the seasoned meat into twelve equal portions. Wrap each part around a bamboo skewer while pressing it with your hand to cover about half the length of the skewer, satay-like.

3. Preheat a broiler or grill for direct heat. Place the skewers in a broiler pan or on the grill grate. Broil or grill, turning occasionally, 5 to 6 minutes or until lamb is barely pink in the center; serve warm.

It is truly a labor of love to make delicate strands of fresh sevai, rice noodles so tender they fall apart in your mouth. No pasta machines in this neck of the woods can expedite the process. "Yennai da paithium, nalla sevai panarthuku nariya time vénum," Amma retorted when asked to make sevai in a hurry. I knew by her response it took time to make these melt-in-your-mouth delicate strands, but I still had to endure her detailed explanation. "First I need to soak uncooked rice for a few hours and then grind it into a very fine batter. Then I have to cook the batter in a vanaali [wok] with oil and make sure all the water is evaporated. The dough cannot be sticky,"

she warned. "I have to let that cool for a few hours. Then I have to steam the dough for a half-hour in my idli paanai [a special mold to make steamed cakes]. While it is still hot, I have to push it through my sevai nari [noodle press], and only then you can have sevai." I rolled my eyes at the process, knowing full well I had to appease myself with something else that evening. "No sevai tonight," I muttered under my breath. But if I kept pushing and begging, maybe tomorrow I could feast on the infamous noodles.

I sit back and think of the laborious process my mother and all those million Tamilian women go through even to this day in making sevai. I realize, with sadness, this endeavor will not be undertaken regularly in my hectic American kitchen. Dried rice noodles are now available at grocery stores all across this country. Specialty stores also carry fresh rice noodles with a consistency and flavor quite similar to the "real deal." As Amma grudgingly said on her one and only visit to Minneapolis, "thévalay"— not bad. I promised myself to come up with an easier version of her noodle-making method, thus freeing those poor steam-ridden, noodle-making women in southern Indian home kitchens all across the world. — RI

Fresh Rice Noodles / Sevai

Raghavan Iyer

Makes about 1 pound, to serve 4

1 1/4 cups rice flour	1 1/4 cups warm water
1 teaspoon salt	2 tablespoons vegetable oil

1. Combine rice flour and salt in a medium bowl; whisk in water a few tablespoons at a time to thin crepe-batter consistency.

2. Add oil and batter to cold wok or nonstick skillet. Heat batter over medium heat, stirring constantly, 2 to 3 minutes or until batter thickens up, starts to leave sides of pan, and comes together into a ball to form soft dough. It should feel silky smooth but not sticky to the touch. Remove dough from wok and cool 2 to 3 minutes. Divide the dough into two equal portions; shape each portion into a 1/2-inch-thick disk.

3. Place dough disks in a lightly greased steamer and steam for 10 minutes. Turn off heat and keep steamer covered to maintain the dough's warm temperature.

4. Remove a dough disk from pan and squeeze it through a noodle press (see note) onto a plate in a single layer; repeat with remaining dough disk.

5. Cool the noodles completely before handling them.

Notes: Unlike Amma's laborious process, this version of noodles is relatively quick to make, especially when you have a noodle press in your kitchen. The Indian *sevai nari* (noodle press), available either in brass, wood, or stainless steel at any Indian grocery store, is usually cylindrical in shape, about four inches long and three inches wide. The bottom of the press has four removable plate-molds with variously shaped perforations. Use the mold with the tiniest holes to extrude these spaghetti-thin noodles.

Take extra care not to handle the noodles when they are freshly extruded as they may stick together and turn gummy. Allow them to cool before using them. Often, they are broken up into one-inch pieces, easy to pick up with fingers—as you know, Indians usually eat everything with our fingers. All the easier to slurp that last bit of noodle left behind on the banana leaf!

This combination is often taken on picnics and long train journeys in southern India because it tastes divine when served at room temperature.

Fresh Rice Noodles with Toasted Coconut / Thenga Sevai

Raghavan Iyer

Serves 4

2 tablespoons *urad dal* (split and hulled black lentils), sorted (see note), divided

2 tablespoons *chana dal* (yellow split peas), sorted, divided

4 dried red Thai, cayenne, or serrano chilies

2 tablespoons ghee or canola oil

1 teaspoon black mustard seeds

1 tablespoon whole raw (not roasted) cashews, coarsely chopped
1 tablespoon dry-roasted unsalted peanuts, coarsely chopped

1 cup shredded coconut (available frozen in Asian markets)

1 tablespoon finely chopped cilantro leaves and tender stems

12–15 medium to large fresh curry leaves (see note)

1 teaspoon coarse kosher or sea salt

1 pound sevai (page 128; see note)

1. In a 10-inch skillet place 1 tablespoon urad dal, 1 tablespoon chana dal, and 3 chilies; heat over medium-high heat, shaking pan occasionally, 2 to 3 minutes or until dal are golden brown and chilies slightly blackened. Transfer roasted ingredients to a plate and cool 3 to 5 minutes; grind in spice grinder until mixture looks like the texture of finely ground black pepper.

2. In same skillet heat ghee over medium-high heat; add mustard seeds. Once seeds begin to pop, cover skillet with lid. As soon as they finish popping, add remaining urad dal, chana dal, dried chili, cashews, and peanuts. Stir-fry 30 seconds to 1 minute or until dal and nuts turn golden brown.

3. Stir in coconut, cilantro, and curry leaves and cook, stirring constantly, 2 to 4 minutes or until coconut is golden brown.

4. Transfer coconut mixture, roasted ground dal-chilies blend, and salt to large mixing bowl with sevai; toss gently.

Notes: If using store-purchased dried rice noodles (but why would you, given how easy it is to make your own—see page 128), cook them according to their package instructions. Take care not to overcook them since they will turn mushy and become unpalatable.

Use an extra 2 tablespoons chana dal if urad dal is unavailable. Eliminate curry leaves if none are at hand.

One school of thought has it that the word *curry* is an anglicized pronunciation of the yogurt- or buttermilk-based dish called *kadhi*. Kadhis have been in existence all around the Indian subcontinent for eons, and they have a reputation as a cure for digestive ailments: a scoop of delicately spiced kadhi over a mound of hot white rice will do the trick. This version, from the northwestern state of Gujarat, uses thick slices of okra fried in clarified butter and simmered until tender in spiced, herbed buttermilk thickened with chickpea flour. One eloquent word describes this combination: *yum*!

Spiced Yogurt with Okra / Bhindi Kadhi

Raghavan Iyer

Serves 6

1 pound fresh okra, rinsed and thoroughly dried	1/4 teaspoon ground turmeric
4 cups buttermilk	2 tablespoons finely chopped cilantro leaves and tender stems
2 tablespoons chickpea flour	
2 teaspoons white granulated sugar	12 medium to large fresh curry leaves
2 teaspoons coarse kosher or sea salt	2 tablespoons ghee or melted butter
1 teaspoon ground red pepper (cayenne)	1 teaspoon cumin seeds
	1 teaspoon fenugreek seeds

1. Trim the caps off the okra without cutting into the pods, and then cut the pods into 1-inch lengths.

2. Whisk the buttermilk, chickpea flour, sugar, salt, cayenne, and turmeric together in a medium bowl, making sure the flour is completely incorporated, with no lumps. Then stir in the cilantro and curry leaves.

3. Heat the ghee in a large saucepan over medium-high heat. Sprinkle the cumin and fenugreek seeds into the pan and cook until they sizzle, turn reddish brown, and are fragrant, about 10 seconds.

4. Immediately add the okra and stir-fry until the slices blister in spots and acquire a light brown coloration on their ridged skin, 8 to 10 minutes.

5. Pour in the spiced buttermilk mixture and stir once or twice to deglaze the pan, releasing any browned bits of spices and okra. Lower the heat to medium and simmer, uncovered, stirring occasionally, until the okra is fork tender and the curry has thickened slightly, 10 to 12 minutes. The transformation from a pale, cream-colored curry to a robust, sun yellow one is beautiful to watch. Serve.

Reprinted with permission from *660 Curries* by Raghavan Iyer (Workman, 2008).

A Japanese-Trained Potter, a Mumbai Chef, and Betty Crocker

When Mumbai native Raghavan Iyer was asked to cater a special management luncheon at General Mills, it occurred to him this would be a good opportunity to pitch an idea he had for an Indian cookbook. The plan worked, and three years later General Mills produced *Betty Crocker's Indian Home Cooking* by Raghavan Iyer. Published in 2001 by Hungry Minds, Inc., the cookbook had another Asian connection—specially designed serving dishes by Japanese-trained potter Richard Bresnahan. It was truly an international collaboration between the Minnesota-based corporation, the writer from India, the potter trained in classic Karatsu ware, and the photographer Valerie Bourassa.

In this, Raghavan's first cookbook, he was drawing on his childhood memories of his mother's home cooking. He also wanted the food to be surrounded by natural-looking dishes and accessories. When editor Kim Walters showed him some of the serving dishes and containers she had from the acclaimed potter Richard Bresnahan, Raghavan knew they would make the food look especially appealing and natural in the photos.

A native of North Dakota, Richard began as a government and social work student at St. John's University in St. Joseph, Minnesota, eventually switching to the art of pottery. By the time he was a senior, Richard's extraordinary talent was obvious and his mentor, Johanna Becker, OSB, arranged an apprenticeship for him with the

Nakazato family of potters in Japan. The father had been named a "living national treasure," and his Karatsu ware was world renowned. For the next three years Richard toiled under the sixteen-hour days of his rigorous training routine; on completion he was named a master potter. On his return to St. John's in 1979, Richard was offered the position of artist in residence and became director of St. John's Pottery. A few years later he built North America's largest wood-fired inclined kiln, which can hold up to twelve thousand pieces of art.

Over the years Richard's work was acquired by collectors and museums throughout the United States and Japan. He received numerous awards, was featured in PBS programs and film documentaries, and was the subject of *Body of Clay, Soul of Fire* by Dr. Matthew Welch, assistant director and curator of Japanese and Korean art at the Minneapolis Institute of Arts.

When the cookbook team got together to discuss the project, it became clear that some of the servingware would need to be specially designed for the photos. For the next year, as Raghavan developed the recipes for each dish, Richard created each piece of pottery to properly showcase the food. The result was a Betty Crocker cookbook featuring the food of India photographed on original, handcrafted pottery created by a master potter trained in Japan.

Viewed as appealing to average American homemakers, Betty Crocker cookbooks traditionally reflected their audience's surroundings. The Betty Crocker Indian cookbook not only presented food unfamiliar to most of its audience but also displayed it on original pieces of art, making it a truly Asian-influenced product from Minnesota that was reissued several times and sold worldwide.

Richard Bresnahan, director,
St. John's Pottery, Collegeville, 2011.

I first encountered Raghavan Iyer when I attended his cooking class at Byerly's School of Culinary Arts in St. Louis Park in 1994. I was impressed with the enthusiasm he brought to the class and to his delicious food. His Indian cooking was so much different from the food I had tasted in local Indian restaurants, and I thoroughly enjoyed it. We became good friends and culinary collaborators, and in 1995 he was a cofounder of the Asian Culinary Arts Institutes Ltd., where he serves as our education director. In 2004, he was named Outstanding Cooking Teacher of the Year by the International Association of Culinary Professionals (IACP). He has written four cookbooks, and we are pleased to have his collaboration on this book. While Raghavan has included some of his own recipes, we also offer the following three dishes that have become favorites in my household. — PLH

Spinach Masala

Raghavan Iyer

Serves 4

2 tablespoons canola oil or ghee

1 medium red onion, halved and thinly sliced

1 teaspoon finely chopped garlic

1/2 cup golden raisins

1 pound fresh baby spinach

1 teaspoon garam masala

1/2 teaspoon coarse kosher or sea salt

1. Heat the oil over medium-high heat in a wok or frying pan large enough to hold the spinach. Add the onion, garlic, and raisins and stir-fry until the onion and garlic are partially golden brown and the raisins swell, 2 to 3 minutes.

2. Add handfuls of the spinach and continue to stir-fry until wilted. Repeat until all the spinach is used up. This will take about 1 to 3 minutes.

3. Sprinkle in the garam masala and salt and serve immediately.

Chopped Tomato Salad

Raghavan Iyer

Serves 4

3 medium tomatoes (about 1 pound), any color, peeled and chopped

1 small cucumber, peeled, seeds removed, and chopped

1/4 cup dry-roasted unsalted peanuts, coarsely chopped

1/4 cup finely chopped fresh cilantro leaves and tender stems

2–3 fresh Thai, serrano, or cayenne chilies, finely chopped (see note)

1/2 teaspoon salt

1 tablespoon vegetable oil

1 tablespoon black or yellow mustard seeds

1/4 teaspoon ground asafetida

lettuce leaves

1. Mix tomatoes, cucumber, peanuts, cilantro, chilies, and salt in a medium bowl.

2. Heat oil and mustard seeds in a 6-inch skillet over medium-high heat. Once seeds begin to pop, cover skillet and wait until popping stops. Sprinkle in the asafetida.

3. Pour hot oil mixture over tomato mixture and toss well. Serve on a lettuce leaf.

Note: Start with half of a chili chopped and then add more to taste. It is often difficult to judge just how hot fresh chilies are until they are combined with other ingredients. Better to start slowly and add more as necessary.

Adapted from *Betty Crocker's Indian Home Cooking* (Hungry Minds, Inc., for General Mills, Inc., 2001).

Grilled Corn with Lime

Raghavan Iyer

Serves 4

4 ears fresh sweet corn

1 teaspoon cumin seeds, toasted and ground

1/2 teaspoon coarse kosher or sea salt

1/2 teaspoon ground red pepper (cayenne)

2 tablespoons finely chopped fresh cilantro leaves and tender stems

2 tablespoons finely chopped fresh mint leaves

1 medium lime, cut into 4 wedges

1. Heat charcoal coals or gas grill to medium for direct heat.

2. Remove husks and silk from corn. Rinse corn. Place ears of corn directly on the grill about 4 to 5 inches above the heat and cook, uncovered, for 15 to 20 minutes, turning occasionally, until the corn is golden brown.

3. Mix cumin, salt, pepper, cilantro, and mint together. Dip lime wedges into the salt mixture and rub evenly over the ears of hot corn. Serve immediately.

Adapted from *Betty Crocker's Indian Home Cooking* (Hungry Minds, Inc., for General Mills, Inc., 2001).

The Flavors of India Continue to Please Minnesota Diners

By 2009 there were an estimated forty-three Indian restaurants in Minnesota and more than a dozen food markets specializing in the flavors of India. While the numbers may not compare to some of the other Asia Pacific Rim cuisines, more and more Indian flavors are finding their way into mainstream American dishes as well. Someday there may even be a McIndia for drive-up curries.

Rice Noodles with Toasted Coconut (page 129) and Grilled Corn.

The flavors of...
Sri Lanka

Raghavan Iyer

The tiny teardrop island of Sri Lanka (formerly Ceylon) off the southern coast of India is home to a cuisine influenced by its neighbor and the variety of foreigners who settled there, including tea growers from Scotland, spice traders from Portugal, Muslims and Malaysians, Moors, Dutch, and British. Here you will find the curries of India alongside lemongrass and other flavors of Southeast Asia. Holiday celebrations take on international dimensions with the traditional fruitcake, Ceylon's Christmas cake, using fifty egg yolks. It should come as no surprise that the enterprising Sri Lankans, welcoming to all foreigners, should seek that same hospitality from Minnesotans as well.

The Sri Lankan Connection

Heather Jansz exudes passion each time she talks about foods from her youthful years. Like many immigrants from Asia, she had no thoughts of coming to Minnesota, but that changed at a tender age when she left Australia, her adopted home, in the fall of 1974. Her parental roots were from Colombo, Sri Lanka, and her childhood favorites—dishes that wove in complex flavors from sweet

cinnamon, sensuous cardamom, toothsome coconut, and vibrant chilies—lay snug in her bagful of memories as she learned to adapt tastes from her new midwestern home. While pursuing a degree at the University of Minnesota, she stayed with a Sri Lankan family to care for their son as a live-in nanny. A visit to the local Bridgeman's ice cream parlor introduced her to certain combinations that made her crave her spiced dishes even more. As she set roots in her community, her expanded circle of friends wanted to indulge in those Sri Lankan flavors as well, and soon she was whipping up her curries, sambols, and coconut flatbreads with a great deal of regularity.

Her foray into the restaurant world began in a small freestanding building in the northeastern part of Minneapolis, on Eighteenth and Central Avenue, in the winter of 1977–78, called Mulligan Stew House. Her most popular dish was, in fact, mulligan stew, that Irish staple of meats, potatoes, and vegetables simmered as a one-dish comfort offering to her not-so-adventurous

Facing page: Curried Lentils.
Right: Heather Jansz.

diners. Pepper and salt was just right; other spices were a wee bit foreign. The first Sunday of every month she catered to friends who continued to hanker for her spicy curries, and soon longtime restaurant critic Jeremy Iggers coaxed her into expanding her menu to include those delectable curries, sambols, coconut rotis, and other Sri Lankan specialties with greater frequency. Her penchant for theater shone in the songs she belted out to provide entertainment for her diners, some of whom were musicians from the United Kingdom. Thus Sri Lanka Curry House was birthed, plump with assertive flavors, in that location, and thrived for five years.

Heather outgrew her location and moved to the Uptown area in Minneapolis, setting up in the old Fingerhut Gallery on Twenty-eighth and Hennepin. She spiced her way into many hearts for seventeen years, working alongside her partner and husband Evan Balasurya. The menu remained steadfast, with seasonal specials peppering their offerings. She and Evan parted ways after seventeen years at that location, and Heather wedged into a corner restaurant, Curry Leaf Deli, on Grand Avenue in St. Paul, collaborating with Steven Sears from 1994 to 1998. The restaurant business took its toll, and she called it quits to focus on catering. Evan Balasurya, meanwhile, opened a short-lived restaurant in Calhoun Village, also called Sri Lanka Curry House, for which Heather continued to make the coconut sambols, chutneys, and condiments. Earlier, while at the original Sri Lanka Curry House, she co-authored a cookbook, *Fire and Spice* (McGraw-Hill, 1989) with *Star Tribune* feature writer Karen Winegar.

Her catering business focused on special dinners, events, and classes as she cooked meals for the likes of Martin Sheen, Deepak Chopra, and many others. She is occasionally a featured chef at the Highland Grill, seasoning her curries, chutneys, and dhals the way she did in years gone by. And she continues to build her business and client list, with hopes of spreading the joy of healthy, organic Sri Lankan foods along with her other passion —music.

Curried Lentils / Dhal

Heather Jansz

Serves 8

1 tablespoon brown mustard seeds	1 tablespoon cumin
2 tablespoons canola oil	1 teaspoon sweet paprika
3–4 dried red chilies, stems removed	1 teaspoon ground turmeric
1 medium onion, thinly sliced	1 (2-inch piece) cinnamon stick (preferably Ceylon)
5–6 cloves garlic, peeled and crushed	6 cups water
10–12 medium to large fresh curry leaves, optional	1 cup unsweetened coconut milk
1 tablespoon ground coriander	3 cups red Egyptian lentils
	salt to taste
	8 cups steamed red or white rice

1. Heat a medium to large saucepan over medium-high heat. Sprinkle in the mustard seeds and toast them until they pop.

2. Pour in the oil and add the chilies along with the onion, garlic, and curry leaves (if using). Stir-fry the ingredients until light brown, 3 to 5 minutes.

3. Sprinkle in the coriander, cumin, paprika, and turmeric and add the cinnamon stick. Stir to cook the spices, 1 to 2 minutes.

4. Pour in the water and coconut milk, stirring once or twice.

5. Stir in the lentils. Heat to boiling. Continue to cook, uncovered, stirring occasionally, until the lentils are tender and yellow, 8 to 10 minutes.

6. Stir in salt to taste and serve with steamed red or white rice.

Curried Pumpkin Squash

Heather Jansz

Serves 6

1 1/2 tablespoons ghee

1 medium onion, finely chopped

5 cloves garlic, finely chopped

10–12 medium to large fresh curry leaves

1 tablespoon curry powder

1 teaspoon ground turmeric

1 teaspoon coarsely ground black pepper

1 (1-inch piece) cinnamon stick (preferably Ceylon)

1 1/2 pounds butternut squash or pumpkin, cut into 1-inch cubes

salt to taste

2 cups water

1 cup unsweetened coconut milk

1/2 cup toasted desiccated coconut

1. Heat the ghee in a medium saucepan over medium-high heat and brown the onions and garlic, 3 to 5 minutes.

2. Add the curry leaves, curry powder, turmeric, pepper, and cinnamon, and stir-fry for another minute.

3. Stir in the squash and salt, coating the squash with the spices and onion mixture.

4. Pour in the water and coconut milk. Heat to boiling and then simmer the squash, covered, on medium-low, stirring occasionally, until tender, 15 to 20 minutes.

5. Stir in the toasted coconut and serve.

Sweet Hot Chicken Curry

Heather Jansz

Serves 6–8

1/4 cup olive oil

1 large onion, chopped

6 cloves garlic, chopped

1 (2-inch) piece ginger, chopped

15 fresh curry leaves

1 tablespoon roasted curry powder

1 teaspoon ground turmeric

1 tablespoon hot chili powder

1 tablespoon paprika

1 1/2 teaspoons salt

2 cups water

1 (13.5-ounce) can coconut milk

2 pounds boneless, skinless chicken, cut into bite-size pieces

1 cup brown sugar

1. Heat oil in a large skillet or saucepan over medium heat. Add the onion, garlic, ginger, and curry leaves and stir-fry until light brown, 5 to 8 minutes.

2. Sprinkle and stir in the curry powder, turmeric, chili powder, paprika, and salt. Allow the spices to cook about 2 minutes.

3. Pour in the water and coconut milk, scraping the pan to release any collected bits of onion and spices. Add the chicken and sugar.

4. Simmer the curry, covered, stirring occasionally, until the chicken pieces are no longer pink in the center and the juices run clear, about 15 minutes.

The food of Sri Lanka has not garnered a large following in Minnesota, probably because of the limited opportunities to try it. While it is similar to Indian cooking, the Southeast Asian influences give it a different flavor that may be confusing to some diners. When Heather and Evan were operating their restaurants, they attracted a following of diners who liked these interesting combinations. While Heather continues to make Sri Lankan food available through catering and special events, currently the only place to find this flavorful cuisine in Minnesota is occasionally on other restaurant menus.

Sambol: A Sri Lankan Oasis in Eagan

Yankee Doodle Road in the heart of Eagan seemed an unlikely place to find Sri Lankan food, but that's what Sambol offered, along with an extensive Indian menu, in 2006. While the restaurant served primarily Indian food during the week, weekenders could savor Sri Lanka's classic string hoppers and egg hoppers under beds of coconut milk–based curries redolent of cinnamon, cloves, cardamom, and peppercorns. In recent years, the ownership has changed hands and now the focus is on flavors from northern India.

This pickle-like Sri Lankan vegetable perks up plain white rice for a simple lunch.

Fried Plantain, Eggplant, and Cashews with Cayenne-Vinegar Sauce / Batu Moju

Raghavan Iyer
Serves 6

vegetable oil for deep-frying

1 very firm medium plantain

1 small eggplant, stem removed, cut into 1-inch cubes

1/2 cup raw cashews

1/2 cup malt or cider vinegar

2 teaspoons white granulated sugar

2 teaspoons black or yellow mustard seeds, ground

1 teaspoon ground red pepper (cayenne)

1 teaspoon coarse kosher or sea salt

1 tablespoon finely chopped ginger

1 tablespoon finely chopped garlic

1/2 teaspoon coarsely cracked black peppercorns

1. Line a plate or a baking sheet with three or four sheets of paper towel.

2. Pour oil to a depth of 2 to 3 inches into a wok, Dutch oven, or medium saucepan. Heat the oil over medium heat until a candy or deep-frying thermometer inserted into the oil (without touching the pan's bottom) registers 375° to 400°. (An alternative way to see if the oil is at the right temperature for deep-frying is to gently flick a drop of water over it. If the pearl-like drop skitters across the surface, the oil is ready.)

3. While the oil is heating, slice off the stem and heel ends of the plantain (1/4-inch slices). Cut the plantain in half crosswise. Using a paring knife, make a lengthwise slit, 1/8 to 1/4 inch deep, in each half. Wedge your fingers just under the slit and peel off the skin in one easy motion. (You can peel the entire skin with a paring knife, but it is slightly more time consuming.) Cut the light beige flesh into 1-inch cubes.

4. When the oil is ready, add the plantain cubes and fry, turning occasionally, until they are sunny-brown and crisp, 5 to 8 minutes. Remove them with a slotted spoon and place them on the paper towels to drain.

5. Add the eggplant cubes to the oil and fry them in a similar fashion, until shriveled and slightly crisp, 5 to 8 minutes. Add the eggplant to the plantains.

6. Add the cashews to the hot oil and roast them until they turn reddish brown, 2 to 3 minutes. Add them to the vegetables.

7. Whisk the vinegar, sugar, mustard, red pepper, salt, ginger, garlic, and peppercorns together in a medium bowl. Add the fried vegetables and nuts, and toss well to coat them with the sweet-hot-pungent vinegar. This mixture will keep in the refrigerator for up to 2 weeks.

Note: If deep-frying intimidates you, try pan-frying the vegetables and nuts separately in a nonstick skillet. They will take a little bit longer—an additional 5 minutes or so—to cook through and brown.

Recipe adapted from *660 Curries* by Raghavan Iyer (Workman, 2008).

The Versatile Coconut

Once upon a time, a coconut washed up on a beach in Sri Lanka, took root in the sand, grew into a tree, and produced more coconuts. Today, coconut palms grow in abundance on the island, providing a nearly endless supply of fruit and water.

The coconut is not a nut, but the fruit and seed of the coconut palm tree. It is believed to have originated around Malaysia, but over the centuries storms, tides, and ocean currents brought coconuts to other Asia Pacific Rim countries where they took root, grew into trees, and became a culinary staple. They are valued for their sweet coconut meat, refreshing coconut water, rich coconut oil, and hairy, hard shells that are often used for non-culinary purposes.

In Sri Lanka young coconuts are popular for their delicious water and sweet, jelly-like white meat. Now available in Asian markets and some general food stores in Minnesota, young coconuts are smooth, white, and fairly heavy for their size and look nothing like the hairy brown ball they will become if left to mature. Young coconuts are cylindrical with pointed tops that look as if they have been sharpened by a giant pencil sharpener. They are filled with sweet water (not coconut milk) and a thin layer of soft, sweet meat that is peeled away with a spoon and eaten. Left to ripen, that soft layer thickens and becomes the firm coconut meat that is shredded for a variety of dishes. Listed as "coconut water" on restaurant beverage menus, young coconuts are now found in Thai, Vietnamese, Indian, Malaysian, and sometimes non-Asian restaurants in Minnesota. They are served whole with the top cut away so the diner can drink the water and then scoop out and enjoy the coconut jell.

Young coconut filled with coconut water.

Mature coconuts become the familiar-looking hard, round ball with a brown, hairy skin. They contain some coconut water, but the recipes in this book call for shredded or grated coconut meat, coconut cream, or coconut milk. All are available in general food markets in processed forms. Often a can of coconut milk contains a layer of coconut cream at the top, so if the recipe calls for cream and milk, do not shake the can before opening. The thick top layer may be scooped out separately from the lighter milk below. If the cream is not required, shake the can to mix the cream and milk together. Use packaged, shredded coconut or open a fresh coconut, remove the white meat from the shell, and grate it. The freshly grated coconut will keep for about one week if it is carefully wrapped and refrigerated. It has a great deal more flavor than the packaged coconut. Fresh coconut cream and milk may be made by mixing freshly grated coconut with an equal amount of boiling water. Pour the mixture through a strainer, pushing all of the liquid out of the coconut shreds. The first extraction yields the most flavorful milk. A second extraction will provide additional milk. To open a mature coconut, wash it, then position it over a bowl or pan to catch the water, and tap the coconut around the middle with the blunt side of a heavy knife, rotating the coconut and tapping until it cracks in half. Remove the coconut meat by prying it away from the shell.

Coconuts, Ceylon tea, and fresh jackfruit are just a few of the flavors of Sri Lanka that have made their way to Minnesota. While there have been limited opportunities in Minnesota to taste the flavorful dishes of Sri Lanka, it is a cuisine that has found fans here and may develop further in the future.

The flavors of...
Vietnam

Some of the tragedies created by the fifteen-year Vietnam War in the 1960s and '70s were the thousands of people left homeless. The lucky ones escaped their war-torn country and found refuge in friendly nations around the world. Le Tran was one of the lucky ones.

I met Le and her husband, Hiew, in 1993 when I wrote about their story for Asian Pages. They were about to celebrate the tenth anniversary of their Lotus restaurant and frozen food operation. While their story is unique, versions of it were played out thousands of times by Vietnamese refugees who settled in Minnesota and throughout the United States. Here is an updated version of that original article. — PLH

Lucky Le Tran

By the time her fourth child was born in Saigon in 1974, Le Tran knew her life was about to change. Gone was the comfortable life she and her husband, Hiew, had worked so hard to provide for their family. North and South Vietnam had been at war for fifteen years. President Nixon had already ordered the withdrawal of the 543,000 U.S. troops from her country, and the communists were beginning to instill radical "social reorganizations." Neighbors were often herded away to holding areas consisting of little more than a floor and roof hastily built on stilts over the waterfront. Private businesses were being appropriated for government operation, and everywhere people feared for their lives. So did Le Tran.

She says she was lucky. And looking at her successes today, it would be easy to explain it all away as luck.

Facing page: Quang's Che Ba Mau, a tricolored dessert with agar, mung bean, and black beans with coconut milk.

But this former teacher and her ex–army captain husband needed more than luck to bring them halfway around the world to create a new life for themselves and their children.

When Le's sister Tra and Tra's two children were among the refugees sponsored by Hope Church in 1975, Le was able to send along her three older children to Minnesota. She felt it was the only way to keep them safe. "It was a very frightening time," she recalled. So frightening, she knew she, her husband, and her baby must also escape in order to survive. Over the next three years they tried to leave Vietnam ten times. Each time they were caught and sent back, often incurring punishment for their efforts. Finally, on the eleventh attempt they succeeded.

"We escaped from Vietnam in a boat eleven meters [thirty-six feet] long by two and a half meters [eight feet] wide. It held fifty people," Le said. "The oldest was seventy and the youngest only one month." Her daughter was just four years old. They had no food, no water, and only the clothes they could wear or carry. But they took that treacherous five-hundred-mile trip across the South China Sea to a refugee camp in Malaysia and freedom. They were just three of 140,000 refugees who made it. Many others were not so lucky.

Seven months later, when they were about to board the airplane to join Le's sister and the other children in Minnesota, her young daughter worried about only one thing. "Will we have water on the plane?" she asked.

In recalling the journey and the years that followed, Le said, "We were lucky." This time luck meant long hours and hard work. Initially Hiew found work in a factory and in 1980 Le joined Tra in opening the Matin restaurant in the Kickernick Building on First Avenue North in Minneapolis. By 1983 Le was ready for her own operation and opened her first Lotus restaurant in the Uptown area. (Later she would move it to Calhoun Square.) "My husband would work at the factory all day, then come in to the restaurant to help me at night," she said. Even the children helped. They did everything. Cooking, cleaning, buying, cashiering: it was truly a family endeavor and successful from the beginning. Within six months she was looking for a new location to open her second restaurant.

With four growing children, something near a college made sense to Le, and soon she opened the Lotus restaurant near Oak and Washington avenues on the University of Minnesota campus. Within four years she was operating six Lotus restaurants in Minneapolis, Edina, Burnsville, and St. Paul. "We were lucky," she said, but she is also quick to acknowledge the important part played by family, friends, and business associates who helped along the way. Her success also meant sixteen-hour workdays with little free time to enjoy her children, something that worried Le. So she began to sell the restaurants as franchises of the original Lotus.

By 1990 Le's older children were in college, so she turned her efforts to a new endeavor, frozen foods. "I called on the food stores myself," she recalled, one by one. The Lotus food line, including vegetarian egg rolls, fried rice, curry, and cream cheese wontons, was created in the restaurant's kitchen during off-hours. Again, the family and staff did everything, including cooking, packaging, freezing, and even delivery. Lotus frozen foods were sold in Byerly's, Lund's, Cub Foods, New Market, and other area food stores. And, while Le eventually worked with a full staff, food broker, and marketing consultant, she continued to oversee Lotus operations while looking for new challenges to conquer.

"I have always loved to cook," Le said, and she was an avid reader and collector of cookbooks. "If a recipe looks good, I try it first at home. If I like it, we test it in the restaurant before adding it to the menu." Loyal Lotus customers were often asked to try new dishes. Only dishes that met with their approval survived the testing process to join the dozens of offerings already on the Lotus menu. Featuring typical Vietnamese stir-fry and noodle dishes plus many house specialties, Lotus attracted a clientele so loyal that when customers moved away from the Twin Cities, they often called Le to ask for their favorite recipes. "It is really too hard to adapt a restaurant recipe for home cooking," said Le, but she did appreciate their requests. Many suggested that she write a cookbook, but she just shook her head and smiled at the thought.

By 1993, when Lotus at Calhoun Square celebrated its tenth anniversary, Hiew was working full-time in the business, and the children were off pursuing independent careers, Le was able to spend less time at the restaurant.

But that didn't mean she spent more time resting. "If I'm not busy, I go crazy," she said as she looked to the future. With more than seventy Vietnamese restaurants operating in the Twin Cities in 1993, Le did not foresee additional Lotus locations in the area, but she did not rule out the possibility of something an hour or two out of town.

Through the years Lotus restaurants won numerous awards, including Best Vietnamese Food from *Mpls. St. Paul* magazine, Best Vietnamese Restaurant from *Twin Cities Reader*, and Best in the Twin Cities in four restaurant categories by *City Pages.*

Le and Hiew sold off all but the Calhoun Square restaurant, which was still successfully operating in 2008 when the new owners of the square notified them to vacate their space. The building was being torn down for a new structure, and Lotus had to go. The restaurant closed and so did a chapter on the growth of Vietnamese flavors in Minnesota. Le Tran died two years later, and Hiew Tran now operates an import/export business.

Chapter Two Opens with Lotus To Go

In 1984 when Le and Hiew Tran began franchising Lotus locations, they sold a Lotus takeout restaurant at West Grant and LaSalle avenues in downtown Minneapolis to Vietnamese staff member Van Vo and her husband, Trung Nguen. Van's specialty was the preparation work, and Hiew trained Trung in Vietnamese cooking techniques. The couple still divides the work this way, but now they are assisted by their children, Toom, Yoom, Hoom, and Joey Nguen.

They originally called their place Lotus To Go but recently shifted the name to Lotus Restaurant. Le Tran had envisioned this Lotus to be a small takeout place where people could run in and order from precooked dishes waiting in a steam table and then quickly go on their way. There were only two tables for dining. After Van took over the operation she decided to eliminate the steam table, add more tables and a counter with stools, and serve freshly cooked dishes to order. It was an immediate hit.

Yoom, who started working in the restaurant at age nine, recently described the family dynamics. "I was assigned to the cash register," he recalled. "We all worked here when school was out and felt it was a privilege. We still do and have a great time working together as a family." Each of the children went on to complete their college education and were starting careers outside the restaurant business when they decided it was time to return to work with their parents. Their customers have come to know them all, often call them by name, and exchange stories about their own families. Customers have also voted Lotus Best Vietnamese Restaurant in the *City Pages* annual polls for more than seven years.

Van, Trung, and their three oldest children came to the United States in 1981 through the sponsorship of Catholic Charities. They landed in Minnesota on a cold winter day with little but the light clothing they were wearing. When they looked at the snow outside they began to shiver and wonder how they would stay warm. Fortunately, the couple who greeted them anticipated their needs and brought warm jackets and boots for the whole family. Van and Trung knew then this was a good place to be. Their fourth child, Joey, was born in Minnesota and named after one of Catholic Charities' patron saints, Joseph.

Yoom says Lotus is busy all day long with downtown businesspeople at lunch, students in the afternoon, takeout for workers heading home, and the locals who come in for dinner. In this densely populated apartment and high-rise area, many customers walk to the restaurant, where there are now a dozen tables and room for more patrons at the counter. During the warm months, people come in for picnic food to enjoy in nearby Loring Park. Yoom reports that today their business is about 50 percent takeout and 50 percent eat in.

While the children have taken over some of the chores, Van still does the daily shopping for fresh ingredients so important to the dishes of Vietnam. The restaurant receives two shipments of fresh ingredients each day, and during the summer Van also shops at the farmers' market, where vendors often save special items for her. This attention to detail shows up in many of the dishes cooked with fresh ingredients. In fact, Yoom says today's diner is looking for fewer stir-fries and more fresh vegetables and herbs. Perhaps that is why Vietnamese noodle salads and fresh spring rolls have become popular with Minnesota diners. They are easy to prepare at home and are truly healthful alternatives to many other fast foods.

Every Vietnamese cook has a favorite *bun bo sao* (noodle salad) which varies with vegetables and herbs available from the garden or farmers' market. Choose the freshest options and create combinations of sweet and savory, hot and mild. Add thinly sliced chili circles to give extra punch and color. The lettuce and noodles help balance out the extra heat.

Rice Noodle Salad / Bun Bo Sao

ACAI

Serves 4

1 (7-ounce) package rice noodles	6 radishes, julienned
1/2 medium head lettuce, finely shredded	2 scallions, julienned
2 carrots, peeled, julienned, and cut into 3-inch pieces	1 cup bean sprouts
	1 cup chopped roasted peanuts
1/2 cucumber with skin, julienned and cut into 3-inch pieces	1/4 cup cilantro leaves
	1/4 cup mint leaves
	2 cups *Nuoc Cham* (page 144)

1. Fill a medium saucepan half full with water. Bring to a boil and add rice noodles. Boil about 4 minutes, until noodles are tender. Drain noodles, plunge into cold water, and drain again. Add to a mixing bowl and cut noodles in quarters with scissors. Set aside.

2. For each serving use a medium salad bowl. Layer one-quarter each of the lettuce, carrots, cucumbers, radishes, scallions, and sprouts in each bowl. Add one-quarter of the noodles off to the side so the vegetables are visible at the bottom of the bowl. Top with a sprinkling of peanuts and garnish with cilantro and mint leaves. Serve with *Nuoc Cham*.

Notes: Tossing the salad before serving begins to soften the vegetables. Let each diner add sauce as needed to keep the flavors and vegetables crisp. Do not store leftover cooked rice noodles in the refrigerator: they will lose their texture. The salad is often topped with egg rolls, pulled cooked chicken or beef, or shrimp. Either of the egg roll recipes in the Philippines chapter (page 54) or Sue's Thai Egg Rolls (page 100) would go well on top of this salad, creating an Asian fusion meal in one dish.

Vietnamese Salad Dressing / Nuoc Cham (see note)

Makes about 3 cups

4 cloves garlic, peeled and crushed	1/4 cup fresh lime juice (about 2 limes)
2 teaspoons chili flakes	1/2 cup fish sauce
6 tablespoons sugar	2 cups water

With a mortar and pestle, grind together the garlic, chili flakes, and sugar until ingredients form a paste. Place paste in a small mixing bowl. Add lime juice, fish sauce, and water. Mix well. Serve at room temperature in individual sauce bowls.

Note: *Nuoc Cham* is available bottled at Asian markets and is used both as a dipping sauce and as a salad dressing.

The Vietnamese salad ingredients show up again as part of several popular dishes, in fresh spring rolls, and as additions to the popular Vietnamese soup, *pho*. Here are two basic recipes, but, of course, every Vietnamese cook has his or her own version.

Vietnamese Fresh Spring Rolls with Shrimp / Goi Cuon

ACAI

Makes 8 rolls

8 (8 1/2-inch diameter) rice paper rounds	8 radishes, thinly sliced
4 Boston lettuce leaves, halved	2 scallions, julienned
2 ounces rice noodles soaked in warm water, drained, and cut into 2-inch lengths	1 cup bean sprouts
	8 medium cooked shrimp, halved along the back
1 large carrot, peeled, julienned, and cut into 3-inch pieces	1/2 cup cilantro leaves
	16 Chinese chive flowers
1/2 cucumber with skin, julienned and cut into 3-inch pieces	1/2 cup mint leaves
	1/2 cup thin jalapeño rings
	Nuac Cham (at left) or Peanut Sauce (page 149)

Prepare a wide bowl of warm water. For each spring roll, soak 1 rice paper round in the water until softened (a few seconds). Pull wrapper out of water, shake off excess water, and blot dry with paper towels. Place the wrapper flat on the working surface. Place 1/2 lettuce leaf over the bottom third of the circle and cover with rows of noodles, carrots, cucumbers, radishes, scallions, and bean sprouts about 1 1/2 inches high. Tightly roll up the bottom portion of the wrapper to the edge of the lettuce. Place two pieces of shrimp, pink side down, and 2 perfect cilantro leaves down the center of the wrap, forming a line across the wrapper. These will be the first things the diner sees when looking at the finished roll. Continue rolling, tucking in the sides to completely cover the ingredients. Position the roll with the shrimp side up. If you are making several rolls at a time, cover the finished rolls with a damp towel to keep moist and continue with remaining ingredients. Garnish with chive flowers and mint leaves.

Rolls may be cut diagonally in half and positioned to show the colorful contents. Serve at once with jalapeño rings and *Nuoc Cham* or Peanut Sauce.

Note: Other vegetables that work well include julienned fresh spinach, broccoli stem centers, celery, daikon, bell peppers, eggplant, and zucchini. Shredded cooked crabmeat, chicken, pork, or beef may also be added. Choose flavors and textures that complement each other.

Beef Noodle Soup / Pho Bo

ACAI

Serves 4–6

2 pounds beef short ribs

1 pound beef bones

1 (1-inch) piece ginger, peeled and sliced

5 large shallots, thinly sliced

1 star anise

1 cinnamon stick

2 tablespoons fish sauce

1 teaspoon whole black peppercorns

1 teaspoon salt

8 ounces dried rice noodles

1 1/2 cups bean sprouts (see page 102)

1 pound (1-inch-thick) sirloin, rib eye, or rump steak, grilled to medium rare, cooled, and thinly sliced into bite-size pieces

variety of raw vegetables and herbs (see previous recipes for suggestions)

1 cup cilantro leaves

16 lemon wedges

6 chilies, sliced into rounds (do not remove the seeds)

1. To a large stockpot add the short ribs, bones, ginger, shallots, star anise, cinnamon stick, fish sauce, peppercorns, and salt. Add at least 12 cups water, covering the beef by 2 inches. Bring to a boil and remove any scum from the surface. Cover and simmer for 4 to 5 hours, until the meat falls off the bones. Add water as necessary to keep contents covered. Remove and discard meat and bones; strain broth and remove any fat from the surface. If necessary, add enough water to make 12 cups of broth. Adjust seasonings to taste. Set aside.

2. Soak rice noodles in warm water 2 hours. Drain noodles and cook in boiling water for 3 to 4 minutes or until just barely tender. Drain noodles, plunge into cold water, and drain again. Set aside.

3. Bring broth to a low boil. For each serving, place about 2 ounces of noodles in the bottom of a large soup bowl. Add a few bean sprouts and 1 ounce of steak slices. Ladle the boiling-hot broth into the bowl. Serve steaming with a plate of assorted vegetables and herbs plus cilantro leaves, lemon wedges, and chili slices for diners to add as they enjoy the soup.

More Minnesota Nice

When Ngoan Dang came to America from Vietnam, he was looking for work to support himself and his two younger brothers. As the eldest son, it was his duty. He started in Pennsylvania and traveled to Ohio and Wisconsin, interviewing for eighty-one different jobs along the way. While he landed a few, including one in a slaughterhouse, nothing offered the kind of future he wanted.

In 1977 he came to Minnesota, where scholarships were available to learn a trade. Shortly after his arrival, late one frigid winter night he was driving along University Avenue in St. Paul's Frogtown neighborhood when his car broke down. Almost immediately several strangers stopped to help him get on his way. "People were so friendly," Ngoan recently recalled, "I knew it was a good place to stay." And stay he did.

By 1990 Ngoan wanted his own business and with his wife, Mai Nguyen, opened Mai Village at 446 University Avenue West in Frogtown. For more than a hundred years, University Avenue has been the main link between downtown St. Paul and downtown Minneapolis, and its profile is constantly shifting. It housed car dealerships, factories, and businesses, but many of them had closed and abandoned the buildings. University Avenue was becoming home to Asian markets and restaurants, community centers, and small businesses—including Mai Village.

Mai Village's award-winning Saigon Salad.
Below: Ngoan Dang and Mai Nguyen with a Vietnamese carved stone pagoda.

Ngoan's goal was to bring some of the culture of his homeland to Minnesota. His grandfather had been a food taster in Vietnam's imperial city of Hue, where Ngoan had lived until he was nineteen. He had vivid memories of the court chefs' elegant cuisine and wanted to replicate the dishes in his new home. His wife was an excellent cook, and he worked with her to tweak recipes until they were exactly to his taste. Mai Village began offering these treasured dishes, and soon the couple built a successful business.

But it was not enough for Ngoan. He wanted to bring more of the Vietnamese culture to Minnesota, and he began a six-year project to build a showcase for the cuisine that would include some of the visual splendor of his childhood.

Frogtown was undergoing many changes, with a seventy-million-dollar housing and commercial development including a new public library rising within a mile of Mai Village. Many abandoned buildings on University Avenue were torn down for these new structures, and Ngoan explored the possibility of building a restaurant just down the block from his original location. The city, looking for a new use for an empty church on the corner of Western and University avenues, was willing to offer Ngoan a $400,000 low-interest loan to build a new restaurant.

Ngoan's vision was a building that reflected Vietnamese architectural designs, but the city wanted something that would match the other new structures on the avenue, looking more like an office building than an Asian restaurant. So Ngoan had a building designed to conform to the city's wishes on the outside but to showcase Vietnamese culture on the inside.

For several years, Ngoan and Mai traveled to Vietnam to meet with architects, engineers, and artisans in Ho Chi Minh City for the art and furnishings that would grace the new restaurant. As they did, the costs grew and in the end the initial loan was just 10 percent of the final four-million-dollar project total. But Ngoan was determined: the couple used their savings and help from family and friends to make his dream a reality.

In 2004 the new Mai Village debuted at 394 University Avenue to rave reviews. Customers entered a spacious foyer that opened into another world filled with elegantly carved wood, silk upholstery, giant Vietnamese urns filled with colorful silk flowers, embroidered silk menu covers, original paintings, and wall reliefs. Diners crossed

the carved wooden bridge spanning a peaceful koi pond and stepped into a carpeted room with embroidered silk ceiling panels. The wooden furniture was hand crafted, the lights designed especially for the room, and the delicate jade-green tableware showcased Hue city in Minnesota. Somehow the noise of the busy street outside melted away and the quiet elegance inside invited relaxed dining. Mai Village is still one of the most elegant restaurants in the Midwest.

During Mai Village's twenty-one-year history it has garnered numerous awards. In 1992 and 2010 it received the Beef Backer Award from the Minnesota Beef Council, the only restaurant to receive this award twice. The council cited Mai Village's creative use of beef, its quality of beef products, and its use of new beef cuts, for example in its seven-course beef dinner and in its Saigon Salad of sliced beef tenderloin on watercress, dressed with Mai Village's Saigon Sauce.

More than a dozen other awards include Best Restaurant 2011 from *Mpls.St.Paul* magazine, Best Restaurant in America 2011, Top 100 Restaurants in 2009, Best Vietnamese Restaurant 2008 from *Mpls.St.Paul*, and the magazine's Best Asian Spice award. In 1993 Mai Village was one of three restaurants in the United States singled out by *Gourmet* magazine for serving "interesting Vietnamese fare" for the adventuresome. The other two were also from Minnesota: Hoa Bien and To Chau in St. Paul.

Ngoan and Mai generously allowed us to capture the splendor of Mai Village's décor and cuisine through photography. Their desire to share Vietnamese culture with Minnesota has given us a taste of Vietnam and made Frogtown an even nicer place to be.

Mai Village's carved wooden bridge, "MAI" carved wood trim décor, and silk embroidered ceiling.

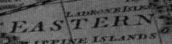

Mai Village's Assorted Meat and Seafood on Griddle lets diners cook their own ingredients and gather them with assorted fresh greens and vegetables in a rice paper wrapper. Add special dipping sauce for a tasty treat.

Mai Village recipes are proprietary, but one of their signature dishes, Nuong Vi Thap Cam, a mixed grill that diners cook at the table, may look difficult but can become a favorite for special occasions or family fun. Over the years ACAI has created recipes for this Vietnamese specialty. We suggest grilling indoors with an electric or butane tabletop grill or outdoors with a tabletop charcoal grill. The charcoal adds a distinctive flavor. Thinly sliced meat and seafood are served with a variety of fresh vegetables, herbs, and rice paper wrappers. A special dipping sauce adds to the variety of flavors for this Vietnamese wrap.

Vietnamese Mixed Grill

ACAI

Serves 6–8

Everything needed for the grill is prepared in advance and then served on large platters for diners to help themselves. The meat and seafood may be grilled with just oil, salt, and pepper but will take on some interesting flavors with traditional marinades. Here are some suggestions:

Chicken:

12 ounces boneless, skinless chicken breast, sliced very thin (about 3 inches long by 1 1/2 inches wide and 1/8 inch thick)

Coat with:

2 teaspoons honey

2 teaspoons fish sauce

1/2 teaspoon salt

1/4 teaspoon freshly ground black pepper

Mix 2 chopped scallions with 18 shredded kaffir limes and 1/4 cup water in a blender. Add to the coated chicken and refrigerate for at least 2 hours.

Beef:

1 pound tender steak, sliced very thin (1 1/2 inches wide by 4 inches long by 1/8 inch thick)

With a mortar and pestle, make a paste of:

2 stalks fresh lemongrass, white part only, peeled and minced

4 shallots, minced

4 cloves garlic, peeled and minced

1 tablespoon sugar

2 small fresh red chilies, seeded and chopped

Stir in:

2 cloves garlic, minced

2–3 small red chilies, stems, seeds, and membranes removed, minced

1 tablespoon sugar

juice of 1 lime (2 tablespoons)

1 tablespoon rice vinegar

1 tablespoon water

4 tablespoons fish sauce

Add to the beef strips and coat on all sides. Set aside for at least 30 minutes.

Shrimp:

24 medium shrimp, shelled and deveined, tails attached

Mix together:

2 cloves garlic, minced

1 tablespoon fish sauce

freshly ground pepper
  to taste

Coat shrimp with mixture and marinate for 10 minutes.

Scallops:

1 pound large scallops, cleaned and muscle removed

Refrigerate scallops until time to grill. Brush with lemon juice and peanut oil and sprinkle with coarsely ground sea salt just before cooking. Grill for less than 30 seconds on each side. Do not overcook.

Additional ingredients for the wraps may be whatever is fresh in the market. Here are some suggestions::

2 ounces cellophane noodles, softened in warm water for 15 minutes, drained and cut into 2-inch lengths

32 rice paper wrappers and a large bowl of warm water

32 lettuce leaves of any type

1/2 cup each: fresh bean sprouts, sliced fresh

mushrooms, daikon sprouts, cucumber sticks, carrot sticks, slivered scallions

2 cups fresh herbs such as mint, cilantro, sweet basil

1 cup fresh pineapple chunks

Heat the grill and lightly brush with vegetable oil. Guests select a few pieces of meat or seafood and place them on the hot grill and turn as necessary. They also soak a rice paper wrapper in the bowl of water to soften, shake off the water, and add whatever ingredients they want in their wrap. When the grilled ingredients are done, usually in a matter of minutes, they are added to the wrap and then rolled up and dipped in a sauce such as a *Nuoc Cham* or Peanut Sauce (recipes follow). The sauces will provide about 1/4 cup for each of four diners or about 1/8 cup for eight. For additional sauce, double the recipes.

Vietnamese Dipping Sauce / Nuoc Cham

ACAI

Makes about 1 cup

2 cloves garlic, minced

2–3 small red chilies, stems, seeds, and membranes removed, minced

1 tablespoon sugar

juice of 1 lime (2 tablespoons)

1 tablespoon rice vinegar

1 tablespoon water

4 tablespoons fish sauce

With a mortar and pestle, mash together the garlic and chilies. Add the remaining ingredients and mix well to dissolve the sugar. Taste and adjust seasonings as needed.

Peanut Sauce

ACAI

Makes about 1 cup

1 tablespoon peanut oil

2 cloves garlic, minced

1 teaspoon chili paste

2 tablespoons tomato paste

1/2 cup water

1/2 teaspoon sugar

1 tablespoon peanut butter

1/4 cup hoisin sauce

1/4 cup roasted peanuts, ground

1 small red chili, stem, seeds, and membranes removed, thinly sliced

1. In a small saucepan, heat the oil over medium-high heat and stir-fry the garlic for 2 minutes; do not burn. Add chili paste and tomato paste, stir and heat, then add water, sugar, peanut butter, and hoisin sauce. Whisk to blend the mixture and bring to a boil. Reduce heat and simmer for 3 to 4 minutes. Remove from heat.

2. Divide the sauce into small dipping bowls and sprinkle each with peanuts and chili slices. Serve warm or at room temperature.

"Build It and They Will Come"

Sometimes the simplest idea creates the most amazing results. Such is the case of Quang Restaurant.

In 1978 Quang Truong, his wife Lung Tran, and their seven children took refuge in St. Cloud, one more Vietnamese family displaced by the war. A local church sponsored their relocation and helped them build a new life in Minnesota. Quang found a job at the local Gold'n Plump chicken processing plant, and Lung worked as a tailor making alterations. She was also preparing traditional Vietnamese food for her family of nine, and it wasn't long before neighbors and friends were stopping by to enjoy her excellent cooking. "Why don't you open a restaurant?" they often asked. In Vietnam, Lung had worked in the family market handling and selling food. The idea of opening her own business began to form.

Unfortunately, Quang died in 1983 and the family moved to California, where Lung went to work in a popular Vietnamese restaurant. Within six months the family knew they wanted to return to Minnesota. They settled in St. Paul.

By 1989 Lung decided it was time to open a food business, and she found a small space off of Twenty-eighth and Nicollet Avenue in Minneapolis. She named it after her late husband, and Quang Deli began selling some of Lung's delicious home cooking. Finding the deli was not easy: located on a parking lot, it was not clearly visible from the avenue. It offered only four tables for dining. But before long business was booming, with lines of people winding out the door waiting to take home Lung's exceptional food, including a variety of pastries and traditional Vietnamese dishes.

Ten years later, Lung was able to expand the deli space, add five tables, and provide more standing room inside. But the deli was still operating in cramped quarters, and within a year it was time to move. Just across Nicollet Avenue from Quang, Palm Brothers restaurant supply company announced it was relocating, and two buildings with a parking lot became available. The family purchased the property and turned one of the buildings into a restaurant with thirty tables and a much larger kitchen. The other they remodeled into small spaces to rent for offices, services, and small businesses. Now Quang Restaurant was easy to see on the busy street and offered plenty of room for its customers in a bright, open dining room. However, Lung and her family did not anticipate the large number of diners who crowded into the restaurant on opening day.

Lung's daughter Sen Reed remembers it well. "We had more space in the kitchen to work and a dining room that could hold 150 diners, but we had the same staff," she said, "just ten of us." They were truly surprised at the number of people who helped to celebrate at their grand opening. It took them a week to make the adjustments necessary to handle the crowds, but through it all their customers remained loyal.

The entire family works at Quang. In addition to Lung and Sen are Khue Pham, Charles Truong, Daniel Truong, Heather Mandanas, Ann McRoy, and My Truong. Cousin James Lam works at the restaurant each day after he finishes at the hair salon next door. Lung has thirteen grandchildren who may also become part of the business someday.

Sen says the Quang menu has evolved in its twenty-two years to keep up with the changing clientele. "Initially, 90 percent of our customers were Asian with just a few non-Asian," she said. "Today the mix is more 60 percent Asian and 40 percent non-Asian." As the ratio shifted, so did the food requests: "Customers began asking for more Americanized Asian dishes such as fried rice." While Quang's menu today may include more Asian combinations familiar to Minnesota diners, it still offers many traditional Vietnamese dishes. Beer and wine were added to meet customer demands, and no doubt the menu will continue to evolve.

Quang Restaurant offers a special weekend menu featuring Vietnamese favorites that require more time to prepare than regular menu items. Rice porridge with pork innards, steamed pork rolls, and sea bass soup are just three of the special items, which have become so popular that many customers plan their visits to Quang on Saturday or Sunday.

The restaurant still has a small deli at the entrance that is busy all day long, offering submarine sandwiches, boiled peanuts, a variety of pastries, bubble tea, and cold desserts. Coconut rice cake, cassava cake, flan, pudding, and tricolor dessert are just a few of the items people choose for a quick take-away.

The restaurant has won more than a dozen awards over the years, including Best Vietnamese, Best of the Twin Cities, Diners' Choice Award, Top Restaurants in Minnesota, Best Soups, Best Noodle Shop, and more.

In 1990 I wrote an article about the new Quang Restaurant for **Asian Pages,** *citing the quality and freshness of its food, its bright open dining room, and excellent service. One weekday afternoon, I was surprised to see so many Asian families having lunch at Quang. One busy mother had five young children in tow, all a little restless about waiting for their order. She went to the deli counter, bought a submarine sandwich, and divided it into five small appetizers. The group was quiet from then on. — PLH*

Quang Restaurant is a family business. Center front: Lung Tran. Left to right: Khue Pham, James Lam, Sen Reed, Daniel Truong, Charles Truong, Heather Mandanas, Ann McRoy, My Truong.

Lung Tran shares two of her favorite dishes served at Quang Restaurant: Sea Bass Noodle Soup and Che Ba Mau, a tricolored dessert. The soup is available only on weekends as it takes some time to assemble. The Tricolor Dessert is available every day in the deli for takeout. Together they make a most interesting Vietnamese meal.

Sea Bass Noodle Soup / Bun Ca Kien Giang

Lung Tran

Serves 4

1 pound chicken, with bones and skin, cut into 2-inch pieces

2 pounds pork neck bones

4 ounces vermicelli rice noodles

4 (8-ounce) sea bass steaks, or substitute walleye

1/4 cup sea salt

1/4 cup dry white wine

2 teaspoons minced chives

1 teaspoon ground black pepper

1 teaspoon salt

1/8 teaspoon sugar

3 (1/2-inch) slices ginger

1/2 cup chopped yellow onion

fish sauce, salt, and sugar to taste

12 jumbo shrimp, peeled and deveined

4 tablespoons minced leeks, divided

4 tablespoons chopped onions, divided

4 tablespoons chopped chives, divided

Garnish:

4 lettuce leaves, broken into 2-inch pieces

1/2 cup mint leaves

4 sprigs cilantro leaves

1/2 cup bean sprouts

8 lime wedges

2 jalapeños, stems and seeds removed, sliced in thin rings

1/2 cup pickled leeks

1/2 cup chopped onion

1/2 cup chopped chives

1/4 cup minced ginger

1. Fill a large stockpot half full of water, add 1 tablespoon salt, and bring to a boil.

2. Rinse the chicken and pork neck bones thoroughly, add to the boiling water, and return to a boil. Lower heat to simmer and cook for about 45 minutes, or until the chicken is tender and falling off the bones. With a wire strainer, remove the chicken and pork pieces and discard. Strain the stock and set aside.

3. Fill a medium saucepan half full of water and bring to a boil. Add the vermicelli noodles and cook until tender, about 5 minutes. Drain the noodles, rinse under cold water to stop the cooking, and drain again. Pour into a bowl and set aside.

4. Rub the fish with sea salt and cooking wine to clean off as much of the film as possible. Rinse and pat the fish dry with paper towel. In a small bowl combine the chives, black pepper, salt, and sugar. Rub the mix generously over the fish to coat all sides. Let the seasoning marinate for at least 10 minutes.

5. Fill stockpot half full of water and bring to a boil. Submerge the fish and boil for 4 to 5 minutes, then scoop out the fish with a wire strainer and set on a plate. Strain the fish stock.

6. Combine the fish stock with the chicken/pork stock. Bring to a boil. Add the ginger and onion and boil for 3 minutes. Taste the stock and add fish sauce, salt, and sugar as needed.

7. Place shrimp in a wire strainer and lower into the boiling broth. Cook just until the shrimp turn pink and are barely done, 3 to 5 minutes. Remove from the broth and set aside.

8. For each serving use a large soup bowl. Add a handful of noodles, 1 cup of fish, 2 to 3 shrimp, and 1 tablespoon each of minced leeks, chopped onions, and chives. Ladle the boiling broth over the bowl of noodles and fish. Serve with a plate filled with lettuce, mint, cilantro, bean sprouts, lime wedges, jalapeños, leeks, onions, chives, and ginger for diners to add as they enjoy the soup.

Tricolor Dessert / Che Ba Mau

Lung Tran

Makes 4 (8-ounce) servings

1 (4-ounce) package agar powder

1/2 cup plus 5 tablespoons sugar, divided

1 teaspoon green food coloring

7 ounces peeled split mung beans

1 teaspoon vanilla extract

1 (14-ounce) can coconut cream

1 (15-ounce) can red kidney beans (Goya)

2 cups crushed ice

4 (8-ounce) glasses at least 6–8 inches tall

1. One day ahead, cook the agar powder as listed on package instructions. Add 1 tablespoon sugar and the green food coloring, stirring occasionally for about 3 minutes until well blended. Remove agar to a covered container and refrigerate overnight.

2. Soak the peeled split mung beans in warm water for 15 minutes. Drain and rinse beans, then add them to a medium saucepan with enough water to cover beans by half an inch. Cook over medium-high heat for 20 minutes. Stir in 2 tablespoons sugar and vanilla extract. Mix together until the beans are the consistency of paste, about 10 more minutes. Remove from heat and cool to room temperature.

3. In another saucepan add the coconut cream, 3/4 cup water, 2 tablespoons sugar, and a pinch of salt. Bring the mixture just to the boiling point over medium heat. Remove from heat and set aside to cool to room temperature.

4. Rinse the kidney beans with cold water. In a small saucepan add 1 cup water and 1/2 cup sugar. Mix together and bring to a boil over medium-high heat. Add the kidney beans, stir, and simmer for 10 minutes or until it forms a paste. Remove from heat and cool to room temperature.

Quang's Che Ba Mau, a tricolored dessert with agar, mung bean, and black beans with coconut milk.

5. Cut the agar gel into julienne strips. In each glass, add a handful of agar strips to the bottom. Add 1 tablespoon of red bean mixture and top off with mung bean paste. Top with a dollop of the coconut cream and chill for at least 2 hours. Serve cold with a mound of crushed ice on top of each glass.

By 2009 there were eighty-seven Vietnamese restaurants in Minnesota, with more opening each year. *Pho* has become such a popular soup that it is now appearing on menus outside of Vietnamese restaurants. And fish sauce, once known only in Southeast Asia, is finding its way into many dishes from non-Asian kitchens to once again change the tastes of Minnesota.

The flavors of...
Korea

Immigrants from Korea came to Minnesota in the early 1900s. The first was believed to be a mineworker on the Mesabi Iron Range. Larger numbers arrived as refugees from the Korean War after 1950. By 1980 the U.S. Census reported there were 6,319 Koreans living in Minnesota, plus Korean students. But there were also a growing number of other Koreans: children adopted by Minnesota families.

Martha Vickery, cofounder and managing editor of *Korean Quarterly*, is very familiar with the differing Korean communities. She explains, "The country's highest concentration of adopted Koreans lives in Minnesota. Children were placed with families here starting in the late 1960s and up to the present." And while their heritage may have been the same as that of the older immigrants, their needs were different. One of the greatest was the children's need to interact with their Korean compatriots to learn more about their heritage and traditions.

Martha saw that the original Korean immigrants, their children (now second-generation adults), and the adopted Korean children needed to find a way of communicating with each other and with the general community. So she and Stephen Wunrow founded *Korean Quarterly* in 1997 to do just that. "We started with a thousand copies, a few ads, and a small grant from the Presbyterian Church," she recalled. The publication was intended to give voice to the Korean communities and to tell their story to

the public in general. Today *Korean Quarterly* is still a nonprofit newspaper run entirely by volunteers with a circulation of ten thousand, mainly in the Twin Cities area. It also reaches Korea-related departments of colleges and universities and has paid subscribers in the United States, Korea, Canada, Australia, and Europe—all countries where Korean children were adopted.

"It has been our intent to give all the Korean communities a voice and to work with some of the country's most informed Korean specialists who write about the ongoing relationship of North and South Korea," Martha said. *Korean Quarterly* is the nation's only English-language newspaper about the Korean American community. It covers local, national, and international news. The paper also highlights Korean food in each issue, with cookbook reviews, feature stories on Korean chefs and restaurants, as well as typical recipes. We turned to one of its contributors to provide us with some of her favorites.

Facing page: An individual serving of Sole Café's Bibimbop topped with a fried egg.

Right: Korean Quarterly, *Summer 2012.*

Finding Korean Food Outside the Twin Cities

While the largest number of Koreans and those of Korean descent in Minnesota live in the Twin Cities, others are scattered throughout the state and in neighboring Wisconsin. Korean native Mary Lee Vance, a contributor to *Korean Quarterly*, was on the staff of the University of Wisconsin–Superior, just across the state line from Duluth. Since there were so few Koreans in the area, she found it difficult to get Korean ingredients and often made buying trips to the Twin Cities.

"For a time there were two small Asian grocery stores in Duluth," she recalled, "but they went out of business shortly before we moved to Montana," where she now lives. The stores carried mostly Chinese, Japanese, or Filipino ingredients, so periodically she would put some coolers in her car and drive to the Twin Cities to stock up on *kimchi* (a fresh vegetable pickle), *gochujang*, seasoned seaweed, toasted sesame seeds, squid, eel, caviar, *japchae* noodles, Korean pears, and other items needed for Korean cooking.

In the Duluth/Superior area there were only two sources for experiencing Korean cuisine: Our Redeemer Church in Duluth, where a small group of Koreans met every Saturday night and served dinner afterward, and home cooks, like Mary Lee, who shared their cooking with friends. The mostly female Korean church congregation was always happy to have Mary Lee contribute to their suppers. So were the seven Asian faculty and staff of UW-S when they got together for potluck suppers at Mary Lee's house. She was the only Korean of the group.

When Mary Lee accepted a position at the University of Montana, she and her husband, Eric,

Mary Lee Vance

moved to Missoula and found the same lack of Korean food. Except for the Korean church in Missoula (where Mary Lee contributes well-appreciated dishes), Mary Lee's cooking at home, and a Korean-owned Japanese sushi restaurant that offers grilled *bulgogi*, there is no place within 150 miles to go for Korean groceries or meals such as traditional *dolsop bibimpob, kimchi chige,* or other favorites. Mary Lee has had to rely on her personal stockpile of Korean ingredients to do her own cooking (with her *Korean Quarterly* pals sending the occasional care package) and the generosity of the local Korean church. Fortunately for her, the women at the Korean church keep her well stocked with fresh kimchi.

Among the recipes Mary Lee likes to share with friends and neighbors is *Chop Chae*, a very tasty noodle dish found on many Korean restaurant menus. Each ingredient is cooked separately and then combined just before serving. This traditional dish is served at many social functions.

Stir-Fried Sweet Potato Noodles / Chop Chae

Mary Lee Vance

Serves 4

Marinade:

1 tablespoon sugar

1 tablespoon low-sodium soy sauce

1 tablespoon sesame oil

1 tablespoon toasted sesame seeds

1/2 teaspoon freshly ground black pepper

1/2 teaspoon finely minced garlic

Beef:

1/2 pound lean beef tenderloin, beef chuck, or other meat, thinly sliced

Other Ingredients:

5–6 dried black mushrooms

1 (2-ounce) package dried black fungus

4 tablespoons vegetable oil, divided

1 1/2 teaspoons salt, divided

1 red bell pepper, seeds and stem removed, julienned

1 small carrot, julienned

1 egg

1 (2-ounce) package sweet potato noodles, or substitute cellophane noodles

2 tablespoons sugar

3 tablespoons soy sauce

2 tablespoons sesame oil

2 tablespoons toasted sesame seeds, plus more for garnish

1 tablespoon finely minced garlic

1/4 teaspoon black pepper

2 green onions, julienned

1. In a medium bowl mix the marinade ingredients together. Cut meat into narrow strips 2 inches long and with your hands combine the meat and marinade, coating each strip. Cover and refrigerate 1 hour for tender cuts, overnight for tougher meat.

2. In separate bowls cover the dried mushrooms and fungus with water and soak until softened, about 1 hour. Pour off water and wash each mushroom and fungus. Dry with paper towels and slice into thin strips. Heat a wok over medium-high heat, add 1 tablespoon vegetable oil to coat the pan, and stir-fry mushrooms and fungus separately for 2 to 3 minutes each. Set aside.

3. Heat a wok over medium-high heat, add 1 tablespoon oil, sprinkle on 1/2 teaspoon salt, and stir-fry the pepper until it turns bright red. Remove and set aside. Stir-fry the carrots separately in the same manner, also adding 1/2 teaspoon salt, until the colors become bright. Set aside. In the same wok add another tablespoon of oil and stir-fry the meat for 2 to 3 minutes, until just barely done. Set aside.

4. In a small bowl beat the egg until mixed but not frothy. Heat a small frying pan, add 1 tablespoon vegetable oil, and pour in egg, tilting the pan to make a thin crepe. Fry for 2 minutes, until the bottom is set, then flip over and fry for another minute. Remove to a cutting board, cool, and slice the egg crepe into thin strips 1/4 inch wide and 3 inches long. Set aside.

5. Fill a medium saucepan half full of water and bring it to a boil. Add the noodles and cook until al dente, 3 to 5 minutes (less for cellophane noodles). Drain noodles and plunge into a bowl of cold water. Drain again and set aside.

6. In a large bowl mix sugar, soy sauce, sesame oil, sesame seeds, garlic, pepper, and remaining 1/2 teaspoon salt together. Mix cooked noodles, vegetables, and meat into sauce and lightly toss to coat all ingredients. Using your hands will help thoroughly mix ingredients. Transfer mixture to a serving bowl and garnish with green onions and egg crepe slices. Sprinkle with additional sesame seeds.

Note: Mary Lee uses all sorts of vegetables and likes to chop each one differently to make a dish with a variety of shapes and colors. This dish may be vegetarian with the elimination of the meat and egg.

Korean Restaurants Come to Minnesota

By the 1980s Korean restaurants were opening in the Twin Cities. They offered moderately priced family-style dining that included many ingredients popular with Minnesota diners. One of them was Shilla, opened in 1989 on Snelling Avenue in St. Paul by Wayne (Won) J. Cho, a man passionate about his work. Wayne had been in the hotel business in Seoul and wanted a location where he could showcase the cooking of his native land. The spot between University Avenue and Macalester College seemed ideal. He brought in professionally trained chef Tom Chung from Korea to head the kitchen staff and created a Midwest-Asian atmosphere. He staffed it with friendly and helpful servers and was soon attracting a loyal following.

Named after Korea's golden dynasty, AD 668–936, Shilla offered a variety of traditional dishes. The most popular with Minnesota diners, according to Wayne, was *galbee* (or *bulgalbi*), charcoal-barbecued beef ribs. Traditionally beef short ribs flavored with soy sauce, garlic, ginger, black pepper, and sesame seeds, *bulgalbi* is charcoal grilled and served with rice, Korean vegetables, and, of course, *kimchi*. Shilla also offered a complete menu of fish soup, octopus, firepots for cooking at the table, and more. In 1994 Wayne was looking into the possibility of opening small fast-food Korean barbecue restaurants around the state, but this plan did not materialize. After a successful twenty-one years, Shilla closed. Shortly afterward another restaurant with a similar name opened in the same location.

Charcoal grilling is a staple of Korean cooking, used for everything from fine steaks to beef brisket and ribs to pork and a wide variety of other meat and fish. *Bulgogi* is a dish that many Minnesotans seem to like from the first taste. And why not! Marinating lean beef rib eye for days in rice wine, sesame oil, soy sauce, garlic, and ginger can only produce amazing flavors. Mary Lee Vance has a favorite recipe that, if you really can't wait two days, may be made with only thirty minutes of marinating.

Below: Every Korean meal includes a variety of pickled vegetables, fresh bean sprouts, deep-fried seaweed, kimchi, and other condiments. Here is an assortment from Sole Café.

Right: Sole Café founder and chef Kimberly Firnstahl.

Korean Grilled Steak / Bulgogi

Mary Lee Vance

Serves 2–4

1 finely grated ripe Korean apple pear, or substitute 1/2 cup sugar

2 tablespoons rice wine

1 tablespoon roasted sesame oil

1/4 cup low-sodium soy sauce

1/2 teaspoon minced garlic

1/8 teaspoon grated ginger

2 green onions, sliced into small pieces

1/4 teaspoon freshly ground black pepper

1 teaspoon toasted sesame seeds

2 tablespoons water

1 pound lean beef rib eye, tenderloin, flank steak, or chip steak, sliced against the grain into thin strips

1. In a medium bowl mix together all of the ingredients except the beef. Add the beef and with your hands thoroughly coat each piece with the marinade. Cover and marinate 30 minutes, or store in a sealed plastic container in the refrigerator for up to 2 days.

2. Heat a charcoal grill until the coals are hot and covered with white ash. Oil the grate and carefully lay the beef strips on the grill. They will cook quickly, so turn after 2 minutes and grill another 2 minutes, until well done but not dry. Serve at once (see note for suggestions).

Note: The bulgogi may also be baked. Heat the oven to 350° and place meat in a covered dish or pan. Bake for 45 minutes, stirring occasionally to make sure the meat stays coated with the marinade. Keep it in a warm oven until ready to serve.

A popular way of eating bulgogi is in a lettuce wrap. Serve a bowl of the beef with a platter of lettuce leaves, chrysanthemum leaves, or perilla, fresh bean sprouts, and kimchi. Diners take a lettuce leaf, add a few pieces of beef, top it with a small ball of hot, cooked sticky rice and some ssamjang, then wrap the leaf around the contents and eat it.

Dreams of Gold Turn to Award-Winning Cooking

When Kimberly Firnstahl was growing up with six siblings in Korea, stories of America's streets of gold seemed very alluring. In 1972 at age nineteen, when she got a three-month visa to visit a friend in Minnesota, she found the image was not exactly as advertised. "As we were driving away from the airport," Kimberly recalled, "and I looked at the surroundings, there was no gold!" In fact, there was nothing but trees and grass and buildings that made her think she was in the wrong place. But she stayed, extended her visa, and eventually married. She soon had a daughter and then a son. Her life centered on caring for them and learning to cook.

"As one of seven children, I never cooked at home," Kimberly explained. She learned to make her mother's home cooking and became very good at it, earning some rave reviews from friends and family. When the children were grown and on their own, Kimberly started looking for work but could find only entry-level jobs. She called

a friend in Los Angeles to talk over the idea of opening a restaurant. Her friend helped her get started, and in 2008 Kimberly opened Sole Café at 684 Snelling Avenue North, St. Paul. A small restaurant with a dozen tables and a tiny counter, Sole offered thirty Korean dishes. Soon the freshly prepared food and the ever-smiling Kimberly were attracting customers who often came in to talk with her as well as enjoy her cooking. Then they began bringing their friends. She expanded the Sole Café menu to forty-three dishes, and the business grew.

In 2011 the readers of *City Pages* voted Sole Café Best Korean Restaurant. And by 2012 Kimberly was offering cooking classes to home cooks. It is quite an accomplishment for someone who had to teach herself how to cook.

Bibimbop is one of the most popular Korean dishes with Minnesota diners. It often comes to the table in a sizzling-hot cast-iron or stone pot and continues to sizzle throughout the meal. The sizzling is from a layer of cooked rice at the bottom of the pot that is getting a very nice crusty layer, adding a smoky flavor to the vegetables above. Every cook has his or her own special recipe for bibimbop. Here is one that is not difficult to make and is a good starting point for creating your own personal combination of ingredients.

Sizzling Rice with Vegetables / Bibimbop

ACAI

Serves 2–4

4 tablespoons vegetable oil, divided	1 cup fresh bean sprouts
2 quarter-size slices fresh ginger	5 ounces fresh shiitake mushrooms, julienned
1 cup julienned carrots	1 tablespoon rice wine
3/4 teaspoon salt, divided	1 tablespoon low-sodium Kikkoman soy sauce
1/4 teaspoon sugar	1–4 eggs (see note)
1 teaspoon minced garlic	1 tablespoon roasted sesame or vegetable oil
1 cup fresh green beans, ends removed, French cut	

3 cups hot cooked short-grain rice

1/2 cup *gochujang* (Korean chili paste; see note)

1. Heat a wok over medium-high heat and coat with 1 tablespoon oil. Add the ginger and quickly stir-fry for 1 minute. Add the carrots and stir-fry for 2 minutes or until they begin to wilt and turn a bright color. Season with 1/4 teaspoon salt and sugar. Stir-fry 1 more minute and dish out. Discard the ginger. Set carrots aside.

2. Heat a wok over medium-high heat and coat with 1 tablespoon oil. Add the garlic to season the oil and stir-fry 30 seconds. Add the green beans and stir-fry for 2 minutes or until the color deepens. The beans should be just barely tender. Season with 1/4 teaspoon salt, remove to a plate, and set aside.

3. Heat a wok over medium high heat and coat with 1 tablespoon oil. Add the bean sprouts and stir-fry 20 seconds. Season with 1/4 teaspoon salt and stir-fry for another 20 seconds. The sprouts should still be crisp. Remove to a plate and set aside.

4. Heat a wok over medium high heat and coat with 1 tablespoon oil. Add the mushrooms and stir-fry 1 minute. Add the wine and stir-fry another minute. Add the soy sauce and stir-fry until all the liquid has been absorbed by the mushrooms, about 2 minutes. Dish out and set aside.

5. Fry the egg(s) sunny side up and keep warm.

6. Heat a 12-inch cast-iron frying pan or stone dish over medium-high heat for about 4 minutes. Be very careful. The pan or dish will remain hot throughout the cooking and dining process. Coat the pan with the roasted sesame oil and completely cover the bottom surface with the cooked rice. Remove the pan or dish from the heat and place on a heat-resistant board or plate. The rice will start to brown, so assemble the rest of the dish quickly. Add the carrots, green beans, bean sprouts, and mushrooms on top of the rice, keeping each ingredient in its own wedge. Cover the pan and steam for 1 minute. Remove cover, place warm fried egg or eggs on top, and serve in the pan. Give guests large spoons to dish up the rice and vegetables, making sure they get the crisp layer of rice, with its wonderful smoky flavor, at the bottom of the pan. Serve with *gochujang*.

Note: You may top the dish with one egg or provide guests with their own eggs. Once the rice and vegetables are served, guests can top them with the egg, breaking the yolk as they eat and distributing it into the rest of the ingredients. Or top the serving dish with one egg, and then the first guest breaks through the yolk to distribute it over the rest of the dish. Often this dish also includes cubes of fried tofu on top of the rice. Shreds of cooked meat or fish may be added. Vegetable choices can vary and may include cooked spinach, asparagus, Chinese broccoli, etc. *Gochujang*, Korean chili paste, is available in Asian markets.

Eagan's First Korean Restaurant

Initially Korean restaurants and markets were located in the St. Paul Midway area, where a number of Koreans had settled, and near the University of Minnesota and Macalester College, where Korean students lived. Opening outside of the Twin Cities meant leaving this established customer base and venturing into the more homogenic "burbs." But Young Tae Lim and his wife, Eun Jin Lim, did that very thing in 1993 when they opened Hoban in Eagan. Song Un Lee wrote about the Lims and their pioneer spirit in an article for *Korean Quarterly*'s Spring 1998 issue. Excerpts from that article are printed with permission of the author and the paper.

Hoban, it means "lakeside" in Korean. The restaurant was named by its owners Young Tae Lim and his wife Eun Jin Lim in 1993 when they opened here in Minnesota ("The Land of Ten Thousand Lakes," get it?) As he is explaining the origin of the name, Lim seems a bit embarrassed by the derivation, as if to say, "What do you think, is it too corny?" This sense of modesty permeates Lim's story as he recounts his life before and after Hoban.

A native of Seoul, Lim had held various jobs there while he was a young man searching for his role in life. When he felt the time had come to settle and find stability, he thought, "What could be more stable than a cooking license?" Lim's inspiration was his father whom he said was always cooking and always asking him to try this or that. His father was

an unconventional person in some ways who challenged the traditional view that men should not be in the kitchen. Through his teaching and example, Lim acquired the joy of cooking and sharing the food with others.

[So Lim decided on a culinary career, earned a cooking license, and came to the United States to become a chef. After several years cooking in different states including Minnesota, he and his wife returned to Minnesota to open their own restaurant and settle down.]

Before he decided on a location, many advised Lim to open his new restaurant in the St. Paul neighborhood of Snelling and University [avenues, with its higher percentage of Korean Americans. Instead] Lim said he chose Eagan because he didn't want to give the wrong impression of taking customers away from existing Korean restaurants. Additionally, he felt that it might be riskier to target only Koreans for his customer base. Instead, Hoban's marketing has a different approach—to bring Korean cuisine to the Twin Cities' middle class suburbs, and win over the average Minnesotan to the tastes of Korea.

As a joke, he often tells people he is in the business of "selling culture," when he is asked what he does for a living.

Young Tae Lim, cofounder of Hoban Restaurant.

I first visited Hoban ten years ago and found it a friendly restaurant where regular diners liked to chat with the owners and often expressed their opinions about a particular dish. Clearly the Lims had accomplished their mission of introducing Korean food to suburban diners who in turn came back for more. Hoban has been redecorated with a bright, open look, and on a recent visit the lunch crowd was enjoying the food and the atmosphere. We tried a thin, crisp kimchi pancake that looked more like a pizza than a pancake and had very little dough holding it together, just the kimchi and slivered vegetables. Served with a dipping sauce, it was a light, delicious beginning to lunch and, I understand, is a popular snack. — PLH

Pancakes are very popular in Korea, come in a variety of forms, and are often served as a snack. Ann Kim of Pizzeria Lola (see page 202) shares her mother's recipe for this mung bean pancake filled with kimchi, scallions, and onions. The photo crew had a very good time taste testing this dish!

Kimchi Pancakes / Bindaeddeok

Ann Kim's adaptation of Young Kim's family favorite
Serves 4–6

2 cups dried mung beans

6 tablespoons short-grain rice

2 teaspoons salt, divided

1 zucchini, julienned

1 1/2 cups water

1 small yellow onion, chopped

4 scallions, chopped

1 cup napa kimchi, chopped, plus more for serving

1 tablespoon vegetable oil

Soy Dipping Sauce (recipe follows)

1. Soak the mung beans and rice separately in water for 4 hours or overnight.

2. Sprinkle 1 teaspoon salt on the zucchini strips and let them sit 1 hour. Squeeze excess water out of zucchini. Set aside.

3. Drain the beans and rice and transfer them to a blender or food processor. Add 1 1/2 cups water and 1 teaspoon salt and blend to a pancake batter–like consistency. Add the chopped onion and blend until smooth.

4. Transfer the mixture to a bowl and add the scallions, zucchini, and kimchi. Mix together until all ingredients are well incorporated.

5. Heat a large nonstick frying pan over medium-high heat until hot and coat with vegetable oil. Add about 1/3 cup of batter to the pan to make a small pancake about 4 to 5 inches in diameter and fry on each side until golden brown. Fry several pancakes at a time, keeping finished pancakes warm in a low oven (see note).

6. Arrange pancakes on separate plates or one platter. Serve warm with individual bowls of dipping sauce and extra kimchi. Diners tear off pieces of the pancake and dip them into the sauce before eating.

Note: The dough may be divided in half to make two large pizza-sized pancakes and cut into slices for serving.

Young Kim's Kimchi Pancakes with dipping sauces.

Soy Dipping Sauce

Makes about 1 cup

1/2 cup low-sodium Kik-
koman soy sauce

4 scallions, finely chopped

3/8 cup rice wine vinegar

2 tablespoons Kadoya
roasted sesame oil

Combine ingredients and serve in small bowls for dipping.

Every Korean Family's Secret Recipe: Rice Wine

Many families in Asia Pacific Rim countries have a traditional recipe for making the rice wine used to pay tribute to their ancestors. It is a closely guarded secret and never shared with people outside the family.

When Mary Lee Vance set out to make her own rice wine, she consulted with Chinese, Korean, and Hmong friends who suggested different versions with distinctly different results. After much research and trial and error, she settled on a *makgeolli* that provides a drinkable wine and edible rice mash after just four to five days of fermentation. She suggests using Asian yeast that comes in powder form or as a small hard ball about the size of a preserved plum. A package of brewer's yeast may be substituted, but it will produce a different flavor. The wine is relatively easy to make and can be adjusted to your own taste.

Before you start making the rice wine, sterilize a two-gallon container. Plan to ferment the rice for no more than two months, at which point it starts to turn to vinegar that is also usable. Wrap the container in a blanket or other covering to keep the temperature constant, and store in a warm but not hot place. Once the fermentation is completed, pour the liquid into a container and refrigerate. Both the wine and mash will keep up to two years.

Korean Rice Wine / Makgeolli

Makes 2 cups wine and 4 cups mash

1 pound (about 4 cups)
glutinous (sticky) rice

1 Asian yeast ball, finely
crushed, or substitute 1
package brewer's yeast

1. In a large bowl place the rice and cover with warm water. Soak for 1 hour. Drain and place rice in a medium bowl. Add 3 inches of water and a short steaming rack to a soup pot large enough to hold the bowl and bring water to a boil. Place the bowl of rice on the rack, cover pan, and steam for 25 minutes, adding boiling water to the soup pot if necessary. Remove the bowl of rice, rinse rice with warm water, and cool to about 95° or until you can put your hand in the rice without burning it.

2. Add the rice to a sterilized 2-gallon container. Add the crushed yeast, mixing it in with your hands to thoroughly blend with the rice. Make a well in the center of the rice with your hand to provide room for the wine to form. Cover the container with plastic wrap and wrap it all in a blanket or quilt. Store in a warm but not hot place. In 4 to 5 days the wine will be ready to use. Transfer the wine to another container and refrigerate to stop the fermenting process. Store the rice mash in a separate container and refrigerate for use in a variety of dishes. Or continue the fermenting process for up to 2 months.

Today a number of markets in the Twin Cities offer a wide variety of the ingredients so necessary for Korean cooking. And while there are only about nine Korean restaurants in the area, they have each attracted a loyal following and continue to provide Minnesota diners with the flavors of Korea.

The flavors of...
Indonesia

Raghavan Iyer

During the sixteenth century Indonesia's more than thirteen thousand islands were known to Europeans as the Spice Islands, the source of expensive, exotic flavorings imported by Spanish and Portuguese traders. Nutmeg, mace, ginger, turmeric, tamarind, caraway, and the other island spices were so valuable to the traders that possession of their source often resulted in battles for control of the islands. Over the centuries Indonesia has been home to conquerors from China, Portugal, India, Holland, and Great Britain. Today only half of Indonesia's islands are inhabited—with enough people to make it the fifth most populated country in the world. Indonesia straddles the equator between Malaysia and Australia and is the birthplace of *batik* (dyed cloth), *wayang kulit* (shadow plays), and some intriguing cuisines blending the flavors of both the Old and New Worlds. Chilies and peanuts from the Americas were introduced to the islands by those early traders and have become so important to Indonesian cooking that they almost seem indigenous. Soy sauce and shrimp sauce are now integral parts of Indonesian cooking, but the flavor sources are not as important as the way Indonesians have used them to create cuisines all their own.

Facing page: Gado Gado with Peanut Sauce.

A Minn-donesian at Heart

Those magical items drew Nancy Coune and Jody Sipe, Minnesota natives, to Indonesia in 1983. Nancy became friends with the ambassador from Indonesia to Argentina, where she was studying at the international school. Upon her return to Minnesota, she secured work at an airline company. She rekindled her friendship with the ambassador, who invited her to Indonesia. "Never offer an international trip to an airline employee unless you mean it," she laughs. She landed in Bali and Java, where she spent a month falling in love with the people, the locale, the artifacts, and, above all, the food.

She carried home a bagful of memories and relics that multiplied when she returned to Indonesia again four years later. This propelled her and her husband, Jody, to open the Chandi Gallery, initially at St. Anthony Main in Minneapolis and later at a stand-alone location on Lake Street. She always felt at home in Indonesia and visited the country with some regularity, providing the locals there an opportunity to create objects that she sold at her gallery. The store became a magnet for the new immigrants to Minnesota from Indonesia, who sought the familiarity of homegrown objects amid folks who could speak the language (even though it was a recent one, developed after the country's 1945 independence from the Dutch) in between sips of fresh-brewed tea and "shrimp" crackers called *krupuk*. The store provided a gathering spot for special Indonesian holidays, when friends from the community whipped up traditional fare from Sumatra, redolent of chilies, shrimp, and assertive spices. Nancy's desire to open a restaurant next to the gallery never materialized, but her love for Indonesia found another outlet at the Minnesota State Fair's International Bazaar, where for eighteen years she successfully ran a booth that sold goods from Bali, Java, and Sumatra.

Nancy founded the Minnesota Indonesian Society in 1996, and it still meets the needs of many in the region's Indonesian community. She was recognized by the organization in 2009 for all the great work she has done and continues to do to keep the culture and foods of Indonesia alive and well in Minnesota.

Indonesian Food Gathers Moss

Penny Moss grew up in Java in the city of Surabaya and came to the state of Virginia in 1989 with her husband David, a software developer, where she lived until 1994, when a job compelled them to move to Minnesota. A new home, new surroundings, and a desire for all things Indonesian led her to Nancy Coune's Chandi Gallery and eventually to the Minnesota Indonesian Society. Even though she owned and operated a day-care center, her love for foods from her childhood kept her hands stirring pots of randang smothered with chilies simmered in coconut milk and skewering strips of chicken for grilled sate ayam. To this day she has not seen any restaurant that serves primarily Indonesian fare, making this cuisine not-so-mainstream among Minnesota diners. She laughed when asked if she would open her own restaurant, emphatically replying that a restaurant was never nor will ever be part of her dream (or nightmare, she giggled). She instead takes pleasure in catering small parties, graduations, and special events for the Netherlands-American Association in Minnesota, a group accustomed to classic Indonesian fare.

The biggest event she cooks for is an annual meal for three to four hundred people for the Indonesian Student Association at the University of Minnesota, with the signature dish being *bak mi goreng* (lo mien style with shallots, garlic, white pepper, Indonesian soy sauce, and vegetables like bok choy, carrots, and cabbage). While her dishes are liberally peppered with potent chilies to perk up chicken and beef, she never cooks with pork for religious reasons since the majority of Indonesians follow the Islamic faith. She now serves as board cochair for the Minnesota Indonesian Society as her way of giving back to the community that continues to enrich her life here.

Tang's Ginger Café

In 1992 an unusual combination of circumstances created a unique dining experience for the Twin Cities. A restaurateur from Hong Kong, Peggy Tang, collaborated with an American chef, Hallie Harron, who was influenced by the flavors of Indonesia. Within the confines of a bright new airy space they turned Tang's Ginger Café in the Laurel

Village complex on Thirteenth and Hennepin in Minneapolis into a Chinese/Indonesian culinary experience. Peggy offered the flavors and techniques of her mother's Chinese kitchen in Hong Kong, and Hallie added her love for the multiflavored cooking of Indonesia to create an international experience for Minnesota diners.

Hallie's interest in Indonesian cuisine began while she and husband Bryan were running an inn in Crookston, Minnesota. Twin Cities visits led them to St. Anthony Main and into the Chandi Gallery, which featured Indonesian folk art. It wasn't long before gallery owner Nancy Coune became a close friend, leading to other Indonesian contacts and, in 1991, a trip to Indonesia. That was followed by Hallie's annual visits to the islands, keeping the flavors in Tang's Ginger Cafe fresh as diners were introduced to *soto yam* (ginger-flavored chicken broth with dumplings, noodles, and sambal), Jakarta-style shrimp, Balinese randang, Javanese meatballs, vegetarian *nasi* (stir-fried brown rice flavored with turmeric and coconut sauce), and a number of other Indonesian offerings. Still, the restaurant closed a few years later, succumbing to the pitfalls of a difficult location.

Enter the Dragon

Evelyn Lee came to the United States in 1965 to spend six years in New York and then at Yale to earn a master's degree in piano performance. Born in Indonesia to Chinese immigrants, she immigrated to Hong Kong shortly after her toddler years. Her familial roots and Indonesian influences followed her throughout her time at Yale and then to Minnesota, where she moved in 1978 with husband David, who had been offered a job as a research scientist at Honeywell. She attributed her ability to conform so easily to Minnesota foods and culture to the colonial influences of her childhood home in Jakarta. With only eighteen families of Indonesian decent living in Minnesota at the time, finding the fresh produce she was familiar with in Indonesia, Hong Kong, and to some extent the East Coast was next to impossible. The one food her body craved that was hard to procure, especially during her college years, in this land of potatoes was rice. Her hypoglycemic state led the doctor to order the commissary to regularly serve rice, a staple among the cooks from Cuba.

Even though Evelyn acclimated to her new tundra-like surroundings, her desire to educate the community in Asian culture grew. What better way than through the medium of culture, sport, and, above all, food? She organized two gamelan orchestra performances with the Indonesian consulate in Chicago, sponsored by the Schubert Club. The second performance, at the Ted Mann Concert Hall on the University of Minnesota campus, attracted over nine hundred people, reputed to be the largest-ever Asian concert in the Twin Cities. She received a certificate of commendation from the State of Minnesota for leadership and outstanding contribution to the Indonesian community as well as a leadership award from the Council on Asian Pacific Minnesotans for organizing the gamelan concert. As a result of these events, the Schubert Club decided to buy a gamelan instrument and to offer gamelan classes, which still are held at the university's Technology Center. Evelyn was a member of the ensemble and her involvement continues today.

In 2001, together with Jose and Tien Cung of the Vietnamese community and Philip Blackburn from the American Composers Forum, she led BambooFest at Landmark Center in St. Paul, showcasing bamboo music and products from Asian countries, including food. In 2005 she took over St. Paul's Dragon Festival and was involved with it until 2010. With a grant from the city, Evelyn organized a Unity in Diversity event at the festival, hiring an emerging Hmong artist to create a painting representing Asian unity. People of all ages were invited to paint parts of the work. At the same time, Theater Mu (now part of Mu Performing Arts) director Rick Shiomi received a grant to create music including instruments from Indonesia, China, Japan, and Cambodia, a composition celebrating the spirit of unity in diversity, which in turn spurred dance performance featuring different Asian communities.

The Dragon Festival at Lake Phalen became a haven for the community to savor dumplings, spring rolls, sambals, and curries, opening a window to the culture of not only Evelyn's Indonesian childhood but also many other Asian countries. Next, she hopes to see the creation of a celebration of Asian foods. She says, "They have food and wine tasting by American chefs; we can have curry celebration by various communities since curry is so prevalent in Asian countries and each country seems to be cooking it slightly different. Asian countries have been ravaged by wars as they were colonized by Western countries and as they fought for territory against each other. Now in this new homeland, we should learn to work together for the common good. As a minority group we have a harder time raising money for various nonprofit organizations. Perhaps this kind of culinary celebration can raise funds for the various participating communities." An ambitious goal that is perhaps easily achieved by the "Dragon Festival Lady."

Dragon boat races, Lake Phalen, St. Paul.

Nancy Coune likes to serve *Soto Ayam* in glass bowls to show off the ingredients' rainbow of colors. This version of the soup is relatively dry, which is common in Indonesia. Prepare more broth by increasing the ingredients for the paste mixture in the same proportions as the increase in broth. The longer the broth cooks, the tastier it will be; Nancy advises simmering for no less than an hour. Other variations include replacing the noodles with *lontong* (compressed rice) or *perkedel* (potato croquettes). See note for vegetarian version.

Indonesian Chicken Soup / Soto Ayam

Nancy Coune

Adapted by ACAI

Serves 8

2 cloves garlic, minced or chopped

1 cup sliced shallots

1 (2-inch) piece galangal, peeled and sliced

1 (2-inch) piece ginger, peeled and sliced

1 (1-inch) piece fresh turmeric, peeled and sliced, or 1 teaspoon dried

1 teaspoon coriander seeds

1 teaspoon salt

1/2 teaspoon white pepper

1 tablespoon vegetable oil

10 cups chicken broth

2 stalks lemongrass

6 kaffir lime leaves, or juice of 1/2 lime

1 1/2 pounds bone-in chicken breast

6 ounces vermicelli rice noodles

2 cups finely shredded cabbage

2 cups bean sprouts, rinsed and drained

2 cups julienne carrots

1 cup thinly sliced green onions

1 cup chopped cilantro

8 lime wedges

4 large hard-boiled eggs, peeled and halved

2 cups potato chips

2–4 fresh hot chilies, minced, or substitute store-bought sambal

1. Combine garlic, shallots, galangal, ginger, turmeric, coriander seeds, salt, and pepper in a food processor. Process mixture to a paste, scraping container sides as needed. Or chop ingredients with a knife and then whirl into a paste in a blender.

2. Heat a 5-quart saucepan or heavy pot over high heat, add the oil, and stir in the paste, cooking until the mixture barely begins to brown, about 3 minutes. Stir in broth and cover to bring mixture to a boil.

3. Trim stem end and any tough leaves from lemongrass and pull off coarse outer layer. Crush lemongrass stalk with the back of a knife and cut it into 3-inch pieces. Add lemongrass and lime leaves or juice to broth. Add chicken breasts to broth, cover, and bring to a boil. Reduce heat to low and simmer until the breasts are no longer pink in the center, about 15 to 20 minutes. (Cut one breast to test.) Remove the chicken and discard skin and bones. Cool the chicken, shred it, and set it aside.

4. Skim any fat from the broth and bring it back to a simmer for an additional 45 minutes. (Broth may be made ahead and chilled, covered, in the refrigerator. Before completing the soup, remove and discard the lemongrass, lime leaves, and any fat on the surface. Bring the broth to a boil.)

5. In a large bowl add noodles and cover with 5 cups hot water. Let noodles soak about 5 minutes, until tender. Drain off water. If desired, cut noodles with scissors into 2-inch pieces for easier eating.

6. In individual bowls layer noodles, shredded chicken, cabbage, bean sprouts, and carrots. Cover ingredients with 1 cup of very hot broth. Garnish each serving with green onions, cilantro, lime wedges, and 1/2 egg. Serve with potato chips and minced chilies or sambal.

Note: This delightful soup can be easily made into a vegetarian dish by eliminating the chicken breasts and eggs and by using vegetable broth instead of chicken broth. It is still beautiful and delicious.

Facing page: Indonesian Chicken Soup.

This wonderful meal can be the only dish served for dinner. The sauce is great when made even two or three days ahead. It will keep in the refrigerator, covered, for up to a week.

Indonesian Mixed Salad with Peanut Sauce / Gado Gado

Nancy Coune

Adapted by ACAI

Serves 8

1 1/2 cups natural peanut butter

3 shallots, chopped

1 clove garlic, chopped

1–2 red chilies, chopped

1 (2-inch) piece ginger, peeled and chopped

1 (1-inch) piece galangal, peeled and chopped

3 tablespoons palm or brown sugar

2 (15-ounce) cans unsweetened coconut milk

1/2 cup rice wine vinegar

1/4 cup water

2–3 tablespoons sweet soy sauce, or substitute regular soy sauce mixed with 1 teaspoon sugar

1 tablespoon fish sauce, optional

2 teaspoons lime juice, or to taste

8 cups assorted steamed vegetables such as green beans, carrots, cabbage, bean sprouts, broccoli, cauliflower, spinach, chard, etc., cooled to room temperature

2 potatoes, boiled and cooled, then cubed

4 cups assorted fresh vegetables such as sliced cucumbers, watercress, or coarsely shredded lettuce or salad mix

3 hard-boiled eggs, shelled and quartered

1. Puree peanut butter, shallots, garlic, chilies, ginger, galangal, and sugar in a food processor. Transfer the mixture to a heavy medium-size saucepan. Stir in the coconut milk, rice wine vinegar, water, soy sauce, and fish sauce (if using). Gently simmer, uncovered, over medium-low heat until sauce is thick and full flavored, about 30 minutes, stirring often. Remove from heat and let sauce cool to room temperature. Once it is cool, add lime juice and adjust seasonings.

2. Arrange steamed, boiled, and fresh vegetables and eggs on a large platter. The ingredients may be layered or arranged in individual sections. Add the peanut sauce in small bowls at either end of the platter. Diners may help themselves to the mixed salad or select ingredients of their choice and top with sauce.

Note: Fried tempeh or tofu may also be added to the platter.

Indonesian Mixed Salad with Peanut Sauce.

A Glimpse of Bali on Eat Street

In October 2008 a bright, colorful restaurant opened at 1410 Nicollet Avenue in Minneapolis featuring the flavors of Indonesia. Bali was a welcome addition to the area's growing number of Southeast Asian restaurants and created some excitement among the local food critics. It also began attracting enthusiastic diners who filled the small dining room and even smaller bar on weekends. Spicy fried taro, shrimp skewered on sugar cane, beef slowly cooked with lemongrass in coconut milk, and traditional Indonesian mussels were among the attractions. Indonesian favorites Daging Rendang and Soto Ayam also found fans in Minnesota. Unfortunately the weekend crowd was not enough to sustain the business and Bali closed in October 2009.

Today, Indonesian food is occasionally available in Minnesota at special events or in your own kitchen with the recipes in this chapter.

Bali restaurant menu.

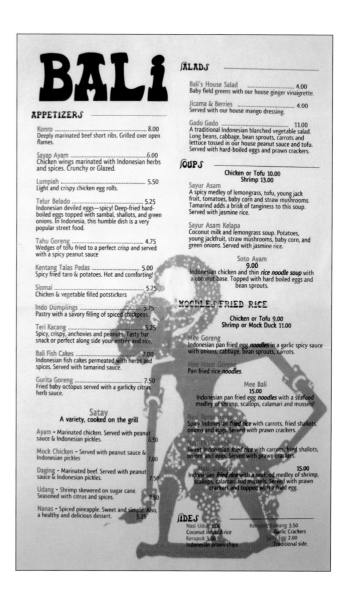

BALi

APPETIZERS

Konro 8.00
Deeply marinated beef short ribs. Grilled over open flames.

Sayap Ayam 6.00
Chicken wings marinated with Indonesian herbs and spices. Crunchy or Glazed.

Lumpiah 5.50
Light and crispy chicken egg rolls.

Telur Belado 5.25
Indonesian deviled eggs—spicy! Deep-fried hard-boiled eggs topped with sambal, shallots, and green onions. In Indonesia, this humble dish is a very popular street food.

Tahu Goreng 4.75
Wedges of tofu fried to a perfect crisp and served with a spicy peanut sauce.

Kentang Talas Pedas 5.00
Spicy fried taro & potatoes. Hot and comforting!

Siomai 5.25
Chicken & vegetable filled potstickers

Indo Dumplings 5.75
Pastry with a savory filling of spiced chickpeas.

Teri Kacang 5.25
Spicy, crispy, anchovies and peanuts. Tasty bar snack or perfect along side your entree and rice.

Bali Fish Cakes 7.00
Indonesian fish cakes permeated with herbs and spices. Served with tamarind sauce.

Gurita Goreng 7.50
Fried baby octopus served with a garlicky citrus herb sauce.

Satay
A variety, cooked on the grill

Ayam - Marinated chicken. Served with peanut sauce & Indonesian pickles.
..............6.50

Mock Chicken - Served with peanut sauce & Indonesian pickles
.........7.00

Daging - Marinated beef. Served with peanut sauce & Indonesian pickles.
.......7.50

Udang - Shrimp skewered on sugar cane. Seasoned with citrus and spices.
.........8.50

Nanas - Spiced pineapple. Sweet and simple. Also, a healthy and delicious dessert.
.......5.25

SALADS

Bali's House Salad 4.00
Baby field greens with our house ginger vinaigrette.

Jicama & Berries 4.00
Served with our house mango dressing.

Gado Gado 11.00
A traditional Indonesian blanched vegetable salad. Long beans, cabbage, bean sprouts, carrots and lettuce tossed in our house peanut sauce and tofu. Served with hard-boiled eggs and prawn crackers.

SOUPS

Chicken or Tofu 10.00
Shrimp 13.00

Sayur Asam
A spicy medley of lemongrass, tofu, young jack fruit, tomatoes, baby corn and straw mushrooms. Tamarind adds a brisk of tanginess to this soup. Served with jasmine rice.

Sayur Asam Kelapa
Coconut milk and lemongrass soup. Potatoes, young jackfruit, straw mushrooms, baby corn, and green onions. Served with jasmine rice.

Soto Ayam
9.00
Indonesian chicken and thin *rice noodle soup* with a coconut base. Topped with hard boiled eggs and bean sprouts.

NOODLE/FRIED RICE

Chicken or Tofu 9.00
Shrimp or Mock Duck 11.00

Mee Goreng
Indonesian pan fried egg *noodles* in a garlic spicy sauce with onions, cabbage, bean sprouts, carrots.

Mee Hoon Goreng
Pan fried rice *noodles*.

Mee Bali
15.00
Indonesian pan fried egg *noodles* with a seafood medley of shrimp, scallops, calamari and mussels!

Nasi Goreng
Spicy Indonesian *fried rice* with carrots, fried shallots, onions and eggs. Served with prawn crackers.

Sweet Indonesian *fried rice* with carrots, fried shallots, onions and eggs. Served with prawn crackers.

15.00
Indonesian *fried rice* with a seafood medley of shrimp, scallops, calamari and mussels. Served with prawn crackers and topped with a fried egg.

SIDES

Nasi Udud 3.00
Coconut infused rice
Kerupuk 3.60
Indonesian prawn chips

Kerupuk Bawang 3.50
Garlic Crackers
Egg 2.00
Traditional side

Malaysia

The flavors of...
Malaysia

When Kin Lee and his wife, Wai Chun, opened Singapore Chinese Cuisine in 1993 near the Maplewood Mall, they thought their customers might be unfamiliar with Malaysian cuisine. "I find most Minnesotans don't know where Malaysia is, while they seem to know something about Singapore," he once said. So he gave the restaurant the more familiar name to attract diners and slowly lure them to the cooking of his native country. It was the first restaurant in the state to offer the very complex cooking of Malaysia, which may include more than twenty-five seasonings in one dish. Singapore is just across the causeway from Malaysia, and its cooking was also part of the restaurant's menu.

Kin came to the University of Minnesota to study finance and earned a bachelor's degree. While in school he used his restaurant training to get a job at the Village Wok on the university campus. He also met Wai at the U. of M., where she majored in international business. After graduation Kin worked as a stockbroker and then decided to open a restaurant. He searched two years for a good location before he and Wai opened Singapore Chinese Cuisine in Maplewood. Wai's training prepared her for the front-of-the-house management, while Kim re-created his home cooking in the restaurant's tiny, efficient kitchen. A Chinese native of Vietnam, Wai was raised in Hong Kong and Paris. With Kin's Chinese heritage and his experience growing up in Ipoh, Malaysia, he might have called the restaurant Malaysian Home Cooking, but he was afraid the name would not attract diners.

Malaysian (and Singapore) cooking combines the influences of Chinese, Indian, Japanese, Portuguese, and Spanish cuisines. *Mee goreng* (wheat noodle) is a typical Malaysian noodle dish stir-fried with bean curd, carrots, scallions, cucumbers, lettuce, bean sprouts, potatoes,

Facing page: Chin Dian's Thomas Gnanapragasam's Nasi Lemak, *a favorite dish in Malaysia.*

eggs, peanuts, peppers, and shallots. Ketchup is used to flavor the oil before the stir-frying begins. *Kway teo* (rice noodle) is another stir-fry noodle dish, featuring seafood, barbecued pork, and eggs. The basic flavor is still spicy but is chicken broth based and much more subtle. Both dishes are good introductions to Malaysian cooking for the timid diner, as are *satays*, grilled meat on skewers served with peanut sauce. Like its Chinese counterpart, the Malaysian egg roll is a filled, deep-fried roll with a very thin wrapper that may hold jicama, taro root, and shrimp paste. The finger-size crisp roll is served on a bed of cold shredded raw vegetables with a side of sweet sauce. A special of the house was Kin's slightly smoky pepper sauce made from white, green, and pink peppercorns.

In 2001 Dr. Jacqueline M. Newman, professor of family, nutrition, and exercise science at Queens College in New York, came to the Humphrey Institute to present a paper on the history of Mongolian food. We spent an afternoon together, starting with lunch at Singapore Chinese Cuisine. She was so pleased with the food that she convinced Chef Lee to package two of his sauces to take with her to New York. Jacqueline is also the editorial director of Flavor & Fortune, *a quarterly publication devoted to Chinese cuisine. In addition, she has collected more than three thousand Chinese cookbooks, now in the permanent holdings of Stony Brook University in New York. When I asked Kin to surprise us with his lunch choices, he selected three of his favorites: silky tofu and stir-fried Chinese vegetables, skate in a multiflavored Malaysian sambal, and Singapore's signature noodle dish,* mee goreng. *They were not only delicious but a nice balance between spicy and mild. Skate, a rather bland flat fish with little meat, was a perfect partner for the very spicy sambal. — PLH*

The restaurant succeeded in attracting diners and in surprising reviewers. Here was a new cuisine that was unique, fresh, and delicious. In 2002 Kin and Wai expanded to south Minneapolis with Singapore! at 5554 Thirty-fourth Avenue South. They partnered with their neighbor from Ethiopia, Tee Balachew, to offer dishes from Ethiopia,

Malaysia, and Singapore. They made the dining room bright and formal, with fresh flowers, tiny lamps, and colorful wall hangings. The tables were set with water goblets and linen napkins. They offered a dozen dishes that changed two or three times a month. One of the first menus included rendang steak, Ethiopian spring stew lamb, captain's curry, sambal sotong, shrimp with lobster sauce, spring scallops, and Ethio/Asian vegetarian delight. A lobster in chili sauce was made from mini-lobster stir-fried with green and yellow bell peppers, onions, scallions, tomato wedges, and ginger slices—all enhancing the lobster's sweet, moist meat. Wai Chun again ran the front of the house while Kin Lee's sister took over the original restaurant in Maplewood.

While the restaurant quickly became successful, Kin Lee was stricken with a severe illness and Singapore! closed. In 2006 Tee went on to open T's Place, featuring Ethiopian dishes, at 2713 East Lake Street in Minneapolis.

Today Malaysian food is available on a few restaurant menus in the Twin Cities, including at Chin Dian (see page 200), where Chef Gnanapragasam offers dishes of his Malaysian homeland, from *nasi lemak* to Indian fried noodles, *kwe tieu goreng* to *sambal chow mai fun*. While his recipes are proprietary, he did prepare the *Nasi Lemak* shown at the opening of this chapter and featuring a pan-fried egg and fried chicken. While every cook has his or her favorite approach, here is a basic recipe for this popular Malaysian dish.

Rice Simmered in Coconut Milk with Anchovy Sambal / Nasi Lemak

ACAI

Serves 4

2 cups long-grain rice	1 1/2 cups water
1 (5.7-ounce) can coconut milk, shaken	1/2 teaspoon salt
2 fresh or frozen *pandan* leaves, optional	4 hardboiled eggs, peeled and halved
Anchovy Sambal (recipe follows)	1 cup fried peanuts
1 cucumber, halved and cut into 1/4-inch-thick slices	

1. Put the rice in a medium saucepan and rinse several times. Drain rice and add the coconut milk, water, and salt. Mix together and bring to a boil over high heat. Boil until there is no water left on the surface of the rice. Place *pandan* leaves tied in a knot on top of the rice. Cover and reduce heat to simmer. Cook about 12 minutes or until there is no steam escaping from the pan. Remove from the heat and let rice steam, covered, for 10 minutes. Remove and discard *pandan* leaves. Fluff rice and keep warm.

2. To serve, fill a rice bowl with warm rice and invert it on a plate, leaving a perfectly formed mound of rice. Top rice with 2 tablespoons Anchovy Sambal and surround rice with half-moons of cucumbers. Add 2 egg halves, yolk side up, and 1/4 cup peanuts to the plate. Repeat with remaining servings. Serve at once.

Anchovy Sambal

Serves 4

6 small dried red chilies	1/2 large onion, sliced into rings
1 cup dried anchovies	2 tablespoons tamarind juice
5 tablespoons vegetable oil, divided	1/4 teaspoon salt
1 teaspoon prawn paste	1/4 teaspoon sugar
4 large shallots, sliced into rings	

1. Place dried chilies in a small bowl and cover with water. Soak overnight. Drain chilies, remove and discard seeds, and mince chilies. Set aside.

2. Rinse anchovies and blot dry with paper towels. In a medium saucepan heat 4 tablespoons vegetable oil to 350° and fry anchovies until crisp, about

2 to 3 minutes. Remove from oil and drain on paper towels. Set aside to cool.

3. Mix the prawn paste, shallots, and chilies together until well blended. In a small frying pan heat remaining 1 tablespoon oil, add the chili mixture, and cook over medium heat, stirring until blended and aromatic, about 3 minutes. Add the onion rings and stir for 3 to 4 minutes, until the onions soften and begin to sweeten. Add the tamarind juice, salt, and sugar. Stir and adjust seasonings if necessary. Add the anchovies, mix well, and cook for 2 minutes to blend the ingredient flavors. Remove from heat and serve at room temperature.

Peninsula Features Food from Home

In 2005 a group of Chinese from Malaysia decided to open a restaurant featuring the food of their homeland. They found an empty building on Nicollet Avenue's Eat Street in Minneapolis and, working with the landlord, spent a year remodeling the street-level space for their restaurant vision, Peninsula. In a modern-looking space carved out of an old building, Peninsula features an open kitchen where diners can watch the chefs at work. In the summer there is also sidewalk dining.

Opened in 2006, Peninsula received favorable reviews from area critics and quickly gained a loyal following with dishes such as the Buddhist Yam Pot made of deep-fried taro root filled with stir-fried shrimp, chicken, mushrooms, snow peas, and baby corn topped with crisp cashews. The restaurant's primarily Malaysian menu offered familiar dishes with unfamiliar seasonings. Rice noodles stray from the pad Thai approach when fish sauce is replaced with a spicy soy chili paste. Malaysian barbecue puts a slightly different twist on this favorite, and while highly spiced food is the specialty here, the restaurant has a number of choices on the milder side as well. Peninsula also offers a variety of rendangs, samabals, satays, and a large assortment of Malaysian beverages.

Peninsula Chef Tong Xu with Buddhist Yam Pot.

Overseeing the kitchen is Chef Tong Xu, originally from the province of Fujian, China. He honed his Malaysian cooking skills first in New York City, then Chicago, and was invited to Eau Claire, Wisconsin, where he continued offering the cuisine of Malaysia. It was here the group creating Peninsula found him and persuaded him to come to Minnesota.

In addition to Peninsula and Chin Dian, Malaysian dishes are also available at Satay 2 Go in Apple Valley. As the taste of Malaysia becomes more familiar to Minnesota diners, there will surely be new opportunities to sample this most flavorful cuisine.

Himalayan Mountains

The flavors of...
the Himalayan Mountains

Raghavan Iyer

Some believe the world's tallest mountains were once covered by a massive ocean. Today we know the area as the Himalayan Mountains, where Tibet is the highest country in the world (elevation 14,800 feet) and was originally settled by people from Mongolia, China, and Burma. Their traditions are among the oldest on earth. Since 1992 the Tibetan population in Minnesota has risen from two to about three thousand. Jigme Ugen is one of that number, a Tibetan who came from Kalimpong, near Darjeeling in northeastern India, where he and his family took refuge from Chinese-controlled Tibet. Armed with a degree in English from the university in Delhi, he sought a better life with aspirations of coming to the United States. He wrote personal letters to Steven Seagal (an actor and Buddhist), Richard Gere (also an actor and Buddhist), and Minnesota's U.S. Senator Paul Wellstone. The letter piqued Senator Wellstone's interest, and he helped Jigme come to Minnesota and establish new roots here.

"Tibet is my fatherland, but India is my motherland," he muses. Jigme's life in the political arena—as an outreach worker and ally for Senator Wellstone's team within the Tibetan community—anchored his career years later as an activist for the reclamation of Tibet from under China's rule. His passion for all things Tibetan propelled him into uncharted territory, but his love for its foods left him seeking to duplicate flavors from his roots in

his kitchen. A curious cook, he soon was able to whip up the noodles and dumplings of his childhood days with ease. But as responsibilities at his job increased, he cooked less at home. His desire for devouring his native food eventually led him to one of Minnesota's successful Tibetan restaurateurs, Gengde Sanpo, who owns and operates Nha Sang in Burnsville, along with his wife, two daughters, and son.

Gengde was a very successful businessman in Ngaba, in Amdo province in eastern Tibet. An automobile broker who was financially thriving as he dealt in Chinese-made cars, Gengde soon felt stymied by the new Chinese authority. He wished for a better life for his family and hoped to live free. He found an opportunity to come to the United States and landed in California in 2001. Friends beckoned him to Minnesota the same year, and he at last found a home, working at first in the restaurants Thanh Do and Azia with his friend and mentor Thom Pham. He took English-language classes in a Lutheran church basement, soon learning to live in the ways of his adopted home and saving enough money to bring his family to Minnesota in 2008.

In 2010 he self-financed his restaurant, a business located amidst a suburban residential neighborhood. Nha Sang continues to build a loyal clientele, and recently Gengde was honored to cook for the fourteenth Dalai Lama, an experience that will remain embedded in his memory forever. He realizes the restaurant is a catalyst for educating his children and also a tool to give back to the Tibetan community for a cause he strongly believes in. Hard work and sacrifice continue to be steadfast squatters in his life, but he has embraced it all in pursuit of his aspirations.

Even though Gengde maintains the essence of Tibetan food culture (son Sheuphen classifies it as strong, thick, plain), his menu also includes dishes from Vietnamese, Thai, Chinese, Japanese, Indonesian, Mongolian, and Himalayan cuisines to represent an amalgam of flavors that can be cohesive. Toward that end Gengde continues the tradition of making many things by hand, including noodles. We asked him to give us a brief demonstration of his technique that can be used in the noodle recipe on page 179.

Facing page: Tibet's famous Momos with tomato dipping sauce.

Top: It is very important to make the dough smooth and pliable. That means while kneading the dough a little flour may need to be added if the dough is too wet or a little water if it is too dry.

Bottom Left: Some noodle dough is pushed and pulled into shape by hand, some stretched with a rolling pin, while others pulled through a noodle machine. Gengde stretched this noodle by hand and gave it a twist, readying it to be cooked in the bubbling broth.

Bottom Right: Chef Gengde's fresh noodles cook quickly and are ready to serve in a matter of minutes.

Pulled noodles, called *thentuk*, from Tibet and the Tibetan communities in Nepal, Bhutan, and Darjeeling, are not as difficult to make as you would think. Reminiscent of the more complex, thin strands of pulled noodles from northern China, this version cuts bite-size pieces of flat noodles directly into a pot of boiling water and cooks them until just tender.

Fresh Wheat Noodles with Vinegar-Kissed Vegetables / Thentuk

ACAI

Serves 4

For the noodles:

1/2 cup unbleached all-purpose flour

1/2 teaspoon coarse kosher or sea salt

1/2 teaspoon garam masala

about 3 tablespoons boiling water

For the vegetables:

1 cup cauliflower florets, cut into 1-inch pieces

1 cup thinly shredded cabbage

1/2 cup frozen green peas

1/2 cup fresh or frozen green beans, cut into 1-inch pieces

1 small carrot, peeled, ends trimmed, thinly sliced at an angle

1 1/2 teaspoons coarse kosher or sea salt, divided

2 tablespoons butter or canola oil

2 tablespoons white distilled vinegar

2 tablespoons finely chopped cilantro leaves and tender stems

2 large cloves garlic, finely chopped

1/2 teaspoon ground red pepper (cayenne)

To make the dough and boil the noodles:

1. Combine the flour, salt, and spice blend in a small bowl. Add 1 tablespoon of water at a time, and stir the spiced flour until it just comes together into a soft ball. Use your hands to knead the dough to a smooth, satin-soft texture. If you feel you have overwatered it, dust it a little with flour and knead it after each sprinkling, until you get the right texture. Cover the dough in plastic wrap and let it rest for 30 minutes at room temperature.

2. Bring a medium saucepan filled three-quarters with water to a rolling boil over medium-high heat. Lightly dust a dry surface with flour. Add the dough and with your hands push and pull the dough into a large circle about 1/4 inch thick. Cut the dough into 1/2-inch-thick strips and slice each strand into 1/2-inch-wide noodles. Drop the noodles directly into the boiling water. Allow them to cook briefly, until the noodles have that wet sheen on their surface and are tender but still firm to the taste or when cut with a fork. Drain into a colander and run cold water through them to prevent further cooking.

To make the vegetables:

1. Add the cauliflower, cabbage, peas, beans, and carrot to a medium saucepan. Cover them with water and stir in 1 teaspoon salt. Bring the vegetables to a boil over medium-high heat. Continue to boil, uncovered, until the vegetables are tender crunchy, about 5 minutes. Drain them into a colander and run cold water through them to stop them from continuing to cook.

2. Heat the butter or oil in a large sauté pan over medium-high heat. Add the vegetables, vinegar, cilantro, garlic, cayenne, and the remaining 1/2 teaspoon salt. Stir-fry the medley until the vegetables are warm, 2 to 3 minutes.

3. Add the noodles and toss the combination to warm up the noodles, 2 to 3 minutes. Serve.

Notes: Store-purchased dried or fresh fettuccini noodles are perfect alternatives. You can steam the noodles, too, but they may turn out tough. Texturally speaking, the boiled ones win hands-down.

Yak meat, so revered by Tibetans, is grown in Minnesota and available at Azariah Acres Farm in Foley and at Hoopers' Yak Ranch in Cold Spring. Visitors to Hoopers' can take a tour in the ranch's yakmobile to see the largest herd of yak in the eastern half of North America and view artifacts from Tibet.

While tea is the favorite drink in Tibet, butter tea is special. In Tibet it is made with yak butter, but you can use local butter in this recipe supplied by the Tibetan American Foundation of Minnesota. A perfect antidote to the bitter cold elements in the Tibetan mountains, this buttery tea is sipped at all times, providing not only warmth but also essential fat to the body.

Tibetan Butter Tea / Solja

Tibetan American Foundation of Minnesota

Serves 4

3 cups water	1/3 cup whole milk
4 tea bags, green or black tea	3/4 teaspoon coarse kosher or sea salt
1/3 cup half-and-half	1 tablespoon butter

1. Combine the water and tea bags in a saucepan and bring to a boil over medium-high heat. Reduce the heat to low to keep the tea hot without boiling. Remove the tea bags. Stir the tea while adding the half-and-half and milk. Stir in the salt.

2. Cut the butter into small pieces, stirring it into the tea. As soon as all the butter melts, remove the tea from heat and whip the mixture until frothy, 2 to 3 minutes. Serve immediately.

A staple among the nomadic population of Tibet, *tsampa*, also considered the country's national dish, is a soft, pliable dough made with roasted barley and warm butter tea. A nutritious powerhouse, it is akin to eating cookie dough, and when accompanied by sips of yak-buttered tea, it provides warm sustenance in the harsh climactic conditions of life in the mountains.

Tsampa

ACAI

Serves 1–2

about 1/3 cup leftover Tibetan Butter Tea (at left), warmed, or warmed milk	1 tablespoon softened butter
	1/2 cup roasted barley flour
tea	

1. Pour the warm tea into a soup bowl and stir in the softened butter. Sprinkle all the flour at once into the bowl. With your fingers, stir in the flour from the edges in one concentric motion, moving the bowl in a circle as you mix, getting the dry and wet ingredients to come together into a soft dough. Continue to mix and gently knead the dough until soft and pliable.

2. Break up the dough into small pieces and shape each piece into a round. Serve as is with tea.

The Nepalese Influence

Growing up in Kathmandu, Nepal, Naveen Shreshta had no inkling of the journey ahead, especially his eventual roles as a cook and restaurant owner. He was busy being a hotel clerk and taking care of his mother, brother, and sister-in-law. Once he turned twenty-five, he had the opportunity to immigrate to the United States, and in 1996 he landed in San Francisco to start a new life. Within months, a family friend beckoned him to come to Minnesota and seek a more peaceful way of making a living. Naveen immediately fell in love with the state and its people, quickly embracing its climate, surroundings, and way of life. After all, the cold was something he was used to, having lived in the mountainous areas of Nepal.

His journey into the restaurant world began at the Highland Café and Bakery in St. Paul, where he learned to cook the American way, preparing meals for breakfast, lunch, and dinner. His reliable customers were curious to try his fare from Nepal, something different from the regular menu of eggs, burgers, and salads. His confidence in cooking foods from his childhood grew and so did his desire to "be his own boss." Driving in Minneapolis's Seward neighborhood, he happened to see a "for rent" sign at a family-run steakhouse. The price was right, and he opened his own restaurant, aptly named Himalayan, on March 28, 2008.

His steadfast menu featured the dishes of his homeland Nepal plus a variety of traditional foods from Tibet and India found in the Himalayan Mountains. The food is mellower than some of the full-bodied flavors of India but more flavorful than many of the soy sauce–based dishes of China. Coconut-chicken curry, chicken saag, and chicken tikka masala are Indian-inspired fare with more mellow tones. Momos, the Nepalese version of Chinese steamed dumplings, tender and tasty, are served with a tomato-cilantro sauce. Aaloo tama, a popular soup of Nepal, features potatoes and black-eyed peas heavily flavored with bamboo shoots and seasonings. Hot from the tandoor, naan speckled with cilantro for color and flavor accompanies plenty of fish and meat dishes, including chicken, lamb, shrimp, and goat. His brother Pravin and sister-in-law Neelima joined him, helping run the restaurant and cook the foods of Nepal. He presents a large selection of vegetarian fare, in keeping with his Hindu upbringing, and offers no beef dishes, substituting yak meat instead, mirroring its wide availability in Nepal. Vegan-friendly dishes appease the neighborhood's clientele, who support his business for lunch and dinner. In 2009 Himalayan was named one of the top ten restaurants in the Twin Cities by City Search.

Naveen has no plans to open multiple restaurants, preferring to maintain a smaller neighborhood-friendly storefront, making the simple foods of his homeland through a limited, easily controlled menu. Once a year, he shares the food and culture of Nepal at the Festival of Nations in St. Paul. Minnesota is now home: he has embraced its people, land, cold climate, and warm hearts.

Tibet's famous Momos with tomato dipping sauce (page 182).

I was fortunate enough to have the opportunity to spend some time with Florence Lin, the grande dame of Chinese cooking, who taught the classic foods of her homeland and authored numerous authoritative cookbooks on the subject. At a series of events for the Asian Culinary Arts Institutes, Florence, along with two master chefs from northern China, shared some great techniques while working with flour to shape, fill, steam, boil, and pan-fry numerous varieties of dumplings. The skills I learned there helped me years later when I created this recipe. — RI

Momos are as common in Nepal and Tibet as dumplings are in the northern regions of China. Most momos swell with spiced ground meat and float in meaty broths or accompany a spiced tomato sauce. These vegetarian momos are great as a snack or even as a substantial starter to any meal.

Boiled Cabbage-Filled Dumplings / Momos

ACAI

Makes 24 dumplings, to serve 4

For the dumpling wrappers:

2 cups unbleached all-purpose flour

1 teaspoon coarse kosher or sea salt

about 3/4 cup boiling water

For the filling:

3 cups shredded green cabbage

2 teaspoons coarse kosher or sea salt

1/2 cup finely chopped cilantro leaves and tender stems

2 teaspoons shredded ginger

1/2 teaspoon ground turmeric

4 fresh green Thai, cayenne, or serrano chilies, stems removed, finely chopped (do not remove the seeds)

4 scallions, green and white parts, thinly sliced

For the tomato sauce:

1 large tomato, cored and cut into 1/2-inch cubes

1 quarter-size piece ginger

1–2 fresh green Thai, cayenne, or serrano chilies, stems removed

1/2–1 teaspoon coarse kosher or sea salt

1/4 cup finely chopped cilantro leaves and tender stems

1. To make the wrapper dough, combine the flour and salt in a medium bowl. Add the boiling water, drizzling in a few tablespoons at a time and stirring with a spoon (since the water is hot, it will be difficult to use your fingers to mix the dough). Add just enough water to bring the flour together to form a ball. It should feel neither sticky nor dry. Remove any dough clinging to the spoon and add it to the dough ball. Knead the dough right in the bowl for 2 to 3 minutes, to form a smooth ball. Shape it into a log roughly 12 inches long. Cut the log into 1/2-inch-wide pieces, cover them with plastic wrap, and set aside.

2. To make the filling, stir the cabbage and salt together in a medium bowl. Set the bowl aside so the salt can leach the liquid from the cabbage, at least 1 hour but no longer than 2.

3. Squeeze handfuls of the cabbage to get rid of the excess water, and place the drained cabbage in a medium bowl. Add the cilantro, ginger, turmeric, chilies, and scallions, and mix thoroughly.

4. To make the dumplings, shape each piece of dough into a 1-inch ball. Flatten it out to form a patty, and then roll it out to form a round that is 2 to 3 inches in diameter (see note). Dust the patty with flour as needed while rolling it out. Repeat with the remaining pieces, stacking the wrappers after liberally dusting each one with flour to prevent them from sticking together.

5. Place a teaspoonful of the filling in the center of each wrapper, and then fold the edge over to make a half-moon shape. Press the edges tightly together with your thumb and forefinger, sealing the dumpling completely. As they are filled and sealed, lay the dumplings on a floured plate. When they are all formed, cover them with plastic wrap.

6. As soon as the dumplings are formed, make the sauce: add the tomato to a blender jar along with the ginger, chilies, and salt. Pour 1/4 cup water into the jar and puree the sauce until smooth. Scrape the sauce into a serving bowl and stir in the cilantro.

7. Fill a medium saucepan halfway with water and bring it to a vigorous boil over medium-high heat. Gently slide six to eight dumplings into the water, stirring gently once or twice to prevent them from sticking to each other. They will sink to the bottom. Once the water comes to a boil again, the dough will start to absorb some of the water and appear puffed up, and the dumplings will float to the surface. All this takes 5 to 7 minutes. As they rise to the surface, scoop the dumplings out with a strainer and transfer them to a plate.

8. Serve the dumplings, still warm, alongside the tomato sauce.

Notes: You can steam the dumplings in a steamer basket instead, but the wrapper's texture may become a bit tough.

For a meat-filled option, use ground pork, beef, lamb, chicken, or turkey instead of the cabbage. There is no need to cook the meat before filling the wrappers, as boiling them will cook it just right. You can also vary the cooking liquid by using chicken or beef broth.

All Asian grocery stores and supermarkets have packages of potsticker wrappers either in the refrigerator section or in the freezer. Use them as a perfectly acceptable alternative.

If you plan to freeze your dumplings for later use, fill and seal them. Then arrange them in a single layer on a sheet of lightly floured waxed paper on a tray. Freeze the tray for 2 to 3 hours. Once they are solidly frozen, lift the dumplings one by one and place them in a self-seal freezer bag; they will keep in the freezer for up to 2 months. Boil them without thawing (otherwise the filling, once thawed, will moisten the wrapper, creating unwanted rips).

For a snack, pan-fry the dumplings: Lightly oil a non-stick skillet or a well-seasoned cast-iron skillet, and heat it over medium heat. Add the dumplings in a single layer, and cook until they are browned on the underside, 3 to 5 minutes. Flip them over and repeat on the other side.

(For a moister result, once both sides are browned, pour 2 to 3 tablespoons water into the skillet and braise the dumplings, covered, until all the water has been absorbed, 2 to 3 minutes—this is the technique used in making potstickers.)

To shape the dumpling wrappers into a perfect round—thin around the edges and thicker in the center to comfortably house the filling—use the type of thin rolling pin that looks like a dowel. First, roll the patty out to form a 2-inch round. Then, to create the perfect wrapper, as Florence Lin says in her *Complete Book of Chinese Noodles, Dumplings, and Breads*, "roll the pin with the palm of one hand while you feed and turn the wrapper with the other hand's fingers. Roll from the edges to the center so that the edges are thinner than the center." It will take a few tries, and slow you down, to master this technique, but with practice your speed will soon pick up and your wrappers will be perfect.

Himalayan cuisine in Minnesota continues to be unraveled as more restaurants feature offerings from this part of the world. One advantage is Indian restaurants' strong foothold in Minnesota, which makes it easier for diners to open up their minds and palates for the subtleties of Himalayan cuisine.

The flavors of...
Tea

It is believed that the practice of drinking tea began over five thousand years ago in China. However, legend has it that the historical event came years later, around 2850 BCE, one day when the Chinese emperor Shen Nung rested by the side of the road under a tea tree. As he heated his water to purify it for drinking, a single tea leaf fell into the boiling water and created a colored beverage. When he sipped the cooled drink, he found he was filled with a sense of peace and calm. This accidental discovery launched an industry that would be felt around the world for centuries to come. Today tea is the most consumed beverage in the world next to water.

Tea has not historically been the most popular beverage in Minnesota, however. European settlers brought with them a preference for coffee. When early Chinese restaurants opened in Minnesota, many did not offer coffee; they only served tea.

Bill Waddington understands that attitude. As the owner of TeaSource, Bill will gladly serve customers any of the more than 250 teas he carries, but no coffee.

While teahouses have been popular in China and Japan for centuries, they were rare in Minnesota. Before the 1990s, except for a few English-style tearooms and cafés offering tea leaf readings, tea was not a popular choice in this region. It was, however, not only Bill's beverage of choice but his passion as well. As director of training for Minnesota-based Supervalu stores, Bill traveled throughout the country, and he would visit each large city's Chinatown and talk with tea merchants to learn all he could about tea. He also wrote to tea growers around the world for information about their particular teas and

often received samples in reply. By 1995 his hobby had become a mail-order business out of his home, and in 1997 he opened his first TeaSource store in the Highland area of St. Paul.

As his business grew, so did his desire to learn even more. Bill began to visit growers in Asia, request samples of unusual teas grown anywhere in the world, and create his own blends. In 2003 he opened his second TeaSource in St. Anthony and in 2012 his third location in Eden Prairie. TeaSource was also named the tea vendor at the Minneapolis–St. Paul International Airport in 2012. Today, he offers more than 250 teas in his stores and through his mail-order and online catalogs. Bill has become such an expert on tea that in 2005 he was invited to be the keynote speaker at the International Tea Exhibition in Beijing, China.

Facing page: A few of the three thousand teas in the world.
Right: Bill Waddington, founder of TeaSource.

He also served on the board of directors of the American Premium Tea Institute and was chairman of the 2004 Specialty Tea Institute and Symposium.

Perhaps because of his teaching background, Bill is adamant about educating the public about tea. He offers tea appreciation and cooking classes in his stores, created a series of free pamphlets on all aspects of tea steeping and selection, and provides tea-tasting opportunities. While 250 teas may seem extensive, they are only a small portion of the three thousand different types of tea in the world.

The 1990s brought additional tea stores and cafés to the Twin Cities; in the 2000s, some specialized in the bubble tea that originated in Taiwan. Today, bubble tea—tea with milk and tapioca balls—is also offered in the stores of Subway, the national sandwich chain.

While tea has been a constant throughout history, its varieties continue to grow. Dark tea that was once shipped only to countries west of western China is now finding its way to the east and America.

The Art of Steeping Tea

Steeping tea can be an art. Steeping it properly is a must. The process is much more complex than boiling water and dunking in a tea bag. In fact, Bill Waddington says that is the worst way to steep tea. Instead, buy loose tea with full leaves that will open in the steeping process to give the richest possible flavor. Heat the water to the proper temperature (from 160 to 212°, depending upon the tea), and time the steeping. And be sure to use good-tasting water: it can make all the difference in the world. Bill offers a variety of information folders in his TeaSource stores. Here are some of his tips:

— Use good tea
— Use good water
— Heat the pot
— Measure the tea
— Measure the water temperature
— Time the steep
— Allow for leaf expansion
— Stop the steeping

The TeaSource "Preparing Tea" folder advises to heat the steeping pot (the serving pot, not the boiling pot) with hot water to warm it, then to pour out the water. Measure the tea—about one rounded measuring teaspoon (3 grams) for each 8 ounces of water—and add it to the warmed serving pot. Then add the heated water to the tea leaves and cover the pot. Black and herbal teas need water at 212° or full rolling boil. Green tea requires 160–180°, oolong 190–200°, and white tea 155–165°. If the water boils and you need to cool it, just add a little cold water. Steeping time differs for each tea, and if it steeps too long the tea will be bitter. It is essential that tea leaves expand during the steeping: giving them plenty of room in the pot is much better than stuffing them into a metal tea ball. Once the tea has steeped, the leaves must be removed: using T-sacs or filters makes that job easiest. Very often steeping is completed in less than a minute, much like that first cup of tea enjoyed by Emperor Shen Nung.

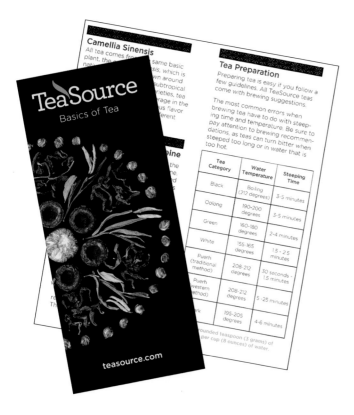

The TeaSource "Preparing Tea" folder.

Cooking with Tea

One of the most popular classes at TeaSource each year is "Cooking with Tea," conducted by Taiwan native Li-Hua Sung MacPherson. The Chinese have cooked with tea for centuries, and Li-Hua brings some of those age-old recipes to Minnesota cooks. She has generously offered to share three of them here.

Marble Devil Eggs with Yunnan Puerh

Li-Hua Sung MacPherson, TeaSource

Makes 20 eggs

10 Marble Tea Eggs (recipe follows), peeled

Mix together:

1/3 cup mayonnaise

2 tablespoons sesame oil

1 tablespoon rice vinegar

1 teaspoon grated ginger

1 teaspoon sugar

2 green onions, finely minced

1/4 cup cilantro sprigs, finely minced

1 teaspoon salt

1/2 teaspoon white pepper

Garnish:

2 tablespoons white sesame seeds

2 tablespoons black sesame seeds

1. Cut each egg in half lengthwise and gently scoop out the yolks into a mixing bowl. Set white halves aside. Mash yolks with a fork until smooth. Mix the mayonnaise mixture together well and mix into the mashed yolks until thoroughly blended.

2. Fill the cup in each white with about one rounded tablespoon of filling so that it forms nearly a ball. Or, place filling in a piping bag or plastic bag with open tip and pipe the filling into white halves, mounding the filling above the whites.

3. Sprinkle with sesame seeds and serve immediately at room temperature. If eggs are to be held for any length of time before serving, lightly cover with plastic wrap and chill in refrigerator.

Marble Tea Eggs with Yunnan Puerh

10 hard-boiled eggs, shells gently cracked but not broken

5 cups water

1/4 cup Yunnan Puerh dry tea leaves

2 whole star anise

5 quarter-size slices ginger

2 teaspoons salt

3 tablespoons soy sauce

1 tablespoon rice wine

1 teaspoon Chinese five-spice powder, optional

Place all ingredients in a wok or saucepan and bring to a boil. Turn down heat to low, cover pan, and simmer for 50 minutes. Remove from heat and let cool to room temperature. Drain eggs and peel. Leave whole and serve warm or at room temperature. For a stronger flavor, leave the eggs in the stewing liquid overnight, then peel and serve.

Li-Hua making Marble Devil Eggs.

Poached Salmon with Oriental Beauty, Pineapple, and Fermented Black Bean Sauce

Li-Hua Sung MacPherson

Adapted by ACAI

Serves 6–8 with rice

1 tablespoon sesame oil

1 (1-inch) piece ginger, minced

3 cloves garlic, minced

5 stalks green onions, halved

2 tablespoons fermented black beans

1 tablespoon rice wine or dry white wine

3 tablespoons soy sauce

1 (20-ounce) can pineapple, cut into 1-inch cubes, juice reserved, or 2 cups freshly cut pineapple

1 teaspoon salt

1/2 teaspoon pepper

1 (2 1/2-pound) salmon, sea bass, or tilapia fillet (choose the middle section)

1/4 cup Oriental Beauty Oolong dry leaves, steeped with 2 cups water at 200°

chopped chives

1. Heat a wok over medium heat and add sesame oil to coat pan. Add ginger, garlic, green onions, and black beans and stir-fry for 1 minute. Add the wine, soy sauce, pineapple chunks, and juice. Cook until mixture starts to boil; season with salt and pepper.

2. Add fish and tea with the leaves. Gently poach for about 8 to 10 minutes, until fish is cooked. Do not overcook. Garnish with chopped chives and serve immediately.

TeaSource was awarded first place in the 2012 Spring Blended White Tea Category for their Jasmine Silver Needle and their 1999 Green Puerh Cake won third place in the 2012 Spring Hot Tea Class in the North American Tea Championships sponsored by World Tea Media.

The Tea Ceremony

By AD 700 tea was most popular with Chinese rulers and the wealthy. It was too expensive for the average person. When the Japanese emperors were served tea by their Chinese hosts, it became a popular drink among Japan's aristocracy as well. Japanese monks found drinking tea beneficial to their long days of studying and meditating, and by the twelfth century they began developing a structured tea ceremony that became popular with the ruling samurai. By the sixteenth century, Japanese tea masters had established a ceremony that became a part of all Japanese life, extending to commoners as well.

In 2001 the Minneapolis Institute of Arts installed a Japanese teahouse, Chashitsu, as part of its permanent Asian collection. Modeled after an eighteenth-century teahouse in Daitokuji Temple in Kyoto, Japan, it embodies the elements designed to teach the four precepts of *Chanoyu* (tea ceremony): peace, respect, purity, and tranquility. Every aspect of the architecture and design were chosen to enhance the Chanoyu experience, from the bamboo to the lighting to the mats and the artwork selected just for the tea ceremony room.

Guests walk through the teahouse garden on a specially designed path to the water area to cleanse their hands and mouths. They then follow a path their host has laid out to the teahouse entry door, where they must bend down to enter through the small opening—a sign of humility. Inside the teahouse, with room for just four guests, they find themselves separated from the outside world and able to focus on the host's tea preparations, including building a fire, making tea, serving it, and enjoying it. The Chanoyu ritual has evolved over centuries until today it is only properly handled by specially trained tea masters. In the sixteenth century, tea masters in Japan were given very high positions where they encouraged the production of paintings, ceramics, lacquerware, and metalwork specific to the tea ceremony. The institute has a collection of such items on display in the adjoining galleries.

Right: Gallery of Tea Ceremony Arts at the Minneapolis Institute of Arts.

One afternoon I met with Dr. Matthew Welch, curator of the MIA's Korean and Japanese art, at the museum's teahouse to talk about the exhibit. It is divided into two rooms, the serving room and the preparation room, where food is sometimes assembled to accompany the tea. Matthew described a Chanoyu that was given in his honor as he was about to leave Japan and move back to Minnesota. "We started as the sun was rising," he recalled, "and were served many courses of food along with the tea." While food is not always served with tea, when it is the portions are small and beautifully arranged on special dishes. The ceremony lasted so long that they took a break after several hours and then returned for the completion of the Chanoyu. "This ceremony started in the early morning and concluded midday when the sun was high in the sky to symbolize the starting of my new life in Minnesota," he explained. Sometimes ceremonies are timed to start when the sun is bright and to end when it has set, symbolizing a closing. — PLH

In an interview on the MIA website, Matthew commented, "the Japanese tea ceremony is the only complete aesthetic experience that I know about. That is, it involves all five senses. Guests come to a tea ceremony, make their way through the garden, slide into the tearoom, and participate in a specially prepared aesthetic experience choreographed by the tea master."

Tea Ceremonies in Minnesota

Perhaps it is not surprising that the tea ceremony, developed nearly a thousand years ago by monks in Japan, intrigued a priest in Minnesota. The Reverend Jim Hermann of St. Raphael's Church in Crystal first became interested in the Japanese tea ceremony in 1989 through Patricia Katagiri. A well-known tea master, Katagiri has been teaching the intricate ceremony for many years and has performed it at a variety of venues, including the teahouse in the Japanese garden at Como Park in St. Paul.

Minneapolis Institute of Arts Teahouse (Chashitsu) made ready for a tea ceremony.

When Jim was assigned to a church in Tokyo in 1983, he continued his studies at the Urasenke Foundation in Kyoto. He received his teaching credentials and tea name, Soki, as well as associate professor status from the sixteenth-generation Urasenke grand tea master. When he came back to the United States he began teaching students himself, and today three are going through the various stages of learning. Since there are 386 ways to present the tea ceremony, attaining the master stage takes fifteen to eighteen years. Students start by learning how to be guests at a ceremony and then move on to the various stages of tea preparation and room arrangements, all designed to achieve peace, respect, purity, and tranquility.

Just a Few of the Three Thousand Teas in the World

Dark Rose from the Hunan Province contains dark tea and rose petals. Until recently dark tea was being shipped only to countries west of China, not to the United States.

Yunnan Mandarin Special is a black tea with spicy, fruity flavors in both the aroma and liquid. Its clarity and freshness are unusual in Yunnan teas.

Long-Life Puerh Brick starts with a small brick of cooked puerh. Break off a small piece of the brick and the tea steeps to a dark, rich, smooth liquid, almost like molasses. It is the choice of many coffee lovers.

Red Flower Jasmine looks like a flower blossom when steeped. Individual green leaves are wrapped and gently tied together by hand. As the leaves are steeped, they expand for a smooth flavor that is slightly sweet.

Jade Oolong Organic steeps to a complex sweet, creamy, silky cup of soothing liquid. It is the only certified organic oolong exported from Taiwan.

Dragonwell is a green tea with a slightly sweet aftertaste. It has a delicious aroma and a mellow floral flavor and is reported to be the most popular tea in China

Fusion Flavors from the Asia Pacific Rim & Beyond

Fusion food has been with us throughout the history of humankind. Any time a dish is cooked with different ingredients, different seasonings, or even water with a different mineral content from the original recipe, the result is a fusion dish—the melding of one cuisine with another, even of one region with another. When Chinese chefs visited Minnesota in 1995 (see page 25) they complained about the taste of our water, our flour, our beef and chicken—all different from what they were used to in Xi'an, China, and all because of the differences in the soil, water, or cattle and chicken feed in Minnesota. To them the differences changed the flavor of their traditional dishes and created fusion food rather than authentic Chinese food. They also objected to pre-ground beef and processed chicken. The growing, processing, and packaging of chickens in Minnesota produces a flavor much different from that of the chickens sold live in Chinese markets to be taken home, killed, and eaten in the same day. The difference was obvious to the Chinese chefs. Even using beef that had been ground the day before was objectionable to them: they always grind beef just before they cook it, giving the finished dish a different flavor.

Even though the first Chinese food in Minnesota in 1883 was called "foreign" food, it was in reality fusion food. Woo Yee Sing and his brother Woo Du Sing could not get every ingredient they needed from China and had to use whatever was available. Their John's Place Chow Mein

(page 3) used locally grown vegetables plus the few canned, bottled, or dried ingredients they could have imported from China or shipped from Chicago or San Francisco. It was not a dish they would have made in China. As Asian flavors became more acceptable to local diners, cooks of other cuisines began using these new flavors in their own kitchens, and soon fusion dishes blending one culinary tradition with others were developed. The number of non-Asian restaurants serving dishes such as teriyaki chicken, spring rolls, pad Thai, fried rice, or sushi rolls continues to grow, and eventually Asian flavors will become an integral part of Minnesota cooking. Even Minnesota-based Betty Crocker's Hamburger Helper line now includes an Asian Helper for Mongolian-style beef.

In this final chapter of our glimpse at the history of Asian flavors in Minnesota, we include a few local chefs who use Asian flavors to alter other cuisines or use Midwest flavors to influence Asian dishes.

The Vietnamese Chef Who Hated Cranberries

When Thom Pham opened his seventh Asian restaurant in the Plymouth Building at Sixth and Hennepin Avenue in downtown Minneapolis in 2010, he did not realize it was just down the block from the former site of the oldest Asian restaurant in Minnesota, John's Place (see page 1). But he did know that some of the recipes he offered on his menu were from the Nankin, a well-known Chinese restaurant that for many years had been located a block from his new Thom Pham's Wondrous Azian Kitchen and in its final years had been just across the street.

Thom was fourteen when he was relocated to Minnesota in 1988 as a refugee from Vietnam. Leaving behind the horrors of his war-torn homeland, Thom lived with a Minneapolis family and set out to learn English. He went on to attend Normandale College and work part time in a Vietnamese restaurant. But his ambition was to own his own restaurant.

Growing up in Qui Nhon, Vietnam, Thom began his culinary career in the kitchen of his grandmother Bo's catering service. His first job at age six was scraping carrots,

Facing page: Thom Pham's Pine Nut–Crusted Sea Bass.

but over the years he learned to cook and to manage a food business. His grandfather traveled throughout Vietnam as a salesman, sometimes taking Thom along so he could sample a variety of restaurants and exciting new dishes. Often young Thom would return from a trip and ask his grandmother how to re-create a dish he found especially interesting.

In 2000 he purchased the Kowloon Chinese Restaurant in St. Louis Park. Owned and operated for many years by Jack Der, a former Nankin chef, the restaurant came with some Nankin recipes dating back to 1919.

Thom went about modernizing the small restaurant and changing the name to ThanhDo, "the new generation in Asian cuisine." He kept some of the Kowloon dishes but added a whole list of new Asian/fusion dishes. Among them were three that would become customer favorites— Cranberry Cheese Puffs, Spanker Soup with Cranberries, and Chicken Cranberry Curry. The neighboring state of Wisconsin is a major grower of cranberries, producing thirty billion every year. The berries are not grown in Vietnam.

I asked Thom why the focus on cranberries. "Because I hate them so much," was his reply. "When I first came to Minnesota, it seemed every holiday included cranberry sauce, cranberry relish, or cranberries in some form. I really did not like them, so I decided to see if I could create some dishes to make them at least tolerable." Apparently he succeeded, because those dishes are three of the most popular in his restaurants. — PLH

After his success with ThanhDo, Thom opened AZIA in the Whittier neighborhood of Minneapolis and added a sushi restaurant next door. In its first year AZIA was selected by *Bon Appétit* as one of the outstanding restaurants in the country. A few years later Thom opened the upscale Temple restaurant in downtown Minneapolis and another ThanhDo in Anoka. At one point he was operating five restaurants.

By 2010 he had closed Temple, sold the Anoka ThanhDo, and moved the original ThanhDo across the street into the Texa-Tonka mall. He then moved AZIA to downtown Minneapolis and renamed it Thom Pham's Wondrous Azian Kitchen, where he featured dim sum on Saturdays and Sundays, live music in the lounge, a sushi bar, and allegedly the largest selection of saké between the east and west coasts. Just a few blocks from Target Center and the Twins' Target Field, in the heart of the Minneapolis theater district, the restaurant is now a gathering place for fans before and after games, audiences before and after performances, and others drawn by the fusion menu and trendy location.

Thom has no culinary boundaries. His fusion food draws inspiration from around the world, and he can often be found visiting other restaurants to gather ideas.

Thom Pham.

Squash Dumplings

Thom Pham

Makes 15–20 dumplings

1 (1-pound) kabocha squash

2 teaspoons dark brown sugar

1/2 teaspoon chili powder

2 teaspoons fish sauce

1/2 teaspoon wasabi powder

1 (15–20 piece) package thick dumpling wrappers

Thom Pham's Squash Dumplings.

1. Quarter the squash, place on a baking pan, and cook in a 350° oven for 20 to 25 minutes, until squash is tender. Remove and discard seeds and skin. Put the squash in a medium bowl and mash. Add the sugar, chili powder, fish sauce, and wasabi. Mix and mash well until the squash is smooth and all lumps are gone.

2. Taking one wrapper at a time, dampen half of the edge with a little water. Add 1 teaspoon of the squash mixture. Fold the wrapper over the filling to form a half-moon and pinch the edges together. Place the filled dumplings on a tray without allowing them to touch, as they will stick together. Keep unused wrappers covered in the package. Continue until all wrappers or filling is used.

3. Fill a large pot half full of water and bring to a boil over high heat. Add one dumpling at a time, pointing them in different directions so they do not stick together. Cook about ten at a time for 2 to 3 minutes, until the dough is completely cooked. Remove cooked dumplings with a metal strainer and place on a plate, again keeping them separate. Cool to room temperature. At this point they can be frozen (see note) or served as an appetizer with a dipping sauce (recipe follows) or used in other dishes.

Note: To freeze, layer dumplings on a plate or pan, covering each layer with a sheet of plastic wrap before starting the next. Cover the entire contents with another sheet of plastic wrap and freeze. To use, thaw dumplings and bring to room temperature.

Dipping Sauce

Thom Pham

Makes about 1 1/2 cups

1 cup Chinese light soy sauce

1/4 cup water

1/4 cup unseasoned rice vinegar

1/4 cup brown sugar

1 tablespoon freshly grated ginger

1 teaspoon dried chili flakes, or to taste

Combine all ingredients in a small bowl and mix well until the sugar dissolves. Serve at room temperature.

Boiled Brown Rice

ACAI

Makes 3 cups

1 cup brown rice

2 1/2 cups water

Wash rice several times and soak the rice in water to cover for at least one hour. Drain and add rice to a medium saucepan with 2 1/2 cups water. Bring to a boil and cook a few minutes, until craters begin to form. Turn heat down to simmer, cover, and cook for 15 minutes. Remove from heat and let rice steam, still covered, for 10 minutes. Remove lid and fluff rice with a fork.

Here are two of Thom Pham's favorite dishes. The key to both is preparing everything in advance of cooking the fish. In the restaurant, all the components are assembled quickly after the order is received, so everything has to be ready for last-minute cooking and plating.

Walleye in Jalapeño Basil Sauce

Thom Pham

Serves 1

1 (8–10-ounce) walleye fillet

Marinade:

1 cup rice wine

1 teaspoon ground white pepper

1 teaspoon garlic powder

1 teaspoon ground ginger

1 teaspoon granulated white sugar

1 teaspoon fish sauce

Coating:

1 cup rice flour

1 teaspoon ground white pepper

1 teaspoon garlic powder

1 teaspoon ground ginger

1 1/2 teaspoons granulated white sugar

Sauce:

2 jalapeños, stems removed, diced (do not remove the seeds)

1 tablespoon Thai basil, chopped

1/2 medium yellow onion, coarsely chopped

1/2 cup heavy cream

1 teaspoon salt

2 teaspoons granulated white sugar

1 teaspoon dashi powder

2 egg whites, beaten until mixed but not frothy

Vegetables:

4 fresh asparagus spears, trimmed and cut diagonally into 1-inch pieces

1/2 red bell pepper, stem, seeds, and pith removed, cut into 1-inch squares

1/2 green bell pepper, stem, seeds, and pith removed, cut into 1-inch squares

1/2 yellow onion, quartered

1 (1/2 inch–thick) ring fresh pineapple, cored, peeled, and cut into 1-inch pieces

1 teaspoon salt

1 teaspoon garlic powder

Additional ingredients:

4 cups vegetable oil

1 cup cooked brown rice (page 195)

1. Place the walleye in a flat dish with sides. In a small bowl mix the wine, pepper, garlic powder, ginger, sugar, and fish sauce together to dissolve the sugar and then pour over the fish. Turn the fish over several times so the marinade coats it well. Cover the dish and refrigerate for 1 to 2 hours.

2. In a small bowl combine the flour, pepper, garlic powder, ginger, and sugar together, mix well, and set aside.

3. Add the jalapeños, basil, and onions to a blender container. Add the cream, salt, sugar, and dashi and blend until smooth. Pour the mixture into a small saucepan and heat over medium heat until hot, about 115°. Stir constantly. Do not boil. Still stirring the mixture, slowly mix in the beaten egg whites and cook for about 2 minutes. Pour mixture into a small bowl and let cool to room temperature.

4. Place the asparagus, bell peppers, onion, and pineapple in a medium bowl. Toss with the teaspoon of salt and garlic powder. Set aside.

5. Place a wire rack over a baking sheet and set aside. Remove the fish from the marinade, shaking off any excess liquid, and place on a clean plate. Sprinkle the fish with the flour mixture, making sure to coat both sides. Heat a large wok (bigger than 12 inches) over high heat and add the vegetable oil. Heat the oil to 375°. Holding the fish at each end, carefully

dip the walleye into the hot oil in a slight swinging motion left to right and back again 2 or 3 times to partially cook the flour coating (see note). Then carefully lay the whole fish in the oil and fry until golden brown, about 5 to 8 minutes. Using a large strainer, remove the walleye and carefully lay it on the wire rack to drain off excess oil and allow the coating to crisp. Keep the oil in the wok hot.

6. Prepare a serving platter with a layer of hot brown rice.

7. Quickly put the vegetables and pineapple into a metal strainer, shaking off any moisture. Carefully add them to the hot oil in the wok and fry for 3 minutes. Remove from the oil, shake off excess oil, and spread the vegetable-fruit mixture out over the rice.

8. Carefully lay the hot fish on top of the vegetable layer and top with the jalapeño sauce. Serve immediately.

Note: While professional cooks can use their hands to dip the walleye in and out of the hot oil, the fish may be held with tongs at each end.

Walleye in Jalapeño Basil Sauce.

The sea bass recipe uses a number of ingredients to achieve a colorful presentation. The squash dumplings should be made ahead of time and refrigerated or frozen. The restaurant always has a supply of handmade dumplings ready for appetizers and to use in other dishes.

Pine Nut–Crusted Sea Bass

Thom Pham

Serves 1

1 (8–10-ounce) sea bass fillet, preferably Chilean

Coating:

1/4 cup pine nuts	1/2 teaspoon salt
3/4 cup panko (Japanese breadcrumbs)	1 teaspoon dark brown sugar
1/4 teaspoon chili powder	2 eggs, beaten
1/4 teaspoon ground cinnamon	

Puree:

6 ounces edamame, fresh or frozen	1/4 teaspoon ground cinnamon
1/4 cup heavy cream	1/2 teaspoon salt
1/4 cup whole milk	1 teaspoon dark brown sugar
1/4 teaspoon chili powder	

Sauce:

1 tablespoon uni (sea urchin roe), fresh or packaged	1 tablespoon butter
	2 palm seeds, each sliced into 3 disks
1 teaspoon dark brown sugar	2 baby leeks, lower bulb portion cut into about 1 1/2–inch pieces
1/4 teaspoon chili powder	
1 teaspoon fish sauce	
1/4 teaspoon wasabi powder	

Additional ingredients:

5 tablespoons vegetable oil	1/4 cup chili powder mixed with 2 tablespoons water to form a red hot sauce, optional
3 squash dumplings (page 195)	

1. Angle-cut the sea bass down through the top into three equal sections. Wash and dry.

2. Dry-roast the pine nuts in a small pan over medium-high heat just until they turn brown. Remove, cool to room temperature, and mince into pieces the same size as the panko. In a small bowl combine the panko, pine nuts, chili powder, cinnamon, salt, and brown sugar until well mixed.

3. In one pie plate add the panko mix. In another add the beaten eggs. Dip each piece of sea bass first into the egg and then into the panko to coat the fish completely. Place on a plate, cover with plastic wrap, and refrigerate.

4. In a small saucepan add the edamame and cover with water. Bring to a boil and cook until soft, about 3 to 4 minutes. Drain and place beans in a small dish. Cool to room temperature.

5. In a blender container add the edamame, cream, milk, chili powder, cinnamon, salt, and brown sugar. Puree and pour into a small bowl. Cover and cool to room temperature.

6. In a small saucepan combine the uni, brown sugar, chili powder, fish sauce, wasabi, and butter. Heat over low heat, stirring, until the mixture begins to caramelize, about 5 minutes. Add palm seed slices and leek. Mix together, then pour into a bowl and cool to room temperature.

7. Remove the fish from the refrigerator. Make a puddle of the edamame puree in the center of a serving platter.

8. Heat a large sauté pan over medium-high heat and add the vegetable oil. Carefully place the fish pieces and squash dumplings into the pan. Cook and turn until the fish and dumplings are golden brown, about 10 to 15 minutes. Center the dumplings in a circle in the middle of the puree. Place one piece of fish just overlapping a dumpling and repeat with the other two pieces. Top each sea bass piece with 1 1/2 teaspoons of the uni sauce, letting it run down over the fish and anything under it. If desired, dribble the chili water around the edge of the platter for additional color and flavor. Serve immediately.

Thom Pham's Pine Nut–Crusted Sea Bass.

In June 2012 Thom opened his eighth restaurant, back in the original location of AZIA on Twenty-sixth and Nicollet Avenue. Azia Market Bar & Restaurant features a market-fresh menu based on the four elements represented in the *kamons* that make up the restaurant logo: vegetables, rice/noodles, seafood, and meat. The fresh focus even extends to the bar, where creative cocktails use fresh fruit and vegetable juices served in a beautiful setting for drinking and dining. Once Thom completes one project another is soon to follow, so this is probably just the beginning of the history of how one teenage immigrant from the Asia Pacific Rim helped Minnesota learn even more about the flavors of Asia.

The Minnesota Melting Pot

Her heritage is Chinese and her homeland was Vietnam. His background is Indian and he was raised in Malaysia. Under different circumstances they may have never met. But Nina Wong's family moved to Minnesota and Thomas Gnanapragasam did, too. It was food that brought them together and eventually led to marriage.

Nina spent eighteen years in the family business, Rainbow Chinese Restaurant on Nicollet Avenue and Twenty-eighth Street in Minneapolis. When she decided to strike out on her own, she chose a location at 500 East Hennepin, between the University of Minnesota neighborhood and an area of industrial companies. In 2005 she opened East River Market, and its limited menu began attracting customers. Thomas was one of them. Soon they were discussing the food of their homelands. Thomas was a self-trained cook specializing in the dishes of India and Malaysia, and when they decided to marry

Thomas left his technical career and became Nina's business partner as well. They changed the market name to Chin Dian and offered a full menu for lunch and dinner.

Nina's idea was to feature noodles in a variety of ways. Not just lo mein and chow fun but also chow mai fun with its curry base, Vietnamese noodle salad, red curry noodle soup, and salsa mai fun soup are offered along with a variety of house entrees. Some sound familiar—chicken pea pods, Madras chicken, shrimp in black bean sauce, Mongolian beef—and some do not. Thomas offers Malaysian dishes such as nasi lemak, kwe tieu goreng, and sambal chow mai fun. A dozen dishes are marked "gluten free," and the assortment of beverages includes Nina's light and refreshing ginger tea, Anna's hot lemonade made with Nina's lemon syrup, and a variety of fruit smoothies as well.

This dish served at Chin Dian is a favorite with diners and a good example of the restaurant's name.

Chow Mai Fun

Nina Wong

Serves 1

2 tablespoons oil

1 egg, lightly beaten

1/4 cup julienne onion slices

1/4 cup julienne carrot strips

1/4 cup cooked shrimp and pork, or substitute chicken

1 ounce rice vermicelli, soaked in warm water 30 minutes

2 tablespoons curry powder

1 tablespoon salt

1/4 cup julienne green onion strips

1/4 cup fresh bean sprouts, washed and dried

1. Heat a wok over high heat and coat the wok with oil. Reduce heat to medium and lightly scramble the egg. Add the onion, carrots, and shrimp and pork (or chicken), and stir-fry until the onion is translucent.

2. Drain the noodles and add them to the wok with the curry powder and salt, and stir-fry until the noodles are limp. Add the green onions and bean sprouts. Stir-fry for 1 minute. Serve hot.

As the business grew, so did customers' requests for some of Nina's special sauces and flavorings. In 2010 Nina created a line of bottled signature syrups and sauces, including black stir-fry sauce, dumpling sauce, egg roll sauce, ginger syrup, lemon syrup, sweet and sour sauce, and white stir-fry sauce. They are available on her website, www. ninawong.com/shop, and in local food markets including Lunds and Byerly's.

Left: Nina Wong and Thomas Gnanapragasam.

Above right: Chow Mai Fun.

Here is a very easy and tasty recipe from Nina's website using her black stir-fry sauce.

Garlic Green Beans with Black Stir-Fry Sauce

Nina Wong

Serves 2–4

1 tablespoon olive oil

2 cloves garlic, minced

1/2 pound fresh green beans, ends removed, blanched

2 tablespoons Nina Wong Black Stir-Fry Sauce

Heat a sauté pan on medium heat. Add the olive oil, garlic, and green beans, stirring until well combined. Add Black Stir-Fry Sauce, tossing until desired consistency. Serve.

Korean Pizza: A Blend of Two Old World Cuisines

When Korea native Ann Kim decided she wanted to run a restaurant, it wasn't because she had trained for it or been brought up in a restaurant family. It was simply because she wanted to do it. "Then I had to decide what kind of restaurant," Ann recalled, and she started looking around for inspiration. She had lived in New York for several years while in college and was back in Minnesota trying to find direction.

"I decided that most people like pizza," Ann noted, but she did not like the pizza available in the Twin Cities. After so many years around New York pizza, she knew there could be something different, and she began looking for the training necessary to create it. She found the International School of Pizza in San Francisco, the only school in the United States affiliated with the Scuola Italiana Pizzaiolo of Italy. She quit her job and became a student. After graduation she was offered a chance to return as an intern, and she is now one of only ninety certified pizzaiolas in the United States.

She and partner Conrad Leifur were ready to launch the new business and needed to find a location. While walking their dog, Lola, one day they spotted a "for rent" sign, and the rest is history. It took nearly a year to prepare the space, with its specially built copper-clad wood-burning oven, and to create the menu she had in mind. In November 2010 Pizzeria Lola opened at 5557 Xerxes Avenue South, in the middle of a residential Minneapolis neighborhood just a few blocks from Edina. It was an immediate success.

"The neighborhood has been very kind to us," Ann commented, and their business has been very good. So good, in fact, that less than a year later they added lunch hours on Saturday and Sunday to their Tuesday through Sunday dinner schedule. Even so, within an hour after opening each night, the line of diners waiting for tables begins to weave around the back wall.

The menu includes house-made pizza crusts designed to have the flavor of bread with a chewy texture enhanced by the smoke from the wood-burning oven. The choice of pizzas includes some that look familiar—Marinara, Margerita, and Old Reliable—and some that are not, such as the Iowan with arugula, the Sunnyside with eggs, the Boise with potatoes, or the Forager with mushrooms.

And then there is the Lady ZaZa, with house-made Korean sausage, serrano peppers, soy chili glaze, and Ann's mother's kimchi. "I wanted to bring something of my heritage into the restaurant," Ann explained, "and I wanted to incorporate some of my mother's exceptional Korean cooking." She could see that combining Korean with Neapolitan cooking actually blended two age-old cuisines. After trying and rejecting several combinations, Ann created a pizza topped with the flavorful sausage and salty kimchi. While she listed it on the original menu, it was not always available to diners. Then she featured it as a monthly special. "It went well as a special," she recalled, "and when the month ended we just forgot about it until customers kept coming back just for the Korean pizza." Now her mother, Young Kim, comes in once a week to make a supply of kimchi.

In addition to pizza there are oven-roasted vegetables, salad, antipasto, and meatballs. Desserts, including ice cream, chocolate chip cookies, and root beer floats, are also house-made. There is a touch of bygone days in the décor, with mismatched dishes that might have come from yard sales, old tin cigarette boxes used to present the checks, and a vintage ironing board doubling as the reception desk.

Left: Ann Kim, Pizzeria Lola's creator, with the restaurant's wood-burning pizza oven.

Right: Harry Singh's restaurant today, and Harry and Annmarie Singh in the early years.

While the restaurant's recipes are proprietary, Ann did provide us with instructions to make one of her mother's favorite dishes, Kimchi Pancakes (page 162). In April 2012 Pizzeria Lola was featured on the cable television show *Diners, Drive-Ins and Dives*, an appearance that increased the restaurant's already-busy dinner business and added to the new lunchtime crowd as well. The restaurant has received "Best" awards, including *City Pages Best Pizza 2012*, and topped the paper's list of best pizza restaurants in 2011. Ann has also been named one of the best new chefs in town. In January she opened a second location at Delta's new terminal at the Minneapolis–St. Paul International Airport. She continues to develop new pizza ideas, including one possibility with Korean barbecued meat. Not bad for someone who had no idea of what kind of restaurant to open.

Caribbean Chow Mein on Eat Street

Chow mein, the first Asian dish commercially served in Minnesota in 1893, opened this book and will be the final dish as well. But this chow mein comes by way of Trinidad.

The Caribbean island was initially inhabited seven thousand years ago, but when Christopher Columbus visited on his third voyage to the New World in 1498, he spent a few days resting there without encountering any natives. He left thinking Trinidad was unoccupied and claimed it for his employer, Spain. The Spanish occupied the island and ruled its inhabitants for nearly three hundred years, surrendering it to the British in 1797. When the British abolished slavery in 1833, they imported workers from China, West Africa, Portugal, and other countries. By 1845 they were bringing in indentured servants from India. This combination of nationalities developed into a wide variety of cuisines that changed

the cooking of Trinidad, leading over the course of five hundred years to the fusion food that exists there today. Trinidad is now an independent, self-governed nation.

When Harry Singh left Trinidad to attend the University of St. Thomas in St. Paul, he brought with him a collection of island recipes including chow mein. After earning his degree in social work, Harry and his wife, Annmarie, went into the restaurant business, opening the first Harry Singh's Original Caribbean Restaurant on Central Avenue in Minneapolis in 1983. The menu included dishes from his Indian heritage such as curry chicken and curry potato chickpea roti and from the island's cuisines such as jerk chicken, Creole stewed fish, and four kinds of fried rice and chow mein.

"I grew up with chow mein," Harry said, a chow mein that shows the island's fusion influences and varies from day to day depending on what is in the kitchen.

I met with Harry to talk about his version of chow mein, which is probably more like the original chow meins served in the United States in the 1800s than today's standardized versions with their celery, onion, bean sprout, bamboo shoot, and water chestnut base. On an early visit to Harry's, I had vegetarian chow mein, filled with crisp slivered red cabbage, lettuce, carrots, and two kinds of beans, served in the center of a ring of white rice and a ring of brown rice. On a later visit I tried chicken chow mein, filled with dark brown, tender chicken pieces, slivered red cabbage, lettuce, carrots, and more, served over a mound of white rice. The chicken had been marinated in something akin to a light jerk sauce and then slowly steamed in its own juices to create a very tender, flavorful, slightly spicy meat. I asked Harry about the differences in the two chow meins, and he said it depends on the seasonings and vegetables available on any given day. He imports his own curry blend from Trinidad along with other special seasonings not available in Minnesota, so the only way to taste Harry's versions of chow mein is to visit the restaurant. They have been on the menu from the beginning. — PLH

Harry and Robyn Singh.

Harry knew his food would be a hit at the Minnesota State Fair, and he began applying for a booth in 1993. After sixteen years, the fair board finally granted him a space in 2009. "We started attracting crowds from the beginning," commented Harry, "and every year the lines are very long at our booth." At the fair he serves jerk chicken, filled roti, and doubles, a chickpea curry served on bread fritters and eaten like tacos: very spicy and delicious. Ginger beer is also popular at the fair.

Annmarie died in 1998, and Harry continued the business, moving the restaurant several times until 2004, when he opened on Minneapolis's Eat Street at Twenty-seventh and Nicollet Avenue. Their son Robyn now works with Harry both in the restaurant and at their state fair booth.

Today the restaurant menu includes a selection of jerk— the island's famous grilled meats and fish—and curries showing the culinary influence of India. Roti, Indian grilled flatbread, is cooked to order and may be filled with a variety of combinations, including curry potatoes and chickpeas. There are also Creole dishes, Caribbean-style rice dishes, goat curry, and Caribbean-style chicken wings. While the menu is not large, it offers a variety of island food that is truly some of the world's oldest fusion cooking. To expand Minnesotans' understanding of Trinidadian cuisine, Harry is planning to open a cooking school one day a week in the restaurant. Before too long, some of Harry's home cooking may be appearing in other restaurants across the state.

Harry Singh's Original Caribbean Restaurant is a bright, colorful space on Eat Street, its walls covered with framed press clippings, restaurant awards, souvenirs from Trinidad, and original island paintings. The music is from the birthplace of calypso and steel bands. It is a cozy, colorful retreat from Minnesota's sometimes bleak weather, and it serves the best Caribbean island chow mein in town.

Restaurants offering Asian fusion dishes have been opening for several years. Chino Latino, in the Minneapolis Uptown area, was one of the first. Wasabi Fusion Restaurant near the Guthrie Theater and Rice Paper with its Southeast Asian fusion in Edina are just two more. Asian fusion is finding its way into myriad restaurant menus throughout the state. Someday, even Minnesota potluck suppers will offer more than tuna casseroles, tater tot hot dish, and mac and cheese. They will include many of the flavors from the Asia Pacific Rim that have become part of the state's culinary history.

When the first Chinese immigrants came to Minnesota in 1875, they brought memories of home cooking, tried to replicate the dishes here, and undoubtedly shared their cooking with their new friends and neighbors. Thousands of Asia Pacific Rim immigrants who followed did the same thing, and soon Minnesota was enjoying a whole new world of cooking. From the state's first Chinese restaurant in 1893 to the more than eleven hundred Asian restaurants today, from Asian farmers to community organizations to home cooks, the flavors of the Asia Pacific Rim have changed Minnesota tastes and will continue to change them in the years ahead.

Asian Pages

ASIAN PAGES   BOX 130593, ROSEVILLE, MN 55113   TEL: 612.223.8351   FAX: 612.223.8604

SEPT 12, 1990 - SEPT 26, 1990

One of the paintings of Cheng-Khee Chee currently on exhibit at the Bloomington Art Center. Story on page

UNITED NATIONS INITIATE PLANS TO END WAR IN CAMBODIA

For more than a decade, Cambodia has been ravaged by a war that shows no signs of ever ending. During Pol Pot's three-year regime, more than a million Cambodians were thought to have perished from starvation, disease, and cold-blooded murder. In 1978, Pol Pot's Khmer Rouge government was driven out by the Vietnamese who installed a new government in Phnom Penh headed by Mr. Hun Sen.

Forced to retreat to the Thai border, Khmer Rouge troops have unceasingly plotted intermittent attacks on the Vietnamese-backed government throughout the 1980s. To make matters worst, two other factions, one led by Mr. Son Sann and the other by Prince Norodom Sihanouk, were also committed to ousting the Vietnamese-backed government.

All these fighting inevitably left the Phnom Penh's economy in shambles. The military soaked up at least 30 percent of the GNP. Inflation is running at 200 percent this year and the Cambodian riel has lost half its value. The recent decision by the Soviet government to end economic aid, which in past years has accounted for up to 80 percent of the government's revenues, is the ultimate blow to the beleaguered Cambodian economy.

Perhaps a much great-er cost is the lost of human lives. This year alone, more than 2000 Cambodians have perished. As the rebels pressed closer to the capital, more casualties are imminent.

The United Nations peace initiative could not have come at a more appropriate time. The Vietnamese are beginning to realize the futility of their attempt to occupy Cambodia. In fact, last year the Vietnamese pulled out some of its troops from Phnom Penh. China, in the face of international pressure, has reduced and may even cut off completely its support for the Khmer Rouge fighters. This would effectively put a cap on further attacks by this strongest of the three factions

Continued on page 6

PUBLIC INTEREST PAROLE (PIP)

-- an alternative to enter the U.S. for those rejected for refugees status

Prior to 1989, individuals applying for entry into the U.S. under the Orderly Departure Program (ODP) qualified for entry into the U.S. either as refugees, as immigrants seeking family reunification, or as Amerasians. Beginning in February 1989, those individuals applying for entry as refugees were tested on a case-by-case basis according to worldwide standards. This case-by-case determination is the implementation of the Attorney General's policy of August 1988. As a result of the new policy, individuals were being denied refugee status.

Public Interest Parole (PIP) is a new channel of entry available to persons who have been rejected for refugee status, but who are of "special interest" to the United States. Individuals offered PIP status are, if otherwise admissible to the U.S., guaranteed automatic and permanent entry to the U.S. and immediate work authorization.

Continued on page 4

MAJOR PROBLEMS FACED BY ASIAN ELDERS
Isolation, loneliness, and a lack of role within the family

A recent survey by the Amherst H. Wilder Foundation reported that Southeast Asian elders are the most vulnerable minority group in Minnesota. The Foundation determined that South east Asian minorities of age 60 and older have needs equivalent to the 85 and older non-minority (i.e. White) population.

Three-quarters of the Asian seniors in the survey reported income levels below poverty and more than 9 in 10 lack home equity and savings. Nearly a quarter rate their health as poor or very poor; half have difficulty performing everyday activities, and two-fifths lack transportation.

Southeast Asian elders have frequent contact with family members but are otherwise socially isolated. About a quarter of those without spouses live with their adult children, and 8 in 10 see their children daily. However, only 15 percent provide volunteer help to organizations, and a third see their friends less than weekly. Nearly a third are lonely, and a quarter reported that depression is a problem. This profile is consistent with other reports that have described isolation, loneliness, and a lack of role within the family as major problems for Southeast Asians elders.

For comparison purposes, among White elders, only 12 percent have incomes below poverty; 16 percent lack home equity, and about a fifth lack savings. Only 8 percent rate their health as poor or very poor; 13 percent report having difficulty performing daily activities, and 6 percent lack transportation. Six

Continued on page 5

Asian Pages

When Gary Liew and Siew Wong created *Asian Pages* newspaper in 1990, they envisioned a voice of and for the Asian community in Minnesota, focusing on its successes. They had grown tired of the mainstream media featuring Asian-related crime and failure stories. Instead, they wanted to report on the many accomplishments of various Asian organizations and individuals. They also wanted to provide information to the Asian community that was not available anywhere else.

Cheryl Weiberg remembers it well: "When Gary interviewed me to be a writer for *Asian Pages*, he wanted to be sure I was comfortable interviewing everyone from the governor to anyone in the Asian community." A freelance writer for many years, Cheryl landed the job and did in fact interview several governors and many members of the Asian community. In 1994 she became managing editor and, along with her husband, Joe, a co-owner of the paper. In 1996 she became editor-in-chief of *Asian Pages*.

Not long after the paper opened, Siew left and C. Ting Insixiengmay became co-owner and publisher. Ting, a native of Laos, and his wife Hieu, who is from Vietnam, were also concerned about creating a positive voice for the local Asian community.

Asian Pages was a free biweekly newspaper supported entirely by advertising sales and initially available on newsstands throughout Minnesota. It grew from 10,000 readers of each issue to 75,000 readers in seven states. In twenty-one years it garnered a number of awards, including the 2008 Minnesota Ethnic and Community Media Award, first place, global/local connections;

Facing page: First issue of Asian Pages.

World Wide News 1999 Newspaper Site Award; 1996 APECD (Asian Pacific Endowment for Community Development) Community Service Award for Journalistic Achievement; and the Typography and Design Award, Minnesota Newspaper Association 1994–95 Better Newspaper Contest.

I met Gary in 1991 when he reprinted an article I had written for the Midwest Asia Center newsletter. We discussed the possibility of Asian Pages *running future center material, and I suggested an ongoing food column to spotlight the food of the Asia Pacific Rim. He discussed the idea with Cheryl, and I began to write "Flavors of Asia." The column appeared in each issue for the next twenty years, providing more than five hundred stories that became the basis for this book. It was also the medium that led me to the granddaughter and great-grandson of one of the founders of the state's first Asian restaurant, John's Place. I had written a column in 2011 titled "Does Anyone Remember John's Place?" hoping I would find some customers who recalled dining at the popular restaurant. Instead, I heard from two members of the Woo family who helped me fill in with amazing stories of the brothers who made such an impact on the history of Asian food in Minnesota.*

While most columns featured Asian food and the people who created it in Minnesota and surrounding states, I also wrote about food in general and Asian food across the nation and overseas. Interviews and onsite research provided interesting material for readers and unique experiences for me. There was the column on Wisconsin's massive cranberry production that found me in the middle of a 6,100-acre marsh filled with the red berries ready for harvesting. I was even invited to put on waders to jump into the knee-high water and help with the process. On a trip to San Francisco, standing in a fortune cookie bakery in Chinatown, I watched workers place paper fortunes on hot, freshly baked cookies and then twist them with their bare hands into the familiar fortune cookie shape. In Las Vegas I watched a Chinese chef stretch and pull a wad of dough into four thousand Dragon Beard Noodles no thicker than a strand of hair.

Asian Pages
207

In lower Manhattan I enjoyed a most memorable lunch of the chef's choice at Nobu, the popular restaurant of the renowned chef Nobu Matsuhisa. In Richfield I got a hands-on lesson in the correct way to form Filipino egg rolls. And everyone I interviewed gave me a new perspective on life. Their stories of overcoming hardships, leaving their homelands, starting again in Minnesota, and persisting until they were successful showed Asian Pages *readers a positive side of the Asian community. They also helped readers understand and appreciate this amazing food that is now part of our whole community.* Asian Pages *was the only medium in the state to devote space in every issue to the food of the Asia Pacific Rim. — PLH*

The August 15, 2011, issue of *Asian Pages* was its final edition. After twenty-one years the pressures of a depressed economy and the growth of electronic communications took their toll, as they had with many newspapers across the country. Its voice will be missed.

Facing page: Last issue of Asian Pages.

Asian Pages®

award winning newspaper

FREE

Volume 21, Number 24   THE LEADING ASIAN RESOURCE SERVING THE MIDWEST   AUGUST 15-31, 2011

YOU ARE INVITED TO THE
SACRED EARTH LAUNCH PARTY!
THURSDAY, AUGUST 18, 5:30-8:00PM

Ragamala invites you to the first in a series of free events leading up to our next performance, *Sacred Earth*! Enjoy drinks and light snacks while mingling with the artists and other friends of the company. We hope to see you there!

Location:
The Calhoun Building
711 W. Lake Street,
Minneapolis
Lower level

Next event:
Open Artist's Studio
Saturday, August 20, 11:00am – 1:00pm

Photo by Ed Bock

SACRED EARTH EVENTS

ALL EVENTS ARE FREE AND OPEN TO ALL AGES UNLESS OTHERWISE SPECIFIED

AUGUST 18 ·   Festival Launch Party 5:30–8:00pm
711 W Lake St., Minneapolis (lower level)

AUGUST 20 ·   Open artist studio. Observe the creation of the Warli paintings for *Sacred Earth* by Anil Chaitya Vangad 11:00am - 1:00pm
711 W Lake St., Minneapolis (lower level)

AUGUST 27 ·

SEPTEMBER 10 ·

SEPTEMBER 14 ·

SEPTEMBER 17 ·

SEPTEMBER 17 ·   *Hands-on drumming workshop led by Mridangam artist Rajna Swaminathan*
6:30–7:30 pm
711 W Lake St., Minneapolis (Studio 306)
$10, free with *Sacred Earth* ticket purchase

SEPTEMBER 23-25 ·

Asian Pages.
P.O. Box 11932
St. Paul, MN 55111
ADDRESS SERVICE REQUESTED

CONTENTS

www.asianpages.com

8/15/11 6

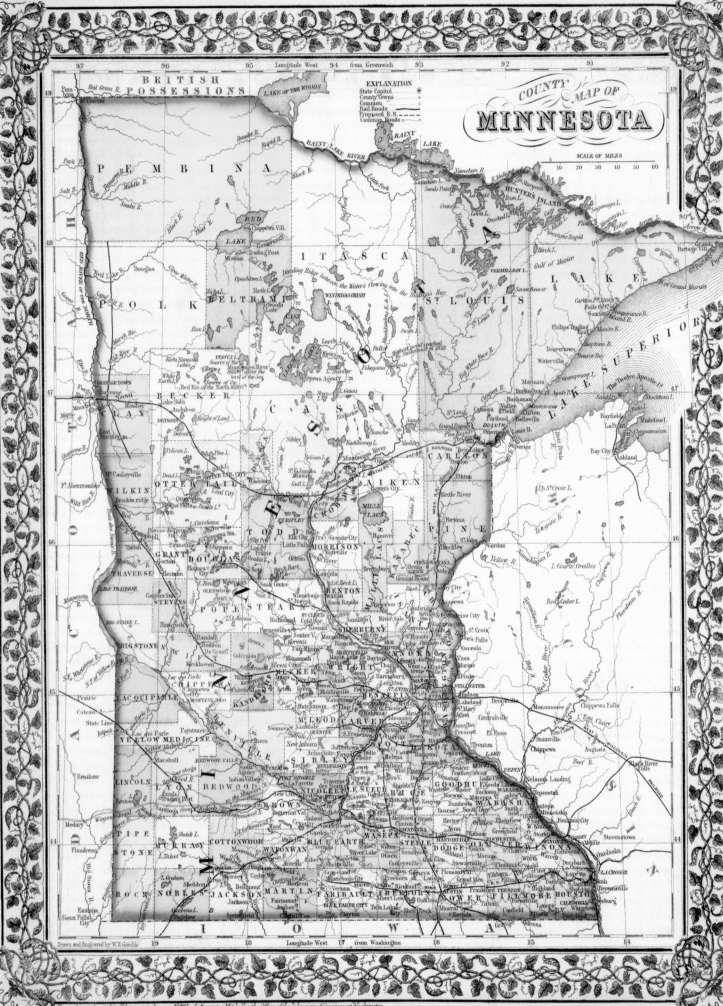

County MAP OF
MINNESOTA

EXPLANATION
State Capitol
County Towns
Common
Rail Roads
Proposed R.R.
Common Roads

SCALE OF MILES
10 20 30 40 50 60

Drawn and Engraved by W.H. Gamble

Entered according to Act of Congress in the year 1877 by S. Augustus Mitchell in the Office of the Librarian of Congress at Washington.

Timeline

A few of the people and events that brought the food of the Asia Pacific Rim to Minnesota

(Some dates are approximate.)

The Area Before 1875

1819 Fort Snelling is established on a bluff one hundred feet above the confluence of the Mississippi and Minnesota rivers to protect the lucrative fur trade. It is the first U.S. military base in the area and is located on land acquired from France in the Louisiana Purchase of 1803.

1837 A treaty with Dakota Indians secures an area along the banks of the Mississippi River to establish the city of St. Paul.

1838 Pierre "Pig's Eye" Parrant, a French Canadian fur trapper, becomes the first foreign occupant of St. Paul and opens its first business, a distillery and tavern in Fountain Cave.

1839 St. Croix Valley lumbering begins and the city of Stillwater becomes its commercial and shipping center.

1849 Minnesota becomes a territory with a recorded population of 4,852. St. Paul is named its capital.

1854 St. Paul is incorporated as a city.

1856 Minneapolis is authorized to become a town.

1858 Minnesota becomes the thirty-second state of the United States with a population of 150,037 whose heritage is primarily English, German, Scandinavian, French Canadian, and Native American.

1867 Minneapolis is incorporated as a city.

Asian Flavors are Introduced in Minnesota

1875 A few immigrants from China settle in Minnesota.

1880 The first Japanese immigrant settles in Minnesota.

1880 Eighteen-year-old Woo Yee Sing, from Canton, China, moves to Minnesota and opens a laundry on Nicollet Avenue in Minneapolis and then an import shop on Glenwood Avenue.

Facing page: A look at Minnesota as the first Asian immigrants knew it, 1877.

Woo Yee Sing (page 1).

1883 Woo Yee Sing brings his younger brother Woo Du Sing to Minnesota and they open the state's first Chinese restaurant in Minneapolis, the Canton Restaurant on Marquette Avenue.

1883 Twenty-five Minneapolis residents form the Minneapolis Society of Fine Arts. A few years later the name is changed to the Minneapolis Institute of Arts.

1900 A mineworker on the Mesabi Iron Range is reported to be from Korea.

1900 There are an estimated fifty-two Chinese immigrants in Minnesota with a total state population of 1.75 million.

1903 Moy Ju Hee from the Taishan area of Guangdong Province opens a restaurant in St. Paul called Kwong Tung Low Co. Café and soon after another Chinese restaurant in Minneapolis.

1903 The Woo brothers change the name of their restaurant to Yuen Faung Low (Café of Exotic Fragrance from Afar) and move it to the second floor of 28 South Sixth Street in Minneapolis. It becomes known as John's Place and operates successfully until 1967 when the building is torn down to make way for a new building and parking lot. Woo Du Sing's son Charles operates John's No. One Son on Wayzata Boulevard until 1979 when it is closed.

John's Place (page 4).

1905 The Minnesota Department of Game and Fish releases seventy pairs of Chinese ring-necked pheasant in Minnesota. None survive, but between 1916 and 1918 the department releases four thousand more pheasant and provides six thousand pheasant eggs to farmers and sportsmen. Raised in China for over three thousand years, pheasant become popular game birds in Minnesota and are considered a delicacy in other parts of the country. By 2012, more than 400,000 birds are harvested each year by pheasant hunters with additional pheasant grown commercially and sold around the country.

1910 The U.S. Census indicates there are two Filipinos in Minnesota.

1914 The University of Minnesota School of Agriculture enrolls its first students from China who use the education they receive here to improve agricultural productivity in their homeland.

1915 The Minneapolis Institute of Arts opens the doors to its museum on Twenty-fourth Street and Third Avenue South in Minneapolis. Its initial collection consisting of eight hundred works of art includes items from Asia.

1918 Chinese immigrant Bernard Wong, known as Bon Wong, and his brother William open the first Chinese restaurant in St. Cloud, the O.K. Café, serving meat and potatoes along with Chinese food. Theirs is one of just two restaurants in St. Cloud that allow women to enter by the front door. The rest were saloons where "ladies" were not allowed. The O.K. Café is open twenty-four hours a day with the staff taking turns sleeping in the back room.

1919 Chinese immigrant Walter James (Kim Wah) opens the Nankin Café next to the Radisson Hotel on Seventh Street in downtown Minneapolis. It becomes a popular Chinese restaurant operating in various locations on the same street for eighty years.

1920 It is estimated that the Chinese population throughout the state now totals nine hundred to one thousand.

1920 Two Korean students enroll at Hamline College in St. Paul.

1928 Filipino students enroll in Minnesota colleges. Other Filipinos in the state are mostly farm workers who were recruited from the Philippines and then stayed on as sharecroppers. These early immigrants become known in the Filipino community as old-timers. Immigrants from the Philippines after the 1930s are known as new immigrants.

1929 Filipino old-timers Filemon and Clara A. Balbuena manage a company restaurant serving Filipino food. It is believed to be the state's first Filipino restaurant.

1934 Chinese American Stanley Chong from Olympia, Washington, moves to Minneapolis and opens the International House to supply Asian food to the expanding Asian restaurants and food stores in the area. With wife Marvel he then opens International House of Foods near the University of Minnesota campus, believed to be the first area food market selling Asian ingredients to consumers.

Marvel and Stanley Chong (page 9).

1940 Japanese "resettlers" come to Minnesota. The U.S. Census indicates fourteen Japanese live in Minnesota outside of the Twin Cities.

1942 Some of the Japanese Americans detained in California during World War II are relocated to Minnesota to provide translation services at the U.S. military base at Fort Snelling.

1944 Jeno Paulucci, an Iron Range resident and son of Italian immigrants, produces the first commercial crop of bean sprouts in Minnesota and begins selling them to East Coast canneries. He learned to grow the sprouts from a group of Japanese in the Twin Cities. Along with his partner Dave Persha he soon begins to can bean sprouts along with other ingredients that could be used to make chop suey. The line was called Foo Young, eventually changed to Chun King and was sold nationally. Paulucci had started the business, headquartered in Duluth, with a $2,500 loan and in 1966 sold the company to R. J. Reynolds Tobacco Company for $63 million.

1946 Stanley and Marvel Chong open Marvel Foods on Nicollet Island in Minneapolis, the first company in America to develop and sell Chinese frozen food products nationally. They begin offering cooking classes that become so popular they have to limit enrollment. By 1961, they are the largest Chinese frozen food firm in the United States and continue operations until the building is destroyed by fire in 1981.

1948 Walter James and Stanley Chong form the state's first organization promoting cooperation between Asian and non-Asian communities. Meetings are held in special rooms at the Nankin Cafe. The organization continues as the Chinese American Association of Minnesota.

1949 A group of Filipino old-timers opens Balbuena Grocery Store in the Selby-Dale area of St. Paul. The store is operated by Filemon and Clara A. Balbuena until 1975.

1950 Refugees from Korea begin to be relocated to Minnesota, and by 1969 there are 157 Koreans in the state.

1951 Chinese immigrant Joe Huie and his two brothers open Joe Huie's Café in Duluth. It is open twenty-four hours a day, seven days a week. Its Chinese and American menu becomes so popular that sometimes they have to hire a policeman to control the lines of diners waiting to get into the café, especially after the bars close. Joe's eldest son Wing Ying Huie opens the Chinese Lantern in 1964, and his youngest son, Wing Young Huie, eventually becomes a nationally acclaimed photographer in the Twin Cities.

Three generations of Fongs (page 18).

1958 David and Helen Fong open Bloomington's first takeout Chinese restaurant at Ninety-eighth and Lyndale Avenue South. David Fong's becomes so popular that a few years later David builds a full-service restaurant and bar at Ninety-third and Lyndale and becomes an active leader in the growing community. In 2005, David Fong is among the first eight people elected to the Minnesota Hospitality Hall of Fame. In 2006 and again in 2007, the restaurant is named one of the top 100 Chinese restaurants in America. In 2008, the family celebrates fifty years in business. Some of the Fong children are also in the restaurant business.

Joe Huie with two of his sons (page 7).

1957 Fargo, North Dakota, native Teddy Wong opens House of Wong, a Chinese restaurant in Roseville, where he offers both American and Chinese food.

1959 Tokyo native Reiko Weston opens Fuji Ya on LaSalle Avenue near Ninth Street in downtown Minneapolis. It is the first Japanese restaurant in Minnesota and offers patrons a whole new dining experience: eating on the floor. In 1961 Reiko purchases a property on the banks of the Mississippi River at 420 South First Street. She builds a 250-seat restaurant and moves Fuji Ya to the scenic site. It operates successfully until 1990, two years after her death.

1960 Reiko Weston opens a second Fuji Ya in St. Paul on Alley 29 and closes it a year later due to demolition to make way for the World Trade Center building.

1962 Abelando Sioson Malicsi begins a journey from his native Philippines that will lead him to a career in metallurgy and establishing his home in Minnesota. After his retirement Abe turns his efforts to one of his favorites hobbies, cooking. Abe becomes known throughout the Filipino community as one of the area's more prolific and generous cooks. A visit to the Malicsi home always includes enjoying some of Abe's favorite foods. He and his wife Lita become leaders in a number of Filipino organizations.

1970 Restaurant broker Daljit Sikka works with Bimla Barar to open one of the first Indian restaurants in Minnesota, the Taj Mahal, on Nicollet Avenue between Tenth and Eleventh streets. He also works with Chander Mehta to open the Bombay House, the first Indian restaurant in Fridley.

Daljit Sikka (page 115).

1971 Former University of Minnesota students open a tofu plant.

1972 Reiko Weston opens Fuji International, a Japanese-style cafeteria at 408 Cedar Avenue on the University of Minnesota's west bank. A self-service restaurant, Fuji International offers freshly cooked Japanese dishes for $0.95 to $1.95, a bargain for nearby students. It is the pilot for a national chain of Japanese cafeterias.

1972 Three partners open United Noodles in Minneapolis to supply locally made noodles to area Chinese restaurants. Teddy Wong, Herb Wong, and Ramon Tan first make chow mein noodles, then grow bean sprouts for restaurants and canneries. They expand to become a major importer/distributor of Asian food to area restaurants and food markets and a full-service Asian food market for consumers. In 2007, their deli is featured on Rachael Ray's television show *Tasty Travels*.

1975 An influx of refugees from Laos, Cambodia, and Vietnam settle in Minnesota over the next six years and create the first Hmong farms in the state, cultivating foods typically grown only in Asia. They establish communities that later expand with the next wave of Hmong refugees settling in Minnesota.

1975 Reiko Weston opens a teppanyaki room on a lower floor of Fuji Ya by the river and introduces Minnesota diners to the Japanese style of specially trained chefs slicing, dicing, and grilling food at the table. It is a method later made popular across the country by the Benihana restaurant chain.

1976 Thai immigrant and science teacher Supenn Supatanaskinkasem Harrison offers the first Thai food at the Minnesota State Fair with her Thai egg rolls. They become so popular that she operates the booth for twenty-five years.

1977 Japanese native Reiko Weston opens Tiaga, a Chinese restaurant in St. Anthony Main just across the river from her Fuji Ya. She is one of the first in the area to feature dim sum on the menu. She imports special equipment and five dim sum chefs from Hong Kong to make twenty different kinds of dim sum every day. The chefs turn out four thousand dim sum wrappers daily, enough to sell to other restaurants and food stores locally and nationally.

1977   Ely and Yvonne Arcilla from the Philippines open Phil.-Oriental Imports on Forest and Maryland avenues in St. Paul. They move locations several times and in 1988 buy the building at 789 University Avenue West where they continue to operate. In 2012 they add a deli on weekends for Filipino takeout food.

1977   Heather Jansz opens Mulligan Stew House on Eighteenth and Central Avenue in Minneapolis where on the first Sunday of every month she prepares Sri Lankan curries for friends. She soon changes the name to the Sri Lanka Curry House. A few years later, with husband Evan Balasurya, she moves the restaurant to the Uptown area of Minneapolis and operates there for seventeen years. When the couple divorces, Heather opens the Curry Leaf Deli in St. Paul and Evan opens another Sri Lanka Curry House in Calhoun Square, Minneapolis.

1979   Supenn Harrison purchases the Gopher Grill on Lake Street in Minneapolis and turns it into the Siam Café, featuring Thai food. It becomes the forerunner to her Sawatdee Thai restaurants in Minneapolis, St. Paul, Bloomington, Maple Grove, and St. Cloud.

1979   The Japanese restaurant Ichiban opens on Nicollet Avenue at Thirteenth Street in Minneapolis, offering a full menu of teppanyaki created tableside by knife-wielding chefs.

1979   After three years of studying with the legendary Nakazato family in Japan, North Dakota potter Richard Bresnahan helps establish St. John's Pottery in Collegeville with a program based on Japanese techniques. He creates America's first

woodburning kiln and uses only all-natural supplies from local sources. Many of his creations are designed for use with food and beverages and include a collection of vessels for use in the Japanese tea ceremony. His work is now in museums around the country, including the Minneapolis Institute of Arts, as well as museums in Japan.

Teapot by Richard Bresnahan (page 130).

1980   Leeann Chin, a seamstress from Guangzhou (Canton), China, opens her first Chinese restaurant in Minnetonka, leading to the first major chain of Chinese restaurants in the Midwest with fifty-two locations in four states. She eventually expands the takeout operations into the Dayton's Department Store food court and into Byerly's food stores. She also opens Asia Grille in several locations, offering the food of several Asian countries, and establishes Chinese takeout operations in Seattle, Washington.

1980   Le Tran joins her sister Tra in opening Matin, a Vietnamese restaurant, in the Kickernick Building on First Avenue North in Minneapolis. It is one of the first Vietnamese restaurants in the state.

1981   Chavhivan (Bou) Haanpaa opens King and I Thai on Nicollet Avenue in Minneapolis in the space vacated by Taj Mahal. She later moves it to LaSalle Avenue.

1981 General Mills publishes *Betty Crocker's Chinese Cookbook* by Leeann Chin. By 2010 it sold an estimated 500,000 copies worldwide.

1981 Reiko Weston is the first to bring in a sushi chef from Japan and opens the first sushi bar in Minnesota at Fuji Ya on the river.

Reiko Weston (page 65).

1981 Some ethnic Chinese from Vietnam are relocated to Minnesota. The Vietnam Hong Kong International store opens in North Minneapolis, selling foods and gifts to consumers and to Chinese and Vietnamese restaurants in Minnesota.

1981 Kim Long's on University Avenue in St. Paul is among the early Vietnamese restaurants in the state.

1981 Minnesota becomes home to 21,000 Indochinese refugees from Laos, Cambodia, and Vietnam. Among them are 9,200 Hmong. Additional immigrants would come to Minnesota, bringing the Hmong population in the state to 66,181. It is the second-largest Hmong community in the United States, behind California.

1982 Bikhalal Patel opens Reshma International Imports in the Minneapolis Phillips neighborhood, featuring food and imports from India. He later moves it to Central Avenue and Eighteenth Street and calls it Asia Imports. In 2004 he opens the Bombay Deli in a corner of the store and continues operation until 2009 when he retires.

1982 Xayasack (Cy) Ratsamy's family opens a small food market specializing in Thai ingredients on Twenty-sixth Street near Nicollet Avenue in Minneapolis. In 1993 they buy the building three blocks away at Twenty-eighth and First Avenue and move their New Orient Market to the new location.

New Orient Market (page 110).

1983 Trinidad native Harry Singh and his wife Annmarie open Harry Singh's Original Caribbean Restaurant on Central Avenue in Minneapolis. He moves it several times, finally locating on Nicollet Avenue near Twenty-seventh Street. His menu features an island version of chow mein, a dish he enjoyed as a child in Trinidad.

1983 Vietnamese refugee Le Tran and her husband Hiew Tran open their first Lotus Vietnamese restaurant in Minneapolis and then add four more locations in the Twin Cities and create a line of Vietnamese frozen foods sold in food markets.

1983 Sunny Kwan and his family open Keefer Court Foods at Cedar and Riverside avenues in Minneapolis, the first Chinese bakery in Minnesota.

Its Chinese fortune cookie division, Golden Plaque, expands to produce millions of fortune cookies annually and ships them worldwide.

Sunny and Pauline Kwan (page 13).

1984 Le and Hiew Tran sell their Lotus To Go restaurant at West Grant and LaSalle avenues in Minneapolis to staff member Van Vo and her husband Trung Nguen.

1984 Reiko Weston opens Fuji Express in the skyway near Seventh and Marquette in Minneapolis. It operates for a year.

1984 Minneapolis-based Lerner Publishing publishes *Cooking the Japanese Way* for young cooks by Reiko Weston. Revised in 2001, it is sold nationally.

1985 The *Hmong Recipe Cook Book* is produced by the New Citizens' Hmong Garden Projects, sponsored by the First Presbyterian Church of South St. Paul. Recipes are from area Hmong cooks.

1985 Asian Foods opens with one pickup truck and by 2002 is providing Asian food supplies to restaurants in five states.

1986 Minneapolis-based Lerner Publishing publishes *Cooking the Thai Way* for young cooks, written by Sawatdee Thai restaurants' founder Supenn Harrison with Judy Monroe.

1987 Calco opens a bean sprout–growing business in Minneapolis on Minnehaha Avenue.

1988 Shanghai native Andy Shun begins to feature dim sum on weekends at his Yangtze Chinese Restaurant in St. Louis Park.

1988 Chinese native Xuong Mau Duong and his family are relocated to Minnesota from Vietnam and open the Truong Thanh (Great Wall) food store on Fifteenth Street off Nicollet Avenue in Minneapolis, complete with hundreds of Chinese herbs. He is believed to be the first commercial Chinese herbalist in Minnesota. In 1993 Xuong and his daughter Huang Lanh purchase a larger building at 2520 Nicollet Avenue South and are able to expand the store.

Huang Lanh Duong (page 11).

1988 Mitch and Sherri Law open Minnesota's first Mongolian barbeque in Dinkytown. Called Khan's Mongolian Barbeque, the restaurant is an immediate hit. The Laws expand to Roseville, Richfield, and Coon Rapids, eventually closing the original restaurant. Their suburban restaurants continue to operate in 2012.

1988 Cora Cayetano, a native of Manila, opens Cora Cayetano's Filipino Fast Foods at 168 Concord Street in St. Paul. It is a food market with a small restaurant featuring the food of the Philippines and is believed to be the first independent Filipino restaurant in Minnesota. After several years she closes the market and opens two chicken wing stores in St. Paul called Cora's Best Chicken Wings at 168 Cesar Chavez Street and 1143 Payne Avenue.

1989 Wayne (Won) J. Cho opens Shilla Korean restaurant on Snelling Avenue in St. Paul.

1989 Lung Tran and her family open Quang Deli on Nicollet Avenue near Twenty-eighth Street in Minneapolis. For ten years they continue to expand the popular deli and then move across the street to a larger space where they can offer a full menu to 150 diners.

1989 Heather Jansz Balasurya and Karen Winegar write *Fire and Spice: The Cuisine of Sri Lanka*, published by McGraw-Hill.

Sakura bento box (page 71).

1990 Miyoko Omori opens Sakura Japanese restaurant in Galtier Plaza in downtown St. Paul. She moves it twice and eventually locates it at 350 St. Peter in St. Paul, where it continues to operate in 2012.

1990 Daniel Lam, a Cantonese-trained chef from Vietnam, takes over Shuang Cheng on Fourteenth Street in the University of Minnesota area called Dinkytown and expands the menu to include a wide variety of Cantonese specialties. The extensive twelve-page menu includes many seafood dishes not found in other Chinese restaurants, and daily specials are listed on the everchanging wall menu.

Shuang Cheng's daily specials (page 21).

1990 Yong Lee opens his restaurant Mirror of Korea on Lake Street in Minneapolis and then moves to Snelling Avenue in St. Paul four years later.

1990 The Science Museum of St. Paul has a house built in the museum by area Hmong elders to give viewers a glimpse of the Hmong lifestyle in Laos and Cambodia. It includes an open fire area for cooking family meals and a giant wok to cook food scraps for the pigs raised by most Hmong families.

1990 Nuntana Erickson brings her Thai food carving skills to Minnesota and begins giving classes in the age-old techniques. In 2009 she produces her first DVD of food carving lessons.

Thai carved squash container (page 112).

1990 Vietnamese native Ngoan Dang and his wife Mai Nguyen open Mai Village at 446 University Avenue West in St. Paul, offering the food of their homeland. They build a new building in 2004 to showcase their collection of Vietnamese art and move the restaurant to 394 University Avenue West.

1991 Twin Cities–based *Asian Pages* newspaper publishes the area's first ongoing food column featuring Asian food and the people who make it. Written by Phyllis Louise Harris, the column, "Flavors of Asia," reaches 150,000 readers each month in seven states. By 2011, when the paper closes, she has written more than five hundred articles.

1992 Peggy Tang opens Tang's Ginger Café in Minneapolis and brings in chef Hallie Harron to add Indonesian dishes to the Chinese menu.

1992 The Mall of America in Bloomington houses a number of national restaurant chains including Panda Express.

1993 Kin Lee and his wife Wai Chun open Singapore Chinese Restaurant in Maplewood, featuring the food of Malaysia. They later open a second restaurant in south Minneapolis called Singapore! and partner with chef Tee Balachew to offer dishes from Ethiopia as well.

1993 Young Tae Lim and his wife Eun Jin Lim open Hoban, the first Korean restaurant in Eagan.

1995 Asian Culinary Arts Institutes brings in two professional chefs from Xian, China, to teach traditional Chinese cooking to culinary students at the Hennepin Technical College in Eden Prairie and at various venues in the Twin Cities. It is the first such endeavor in Minnesota. They also invite legendary cookbook author and nationally acclaimed Chinese cooking teacher Florence Lin to conduct classes at the college.

Pulling Chinese noodles (page 25).

1996 Foodsmart at 995 University Avenue West in St. Paul specializes in Hmong ingredients including fresh Hmong herbs and homemade Hmong sausage. It is later called Sunrise Market and eventually houses Destiny Café with a full menu of Hmong dishes.

1996 Hormel Foods, headquartered in Austin, Minnesota, sets up a joint venture with Patak Spices Ltd. to market Indian food products in the United States.

1997 Bill Waddington opens his first TeaSource store in St. Paul, importing more than 250 teas from all areas of Asia. It is the first store of its kind in the state. He later expands with stores in St. Anthony and Eden Prairie. He creates a tea catalog, produces an informative website, and offers classes in the stores.

1997 Kunrath Lam and Kevin Lam open Cheng Heng at 448 University Avenue West in St. Paul, the first Cambodian restaurant in Minnesota.

1997 *Korean Quarterly* is founded by Martha Vickery and Stephen Wunrow. The paper features an article on Korean food in each issue.

Korean Quarterly *(page 155).*

1999 Thai native Supatra Johnson and her husband Randy Johnson open Jasmine market in Burnsville, where they offer many of the ingredients necessary for Thai cooking and she offers classes on how to use them.

2000 Leeann Chin and her daughter Katie Chin write *Everyday Chinese Cooking for Families* to help families share the fun of cooking Chinese food. Published by Clarkson Potter, it is sold nationally.

2000 Japanese native Koshiki Yonemura Smith and her husband Benjamin Smith open Tanpopo Noodle Shop on Selby Avenue in St. Paul. She offers the comfort food of Japan that she enjoyed throughout her childhood. In 2003 she changes the name to Tanpopo Restaurant and moves it to a larger space at 108 Prince Street in Lowertown St. Paul, a block from the farmers' market.

2000 Vietnam native Thom Pham purchases the Kowloon Chinese Restaurant in St. Louis Park, modernizes the décor, creates a menu of Asian fusion dishes, and names it ThanhDo. It is one of six restaurants he will open in the Twin Cities by 2012, including Temple, AZIA, and Thom Pham's Wondrous Azian Kitchen. His approach to Asian fusion draws national attention and influences other chefs.

Thom Pham's Wondrous Azian Kitchen (page 194).

2001 Minnesota-based General Mills releases *Betty Crocker's Indian Home Cooking,* written by Minnesota author from Mumbai, India, Raghavan Iyer and published by Hungry Minds, Inc.

2001 The national chain P. F. Chang's China Bistro opens its first Minnesota location at the Southdale shopping mall in Edina.

2001 The Minneapolis Institute of Arts has an authentic teahouse (*chashitsu*) built in its Japanese galleries in the museum on Twenty-fourth Street and Third Avenue.

2002 Raghavan Iyer writes *The Turmeric Trail.* Published by St. Martin's Press and sold nationally, it captures memories of his childhood in India and offers traditional Indian recipes for American cooks. It is a finalist for a James Beard Award for Best International Cookbook in 2003.

2004 Carol Weston Hanson and her husband Thomas Hanson open Fuji Ya in St. Paul at Seventh and Wabasha. The Minneapolis Fuji Ya is now located on Lake Street just off Lyndale Avenue South.

2004 Thai immigrant, cooking teacher, and St. Paul restaurant owner Supatra Johnson publishes her cookbook, *Crying Tiger*, filled with recipes for Thai home cooking, and sells it through her website and local retailers. Her website also offers extensive information on Thai food.

2004 Minnesota-based cooking teacher and Mumbai native Raghavan Iyer receives the International Association of Cooking Professionals award for Outstanding Cooking Teacher of the Year. He has been teaching the classic foods of India in culinary schools and organizations throughout the United States and in Canada for more than seventeen years, reaching an estimated 25,000 students.

2005 Nina Wong opens the East River Market on East Hennepin in Minneapolis to offer some of China's best comfort food. A few years later, with husband Thomas Gnanapragasam, she changes the restaurant name to Chin Dian and adds dishes from Malaysia and India. Nina also creates a line of bottled sauces that are sold in area food stores.

Nina Wong and Thomas Gnanapragasam (page 200).

2005 A group of Malaysian immigrants open Peninsula restaurant on Nicollet Avenue near Twenty-sixth Street in Minneapolis to offer the food of their homeland.

2006 Toua Xiong opens the Hmong International Marketplace in a former lumberyard on Como Avenue in St. Paul to meet the growing needs of the expanding Hmong population in Minnesota. It houses several hundred vendors selling imported items along with locally grown products and becomes a weekly meeting place for many Hmong immigrants.

2006 Sambol, an Indian restaurant in Eagan, offers the food of Sri Lanka on weekends.

2007 Supatra and Randy Johnson move Supatra's Thai Restaurant to 967 West Seventh Street in St. Paul, where they are able to add patio dining.

Mhonpaj's Garden (page 81).

2007 A Hmong family farm, Mhonpaj's Garden, begins operation in Oakdale, selling its produce at local farmers' markets and food stores. It is one of many Hmong farms operating in the state. In 2009 it becomes part of the growing community-supported agriculture (CSA) movement, where farmers sell shares in their crops, and is the first Hmong farm in the program to be certified organic. In 2009 the family is selected as the University of Minnesota's Farm Family of the Year for Ramsey County.

2008 Raghavan Iyer writes *660 Curries*. It is published by Workman Press and named Outstanding Asian Cookbook in the U.S. by the Gourmand Awards.

2008 Bali restaurant opens at 1410 Nicollet Avenue in Minneapolis, offering the food of Indonesia. It closes a year later.

2008 Naveen Shreshta opens his Himalayan restaurant in Minneapolis's Seward neighborhood and features the dishes of his homeland Nepal.

2009 The University of Minnesota Press publishes the first hardcover Hmong cookbook distributed nationally, *Cooking from the Heart*, bringing to print the culinary traditions of a culture without a written history. Recipes that for centuries had been passed verbally from one Hmong generation to the next are now available in this informative edition.

2009 Neil Guillen, with a background in Filipino cooking, becomes the chef of the newly opened Subo restaurant at 89 South Tenth Street in Minneapolis. He is followed by another chef with Filipino ancestry, Geoff King, who continues the restaurant's continental approach to the traditional dishes of the Philippine Islands. The restaurant closes a year later.

2009 Sawatdee founder Supenn Harrison publishes *Awaken to Thai Cooking*.

2009 *Asian Restaurant News* estimates there are now 1,091 Asian restaurants in Minnesota, including 697 Chinese, 61 Japanese, 97 Thai, 87 Vietnamese, 43 Indian, 7 Korean, and 99 Pan Asian.

2010 Korean native Ann Kim opens Pizzeria Lola in south Minneapolis and features a Korean pizza on the menu.

2010 Hmong immigrant Yia Vang opens Hmong Village at 1001 Johnson Parkway in St. Paul with thirty-five fresh produce booths, seventeen food stands, 230 import shops, and forty offices.

2010 Gengde Sanpo and his family open Nha Sang in Burnsville, offering the food of their Tibetan homeland.

Geoff and Aimee King (page 61).

2011 Geoff King opens Scratch, one of the growing number of food trucks in the Twin Cities, and offers foods of the Philippines. Along with his wife Aimee, Geoff develops a menu of lunch items drawing on Filipino classics and incorporating some of the ingredients from the islands. In its first season, Scratch earns an award for the best Food Truck Food in 2011.

2012 Mena-li Docto Canlas (also known in the Filipino community as the cake lady) begins offering a Pinoy Brunch and Merienda at the Pines Market in Circle Pines. Filled with a variety of her favorite foods of the Philippines, the brunch is one of the few regularly scheduled opportunities in Minnesota to taste this delicious cuisine.

2012 The Minnesota Historical Society Press publishes *Asian Flavors: Changing the Tastes of Minnesota since 1875*. It is the first book to feature the history of Asia Pacific Rim food in the state.

Recipe List

The dishes of the Asia Pacific Rim do not fall neatly into American menu categories. There are no appetizers, just one of several dishes served at a meal. Soups or salads may be complex enough that they are more a main dish than additions to a meal. Rice and noodle dishes can be considered sides or entrees. While we have indexed the recipes in relatively descriptive categories, many may just as easily fit into another category.

(🌿) Vegetarian recipes as written, or they may become vegetarian by using only vegetables, by substituting Thai light soy sauce for fish sauce, by substituting eggless noodles for egg noodles, or by using vegetable broth in place of chicken or beef broth.

Appetizers

Abe's Egg Rolls with Pork	Philippines	54
Abe's Vegetarian Egg Rolls 🌿	Philippines	54
Empanadas	Philippines	57
Futomaki	Japan	73
Jellied Lamb	China	36
Marble Devil Eggs with Yunnan Puerh	Tea	187
Marble Tea Eggs with Yunnan Puerh	Tea	187
Pearl Balls	China	40
Sue's Thai Egg Rolls	Thailand	100
Tempura 🌿	Japan	69
Vietnamese Fresh Spring Rolls with Shrimp 🌿	Vietnam	144

Facing page: Fresh greens at the Hmong market.

Soups

Beef Noodle Soup	Vietnam	145
Chicken Broth	Hmong	90
Chicken with Bean Thread Noodles	Philippines	55
Indonesian Chicken Soup	Indonesia	168
Pepper Soup with Tamarind 🌿	India	121
Pumpkin Coconut Soup 🌿	Thailand	105
Pumpkin Soup/Drink 🌿	Hmong	90
Sea Bass Noodle Soup	Vietnam	152
Silver Bean Thread Noodle Soup	Thailand	104
Tom Yum Soup	Thailand	101
Velvet Chicken and Cream of Corn Soup	China	34
Winter Soup	Cambodia	94
Yia Moua's Glass Main Dish Noodle Soup	Hmong	88

Salads

Bean Sprout Salad 🌿	China	10
Broccoli Stem Salad 🌿	China	30
Chopped Tomato Salad 🌿	India	132
Egg Salad	Hmong	86
Green Bean Salad with Mustard Sauce 🌿	China	29
Indonesia Mixed Salad with Peanut Sauce 🌿	Indonesia	170
Meat Salad	Hmong	85
Rice Noodle Salad 🌿	Vietnam	143
Silver Bean Thread Noodle Salad 🌿	Thailand	104
Summer Salad	Cambodia	95
Sunomono Salad 🌿	Japan	68
Watercress Salad 🌿	China	34

Sauces, Stocks, and Garnishes

Vegetables and Lentils

Eggs

Chicken, Duck, and Pheasant

Cambodian Chicken-Vegetable Stir-Fry	Cambodia	95
Chicken Adobo	Philippines	61
Chicken Almond Ding	China	20
Chicken Chow Mein	China	8
Chicken with Chestnuts	China	36
Dar Cheen Chicken	China	8
Grilled Chicken	Thailand	105
Holy Basil Supreme	Thailand	102
John's Chicken Subgum Chow Mein	China	3
John's Special Chow Mein	China	4
Leeann Chin's Stir-Fry Chicken with Mango	China	17
Siam Café Chow Mein	Thailand	101
Smoked Duck	China	43
Smoked Pheasant	China	43
Sweet Potato Chicken Curry	Sri Lanka	137
Tandoori Chicken	India	117
Thai Chicken with Lemongrass	Thailand	111
Udon	Japan	75

Meat

Boiled Pork and Mustard Greens	Hmong	87
Korean Grilled Steak	Korea	159
Lamb Curry	India	124
Mongolian Fire Pot	China	24
Pea Vines and Sausage	Hmong	87
Ribs in Special Sauce	China	42
Roasted and Marinated		

Pork Loin	Japan	78
Sautéed Meat and Broccoli Greens	Hmong	86
Skewered Lamb Kabobs	India	128
Spicy Ground Beef with Chilies	India	117
Sukiyaki	Japan	67
Supenn's Thai Red Beef Curry	Thailand	100
Sweet Potatoes with Pork or Chicken	Hmong	88
Sy Xiong Vang's Sweet-Sour Pork with Eggs	Hmong	88
Tonkatsu (Pork Cutlet)	Japan	74
Vietnamese Mixed Grill	Vietnam	148

Fish and Seafood

Cantonese Shrimp in the Shell	China	38
Fong's Chow Mein (with Shrimp)	China	20
Joe Huie's Shrimp	China	7
Poached Salmon with Oriental Beauty	Tea	188
Periwinkles with Black Bean Sauce	China	12
Pine Nut–Crusted Sea Bass	Fusion	198
Red Snapper with Pepper Sauce	Philippines	62
Star Prairie Trout	Japan	80
Steamed Fish with Black Bean Sauce	China	37
Steamed Walleye with Vegetables	Thailand	106
Stir-Fried Scallops and Mushrooms	China	39
Walleye in Jalapeño Basil Sauce	Fusion	196

Facing page: Fresh produce at the Hmong market.

Index

Page numbers in *italics* refer to figures.

Facing page: Longans and lychees at the Hmong market.

C

Image Credits

All food photography, unless otherwise noted, by tnphoto.com

pages iv–v	1856 Desilver Map of the World
pages vi, 15, 75, 131, 187, 224, 229, 231, 250	jedlicka.com
pages vii (left), 1 (right) 7, 9, 210, 213, 214 (left)	Minnesota Historical Society
pages vii (right), 11, 13, 21 (top and bottom), 53 (bottom), 58, 70, 72 (all), 76, 80, 82, 83, 93, 99, 112 (top), 113, 146 (bottom), 147 (all), 159, 175, 178 (all), 185, 194, 200, 202, 218 (left and right), 219 (all), 221 (right), 222 (left and right)	tnphoto.com
pages 1 (left), 211	George M. Dempsie, Minnesota Historical Society
pages 2, 14 (bottom), 25, 44, 49, 66, 96, 110, 111, 217 (right), 220	ACAI
pages 4, 6, 212	Courtesy Wing Ying Huie
page 14 (top)	Roger W. Kline
page 16	2003, First Daughter Media Work
pages 17, 18, 19, 214 (right)	Courtesy David Fong's
page 22	Courtesy Shuang Cheng
page 23	Courtesy Yangtze
page 27	©2004 Alan Richardson
pages 46, 60, 89, 114, 124, 133, 134, 164, 184, 216	Pottery by Richard Bresnahan, St. John's Pottery, tnphoto.com
page 52	Phil.-Oriental Imports
page 53 (top)	Yvonne Arcilla
pages 61, 223	Geoff King
pages 65, 217 (left)	*Pioneer Press*, Sully Doroshow, August 4, 1984
page 94	Courtesy Cheng Heng
page 97	©Wing Young Huie
pages 104, 108	Randall Johnson
page 112 (bottom six)	Nuntana Erickson
pages 115, 215	Daljit Sikka
pages 125, 126	Raghavan Iyer
page 135	Liz Welch & Nick Lethert
page 151	Quang's
pages 155, 221 (left)	Courtesy *Korean Quarterly*
page 156	Mary Lee Vance
page 161	Stephen Wunrow, *Korean Quarterly*
page 167	Mark Huss 2012, markhuss.zenfolio.com
page 171	Courtesy Bali restaurant
pages 186, 191	Courtesy TeaSource
pages 189, 190	Yasuimoku Komuten Company Ltd., Gift of the Friends of the Institute, the Mary Livingston Griggs and Mary Griggs Burke Foundation, the Commemorative Association for the Japan World Exposition (1970), the James Ford Bell Foundation, Patricia M. Mitchell, Jane and Thomas Nelson, and many others Minneapolis Institute of Arts accession number: 2001.204.1
pages 203 (both), 204	Harry Singh
pages 206, 209	*Asian Pages*

Phyllis Louise Harris
Author

Author Phyllis Louise Harris was food editor of *Asian Pages* newspaper from 1991 to 2011 and wrote more than five hundred articles reaching 150,000 readers each month in seven states.

She wrote two cookbooks, is a contributor to Grolier's *Americana Encyclopedia*, and was the primary researcher on 6,000 years of spice history for *660 Curries*. Phyllis also served as executive director of the Midwest Asia Center from 1990 to 1992, where she created, produced, and managed the center's Kite Festival with kites and flyers from China, Japan, and the United States, and additional kites from India and Malaysia. The festival brought the centuries-old traditions of Asia's kite making and kite flying to more than a million people in Minnesota through twenty-six venues including the Minneapolis Institute of Arts, Science Museum of Minnesota, Minnesota Landscape Arboretum, Hennepin County Libraries, and St. Paul and Minneapolis grade schools.

In 1994 she founded the Asian Culinary Arts Institutes, Ltd., dedicated to the preservation, understanding, and enjoyment of the culinary arts of the Asia Pacific Rim. One of the center's first programs was to bring in two chefs from China to teach culinary students at the Hennepin Technical College and other venues in the Twin Cities. Phyllis earned a bachelor's degree in broadcast/journalism from the University of Minnesota and has culinary certificates from the Culinary Institute of America, Chinese Institute in America (NYC), California Culinary Academy, and Disney Institute. She had additional culinary training with master chefs in China and is currently teaching Chinese and other Asia Pacific Rim cuisines.

Phyllis operated her own advertising and marketing agency for thirty years with clients in Minneapolis, New York City, and London. Her work in business, retail, and financial advertising received a number of national and international awards.

Raghavan Iyer, CCP
Contributor

Collaborator Raghavan Iyer is the author of *Betty Crocker's Indian Home Cooking, The Turmeric Trail: Recipes and Memories from an Indian Childhood*, which was a 2003 James Beard Awards Finalist for Best International Cookbook, and *660 Curries. 660 Curries* was listed among the Top Cookbooks for 2008 by National Public Radio, the *New York Times, Boston Globe*, and *Food and Wine* magazine. The book was named the 2008 Best Asian Cookbook in the USA by World Gourmand Awards. Raghavan received the highly coveted 2004 International Association of Culinary Professionals' Award of Excellence (formerly the Julia Child Awards) for Cooking Teacher of the Year and was a finalist for a 2005 James Beard Journalism Award as a contributing writer for *EatingWell* magazine. His numerous articles have appeared in national and international food publications.

For the past seventeen years Raghavan has conducted culinary classes in schools and venues across the United States and in Canada, reaching more than 25,000 students. He is also cofounder of the Asian Culinary Arts Institutes, Ltd.

Team Profiles

Wendy Jedlička, CPP
Book Design

An Institute of Packaging Professionals Lifetime-Certified Packaging Professional, Wendy is president of Jedlička Design Ltd. (jedlicka.com), with several decades of packaging and print design experience. As a design and business strategy vendor, she has served clients from Fortune 100 corporations to three-person startups. An internationally known speaker, Wendy also writes on the topics of sustainable design and business. Her two books on sustainable design, business, and marketing for Wiley Publishing, *Packaging Sustainability* and *Sustainable Graphic Design*, are required reading for many college programs in North America.

Working to change minds in higher education, Wendy is part of the founding faculty for the groundbreaking Sustainable Design Program at Minneapolis College of Art and Design (mcad.edu) as well as sustainability faculty for design and business programs at the University of Wisconsin–Stout and University of Wisconsin–Extension.

As an advocate for sustainability in industry, Wendy is the o2-USA/Upper Midwest chapter chair and Chapter Co-Coordinator for the o2 International Network for Sustainable Design in the United States.

An avid appreciator of Asian culture and Japanese music, art, and martial arts in particular, Wendy has been practicing origami since age eight, studies and works in the Edo style for illustration, studies and performs Taiko (Japanese drumming) with several ensemble groups in the United States including the Mu Community Taiko Group in Minneapolis and Triangle Taiko in North Carolina, and lends a Taiko hand for Twin City Metro Japanese dance group Sansei Yonsei Kai. She also studies Kyudo (Japanese archery) with the Minnesota Kyudo Renmei (mnkyudo.org).

Tom Nelson
Photography

Tom Nelson earned his bachelor's degree in political science from Macalester College in St. Paul. An Upper Midwest native, Tom has traveled extensively around the world, adding to an impressive catalog of both captured and created photographic and digital art. Tom invites you to see samples of his work at tnphoto.com.

Tom is a board member and serves as the photo industry liaison for the o2-USA/Upper Midwest chapter of the o2 International Network for Sustainable Design.

Robin Krause—*Food stylist*

Special Thanks

Cretia Jesse for recommending me for a job that became the first step on my twenty-two-year journey to this book.

Frank Jesse for giving me the position of executive director of the Midwest Center where my involvement with Minnesota's Asian community provided me with the opportunity to become food editor of *Asian Pages* newspaper.

Cheryl Weiberg, former managing editor of *Asian Pages*, who for twenty years allowed me to pursue a wide variety of subjects for and about the Asian community and to write about them in every issue. Those five hundred articles were the inspiration for this book.

Florence Lin, whose teaching and encouragement led me down a path I never knew I would take and who continues to help me improve and expand my Chinese cooking skills.

Pamela McClanahan, director, and Shannon Pennefeather, managing editor, of the Minnesota Historical Society Press for believing in the book and making it happen.

Wendy, Tom, Raghavan, and Robin, whose creativity and dedication brought the idea to life in a fashion I could have never imagined.

The many wonderful people who shared their food, recipes, and stories with me over the years and showed me over and over again what amazing results come from talent, hard work, determination, and perseverance. I only wish we had room to include every one of their stories.

Phyllis Louise Harris

Facing page: Fresh ginger and produce at the Hmong market.
Following page: Produce organically grown in Minnesota at the St. Paul Farmers' Market